CW00829093

# UNDERCOVER SAILORS
Secret Operations of World War II

# UNDERCOVER SAILORS

## Secret Operations of World War II

A. Cecil Hampshire

WILLIAM KIMBER · LONDON

First published in 1981 by
William Kimber and Co. Limited
Godolphin House, 22a Queen Anne's Gate,
London SW1H 9AE

© A. Cecil Hampshire, 1981
ISBN 0-7183-0368-7

Photoset in Wales by
Derek Doyle and Associates, Mold, Clwyd
and printed and bound in Great Britain by
The Garden City Press Limited
Letchworth, Hertfordshire SE6 1JS

# Contents

# List of Illustrations

## MAPS

# Foreword and Acknowledgments

In my book *The Secret Navies*, published by William Kimber in 1978, I wrote about the activities of certain 'irregular' naval formations which came into being during the Second World War. They included the Fifteenth Motor Gunboat Flotilla, which ran a clandestine shuttle service between this country and occupied France and Norway; the Royal Marine Boom Patrol Detachment, from which were drawn the famous 'Cockleshell Heroes'; and 30 Assault Unit, a team of armed and expert looters who operated against the enemy from North Africa to the final collapse of the Third Reich.

In this volume I have related the experiences of more of these 'irregular' formations, largely seaborne although composed of representatives of all three Services, whose activities played no inconsiderable part in bringing about final Allied victory.

For help in compiling their stories I owe thanks to Commander T.H. Maxted, DSO, RD,* RNR; Colonel Andrew Croft, DSO, OBE, MA; Lieutenant-Commander P. Whinney, DSC, RNR; Captain E.B. Clark, RNR; Commander A.C. Seligman, DSC, RNR; Professor M.R.D. Foot; R.M. Coppock, Esq; J.D. Ladd, Esq; and P.F.G. Wilton, Esq.

A.C.H.

# I

## Corsairs of the Aegean

One November evening in 1941 the British submarine *Perseus* sailed unobtrusively from Malta. Her orders were to establish an offensive patrol south-west of enemy-occupied Greece, on completion of which she was to continue on to Alexandria. Her captain was Lieutenant-Commander Edward 'Ted' Nicolay, RN, an experienced submariner who had served in 'the Trade' since before the war. In addition to her normal crew of fifty-three officers and men, the *Perseus* carried a passenger, albeit a working one. He was Stoker First Class John Capes, also a submariner, who was returning to Alexandria to rejoin his own flotilla.

The *Perseus* was a vessel of the *Parthian* class, launched at Vickers Armstrong's Barrow yard in May 1929 and completed in 1930. 260 feet long, with a surface displacement of 1475 tons (2040 submerged), she had a surface speed of 17½ knots, and was armed with one 4-inch gun and eight 21-inch torpedo tubes, six bow and two stern. She and her sisters were designated 'overseas patrol submarines', and as each was commissioned she was sent to join the Fourth Submarine Flotilla on the China station.

In June 1931 one of their number, the *Poseidon*, hit the headlines when after colliding with a Chinese steamer while exercising off Wei-hai-wei she sank in twenty fathoms of water. At that time a new form of personalised escape gear, known as the Davis Submerged Escape Apparatus (DSEA), enabling the wearer to breathe under water, had recently been developed for British submarines, and all submariners were being trained in its use. With the aid of their DSEA gear, and under the inspired leadership of a courageous petty officer, several members of the crew of the *Poseidon* who had been trapped in the forepart of the wrecked submarine and given up for lost, successfully made their escape. It was the first time that the apparatus had been used in an actual disaster situation. Like all other British submarines, the *Perseus* was equipped with DSEA; although under wartime conditions the chances of escaping from a submarine badly damaged by enemy action were not considered to be very high.

In 1940 all China Fleet submarines were recalled from the Far East to serve in the Mediterranean where the Royal Navy was becoming hard-pressed. At that period of the war when the *Perseus* left Malta, British submarines in the Mediterranean were engaged in an unrelenting campaign against enemy supply traffic striving to reinforce their armies in North Africa. By September 1941 enough of them had been concentrated in the eastern Mediterranean to form two separate flotillas: the First based at Alexandria, and the Tenth at Malta.

The latter was composed of smaller but newer U-class boats, bearing such names as *Urge*, *Upholder* and *Unbeaten*, later to become famous for their exploits against the Axis supply routes. The former comprised larger vessels of the 'P', 'R' and 'T' classes, which operated in the Adriatic and Aegean. The latter were also used when they could be spared to carry vital supplies from Alexandria to Malta. These ferrying runs, which maintained along with other urgently needed stores a supply of aviation spirit to enable the Fleet Air Arm and the RAF to conduct operations from that island, became known as the 'Magic Carpet Service'.

Despite the continual enemy bombing of beleaguered Malta, social and business life in the island had somehow managed to adjust to these hazardous conditions and were being conducted much as usual. Thus it was that Captain Simpson, in command of the Tenth Submarine Flotilla, began receiving letters from a Maltese solicitor asking him to produce a certain Stoker John Capes who, it was alleged, while driving a car in Malta just prior to the outbreak of war, had collided with a local *carozzi* (horse cab) and wrecked it. The owner of the *carozzi* was his client, and he now wished to effect a settlement of the case.

Having ascertained that Capes was serving in the First Flotilla at Alexandria, Simpson accordingly contacted his opposite number, Captain Raw, who commanded that flotilla, and asked him to allow the man to be sent over via the 'Magic Carpet Service'. As soon as the court case had been decided, he would be returned by the same means. Capes duly arrived in the island, but after a month had elapsed and still no settlement appeared to be in sight, Simpson arranged for him to return to Alexandria and his own boat in the *Perseus*. Capes embarked shortly before she sailed, and the submarine set out on her mission.

At dawn on 3 December Nicolay sighted and attacked an escorted enemy supply ship. He managed to get off two torpedoes, which may or may not have hit. But he was given no opportunity to come up for a look as the convoy's escort vessels promptly drenched the area with depth charges. Hastily making herself scarce, the *Perseus* continued on her way for her appointment with destiny.

Late in the evening of 6 December, while she was cruising in the channel between Zante Island and the island of Cephalonia, in the Ionian Sea, a terrific explosion blasted the submarine. She had struck an enemy mine which tore a huge hole in her starboard bow. Diving straight to the bottom, she remained balanced perpendicularly on her buckled fore ends for a few brief moments before gradually settling at full length on the sea bed with an acute list to starboard.

Capes, who was in the after compartment of the submarine, was knocked off his feet by the force of the explosion, receiving a terrific blow on his backside. When he picked himself up, the compartment had been plunged into pitch darkness, all lighting having failed and every valve and pipeline broken. Groping about, he eventually found a couple of emergency torches, and by their light discovered that five other stunned and shaken stokers were alive with him. Everyone else in the submarine had apparently been killed by the explosion and consequent flooding.

With difficulty he managed to secure the watertight door, through which water was seeping, thus isolating the compartment. Next the DSEA sets were retrieved from their stowage lockers and donned, for already he and his companions were beginning to feel the effects of the rapidly diminishing supply of air. To make matters worse, the atmosphere was heavily tainted by fumes from some drums of oil and enamel paint stowed in the compartment which had burst under the force of the explosion. The resulting oil and grease mingled with water got on to their hands and faces and made it difficult to fit and retain the nose-clips of the DSEA gear in position.

Aware of the necessity to work fast, since they would all soon become badly affected, Capes managed to undo the escape hatch clips, pull down the canvas trunking and secure it to the deck,*

* Special flood valves were fitted in submarines and escape hatches with twill trunks – canvas cylinders which could be pulled down beneath the escape hatch. The twill trunk made it possible to equalise the pressure and open the hatch without a large bubble going out and letting it slam down again.

tasks made infinitely harder because of the acute angle at which the submarine was lying, the ship's side having become the deck. Floundering about in the oily water, he finally located the flood valve, only to discover that it was bent and immovable.

Desperately racking his brain for some alternative means of flooding the compartment, since he knew that only by equalising the internal air pressure with the outside sea pressure could the escape hatch be opened, it occurred to him to try the underwater gun. Resembling a small, vertically sited torpedo tube, this was a device normally for use by a submarine in distress to send flares to the surface to indicate her position. It worked and the water began to rise rapidly.

By now only one other rating besides himself appeared to be alive, the others having lapsed into unconsciousness or death. Since this man had thus far performed his escape drill correctly, if increasingly feebly, Capes hoped that the latter would be able to follow his own example. But at his first attempt to pass through the escape hatch, he was forced back by the blast of air coming through the trunking. Fixing his nose-clip more firmly, and clutching a DSEA torch, Capes tried again and this time emerged successfully without fouling the submarine's jumping wire.

Yet if war orders had been properly carried out in the *Perseus*, all escape and other hatches except the conning tower hatch would not only have been clipped internally, but also secured by a steel bar externally to prevent any hatch jumping its clips due to depth-charging. Escape would then have been impossible for the men in the after compartment.

As he began to ascend through the inky and freezing water, stabbing pains from his bursting lungs warned Capes that he was rising too rapidly and would soon lose consciousness. He unrolled the small rubber apron which formed part of the DSEA gear to act as a drogue, and was thus able to control his rate of ascent. On his way up he noticed by the light of his torch, floating some fifteen feet from the surface, a sinister looking canister with wires trailing from it, and realised with a shock that it was an acoustic mine.

After what seemed an eternity but in fact was only some ninety seconds, he reached the surface, still pain-racked and gasping. Gazing round, he found himself alone on a calm sea, surrounded by bubbles rising and bursting soundlessly from the wrecked submarine far below. No one else had apparently survived. When his vision finally cleared he could make out a darker shadow on the horizon to the northward which could only be land, and he began to flash the letters 'SOS' with his torch. But there was no response. Despite the crippling pain in his chest and lungs, he struck out towards it.

Some seven hours later Capes crawled wearily ashore. Although he did not know it then, he had reached the Italian-occupied island of Cephalonia. Fearful lest an apparent watcher or sentry he spotted on a distant hill should have seen him, he crabbed his way up the beach on his elbows and concealed himself in a small cave, where he fell into an exhausted sleep.

Around mid-morning two Greeks appeared and were surprised and alarmed to discover the bearded stranger, whom they at first took to be an enemy spy. Eventually Capes managed to make them understand who he was and how he came to be there, and one of the men went off to fetch him some dry clothing. Then, after digging a shallow hole in which they told him to conceal himself, they departed, returning after nightfall with a donkey on which they took him to a village about two miles away.

John Capes was now about to embark on an odyssey which would last for eighteen months, during which time patriotic Greek islanders kept him out of the clutches of the Italians until he was finally snatched to safety from under their noses. For, on the other side of the Aegean, there existed an Allied organisation whose seaborne raiding activities were spreading fear and dread among the Axis garrisons of the numerous islands, to whom news of the existence of the solitary survivor of the missing submarine *Perseus* would eventually be conveyed. His rescue by these corsairs of the Aegean was a minor epic in itself.

\*

To explain how this organisation and the units of which it was composed came into being, it is necessary briefly to outline the course of events following the collapse of France in 1940 and the entry of Italy into the war as they affected the Middle East.

Since the French colonies in North Africa had also capitulated, the Italians were freed from any threat on the Tunisian frontier and able to concentrate their whole North African military strength against the British defending Egypt. Under command of Marshal Graziani, former Governor-General of Libya, this was considerable, totalling in all some 250,000 men, including armoured divisions and a strong air force. Against this General

Wavell, the British Commander-in-Chief, Middle East Command, could muster only a much smaller army, which was also threatened by another large Italian force in East Africa.

The North African desert over which the forthcoming campaigns in the Middle East were to be fought is, except for the coastal strip, a vast area of naked and lifeless ground upon which rain falls at infrequent intervals. In widely spaced localities where underground rivers and springs have worked to the surface are a number of oases. Three of the most strategically important of these were Siwa, Jarabub and Kufra, the former in Egypt and the two latter inside the Libyan border, Kufra being more than 300 miles to the south. Since there was always the chance that Graziani would make use of these oases to outflank our forces in the Nile delta, a special British deep reconnaissance unit was brought into existence to keep an eye on the enemy's movements.

Operating in unarmoured vehicles directed from Cairo, headed by Major Ralph Bagnold, an officer who had organised and led numerous desert motor expeditions and explorations in peacetime, the unit was composed of specially selected volunteers from the New Zealand division attached to Wavell's army. Under the title 'Long Range Desert Group' (LRDG), it was later expanded with officers and men from British and Rhodesian forces.

The basic unit of the Group was the patrol, which normally consisted of five vehicles and twenty men. Each was commanded by an officer and included an expert navigator since, like sailors, the patrols had to navigate their way over a landscape as trackless and featureless as the ocean itself. They carried with them food and water to last a month, and petrol for a round trip of more than a thousand miles, contact with base being maintained by wireless. During the first five months of hostilities the cars of these patrols, based either on Siwa or Kufra, travelled a total of more than half a million miles back and forth across Libya, relaying back valuable information regarding enemy troop movements, collecting topographical data, destroying water pipe lines and cutting enemy communications.

Meanwhile, harassed by British land, sea and air forces, Marshal Graziani at last began his cautious advance along the coast towards Egypt on 13 September, finally halting at a point east of Sidi Barrani, a few miles inside the Egyptian frontier, in order to build up his strength. But early in December Wavell, who had received some much-needed reinforcements including heavy tanks, struck first at his foe in a surprise offensive. In less than ten days he had driven the Italians back into Cyrenaica. Confounding the enemy by the speed of his advance, he followed this up with a series of brilliant victories until, in February 1941, British advanced guards had reached El Agheila, on the Gulf of Sollum, and more than half of Graziani's army had been taken prisoner.

It was at this point that the pendulum of fortune began to swing back.

In the previous October Mussolini, having conquered Albania, invaded Greece, only to have his nose bloodied by the valiant little Greek army who drove the Italians back over the Albanian border. Then Hitler came to the help of his floundering ally, and Jugoslavia and Greece were simultaneously invaded by German mechanised divisions. By then the decision had been taken to send a British expeditionary force to the aid of the Greeks, Wavell being denuded of some of his best units for the purpose. At the same time another of his divisions was withdrawn to the Sudan. Thus when General Rommel and his Afrika Korps arrived in Tripolitania to reinforce the Italians and began his advance eastwards, the weakened British Army of the Nile was compelled to fall back as far as the frontier of Egypt. But they left in their rear the fortress of Tobruk, which was to hold out for the next eight months, an effort to relieve the place in May having failed.

While the new British Commander-in-Chief, General Auchinleck, who replaced Wavell in July 1941, was preparing a counter-offensive against Rommel, the LRDG was especially active. Operating unhindered from Siwa and Kufra, their patrols ranged over an area inside Libya approximately 500 miles from north to south, and 600 from east to west. As a result of their work existing inaccurate maps of this area were revised, and much information collected as to the suitability of the country for the passage of motorised forces.

Small parties stationed themselves on the coast road some 300 miles behind the enemy lines for long periods to take a complete census of and report enemy traffic travelling between Tripolitania and Benghazi. Both in Cyrenaica and Tripolitania enemy convoys were attacked by LRDG patrols and prisoners taken, from whom much information was obtained. Numerous wells and waterholes were located, their quality and yield being determined by a qualified officer attached to each patrol for the purpose, and the sites of suitable landing grounds for aircraft mapped. In spite of considerable air activity and the fact that the country offered little concealment for vehicles, the patrols were not detected. Help was frequently afforded them by Libyan Arabs, who in general detested the Italians. Under Graziani's rule a twelve-foot high wire fence running southwards for hundreds of miles had been erected along the border to prevent the oppressed natives from escaping into Egypt, and was later strengthened by fortified posts at close intervals. They proved no barrier to the patrols.

Subsequently the scope of the Group was expanded. Originally designed and equipped 'to operate against the desert and not primarily against a living enemy', it was now to go further afield and be equipped with striking power as well. Units were to operate over as much as 1,500 miles of territory and for several weeks at a time. Numbers were to be small and not to exceed twelve vehicles. Sub-units were to be self-contained as regards defence, light maintenance and repairs, wireless, medical and navigation, and independent of the rest of the force. The objects of the Group would be to obtain information, carry out raids to compel the enemy to divert forces to protect his lines of communication, destroy laden vehicles, aircraft on the ground, depots and installations and communications.

At this time the LRDG consisted of a headquarters and two squadrons, each of three fighting patrols, the total personnel numbering less than 200, of whom nineteen were officers. In overall command now was Lieutenant-Colonel Guy Prendergast of the Royal Tank Regiment, who had been Bagnold's second in command, the latter having been promoted and appointed to a desk job in Cairo. Their vehicles consisted of 15-cwt trucks, 30-cwt lorries and a number of 3-tonners; and their weapons included Breda machine-guns, captured German twin light machine-guns on AA mountings, Vickers .303-inch machine guns, mortars and incendiary ammunition. As personal arms they carried Thompson machine carbines and .38" pistols. Each unit had its own wireless set, was equipped with a theodolite and prismatic and sun compasses for navigational purposes, watches, torches and binoculars.

The Group had two aircraft of its own known as 'WACOs' (Western Aircraft Corporation of Ohio), the RAF having refused to provide any. They were single-engined cabin aircraft purchased from their Egyptian owners, piloted by Prendergast and Trooper Barker, a New Zealander who had flown with Kingsford-Smith, and they greatly simplified the problems of supply. Thus when on one occasion a patrol left Kufra for an extended reconnaissance into Libya and ran into mechanical trouble next day when two of its lorries developed defective fan belts, a signal was sent to headquarters asking for four new fan belts to be flown out. These were duly dropped a few hours later at the stipulated latitude and longitude.

Early in 1942 four LRDG patrols were detached to work under the command of General Leclerc, the Free French military governor of Chad, whose forces were later to fight their way up from the south to join with the Eighth Army in its triumphal advance after the victory at Alamein. As a measure of the LRDG's reputation, the task given them was 'to carry out a tip and run attack in the Fezzan to cause all possible damage to enemy material and installations; to engage the enemy, whether infantry, motorised, or in the air, wherever and whenever encountered; and obtain information of enemy positions and methods.' For this purpose they were equipped with armoured vehicles and supported by French ground and air forces.

When, after its long pursuit of the retreating Rommel, the Eighth Army was finally poised to drive into southern Tunisia, and the fate of the Axis forces in North Africa clearly only a matter of time, the future of the LRDG came up for discussion at a special staff meeting held at GHQ, Middle East. One recommendation was that, following the conquest of Cyrenaica and Tripolitania, it should be employed helping the Occupied Enemy Territories Administration (OETA); another that it should be attached to the Ninth Army in Syria.

In any event, opinion at the meeting was strongly opposed to disbandment of the Group, to whom the Director of Military Intelligence, Middle East paid a handsome tribute:

> As the only trained road traffic observers, familiar with enemy vehicles and weapons, the LRDG has provided, and still provides, an indispensable groundwork of facts on which calculations of enemy strength can be based. Without their reports we should frequently have been in doubt regarding enemy movements when knowledge of them was all-important, and our estimate of enemy strength far less accurate.

In the event the LRDG, along with certain other 'irregular' units, was to become part of a new force yet to be formed, whose offensive activities would be mainly seaborne.

Following the defeat by General Wavell of Mussolini's army in Libya, it had been intended that we should occupy the large Italian-owned island of Rhodes which, with its harbour and twin airfields, was regarded as being the key to control of the Aegean. Thus, early in 1941, a special force of Commandos and landing craft began assembling at Alexandria with the object of taking over, not only Rhodes, but also the smaller Dodecanese islands of Leros and Cos, and thus open the sea route to Turkey and the Dardanelles.

But after the Germans had intervened, overrun the Greek mainland and captured Crete, the Rhodes expedition faded away. The Germans then proceeded to occupy the more important islands in the Aegean, reinforcing the garrisons of those such as Rhodes, Scarpanto, Stampalia, Cos and Leros which belonged to the Italians and fortifying the latter. Thereafter Axis aircraft, operating from airfields in Crete and the southern Dodecanese islands, were able virtually unhindered to harass British convoys and fleet movements in the eastern Mediterranean.

Included in the force originally intended for the assault on Rhodes was a small unit known as the 'Special Boat Section'. The latter had come into being in the United Kingdom in mid-1940 when the possibility of using collapsible canoes for landing agents in enemy territory, and for special reconnaissance and sabotage work, was first suggested. Approved by Admiral Keyes, then in charge of Combined Operations, the unit consisting of two army officers and seven other ranks was formed and trained on the Isle of Arran.

In command was Captain Roger Courtney, a peacetime big-game hunter and small boat enthusiast, who earlier on had personally demonstrated to a group of sceptical senior officers the ability of one man in a canoe to sabotage an anchored ship by attaching explosives to her hull.

Training consisted of canoe handling and navigation, demolition, cliff-climbing, swimming, boom crossing, etc., and the use of limpet charges. The Section was then attached to No 8 Commando of the Special Service Brigade, its officers and men having been drawn from the Commandos.

Among early proposals for the employment of the Commandos of the then newly formed Combined Operations Command was an assault on the heavily defended island of Pantelleria, north-west of Malta. Although Winston Churchill was strongly in favour,

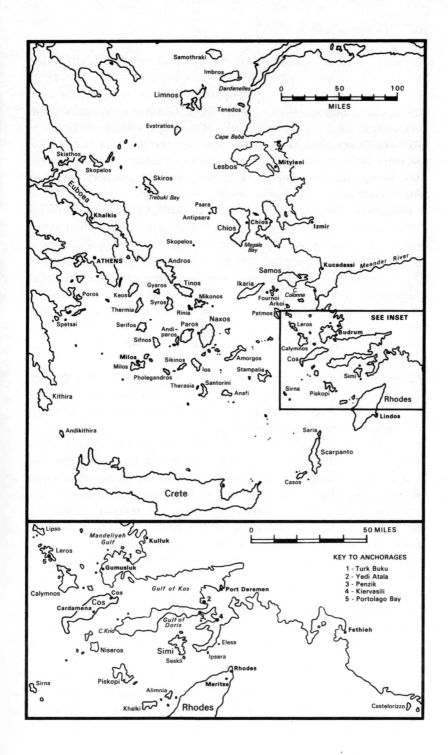

Samothraki

Imbros

Limnos

Dardanelles

Tenedos

Evstratios

Cape Baba

Skiathos

Skopelos

Lesbos

Mityleni

Skiros

Euboea

Trebuki Bay

Khalkis

Psara

Antipsara

Chios

Chios

Izmir

Skopelos

Megala
Bay

ATHENS

Andros

Samos

Kucadassi

Meander River

Gyaros

Tinos

Ikaria

Poros

Keos

Mikonos

C.
Colonna

Fournoi

Thermia

Syros

Rinia

Arkoi

Spetsai

Serifos

Andi-
paros

Paros

Naxos

Patmos

SEE INSET

Leros

Budrum

Sifnos

Calymnos

Milos

Sikinos

Amorgos

Cos

Milos

Ios

Stampalia

Pholegandros

Simi

Therasia

Santorini

Sirna

Piskopi

Rhodes

Kithira

Anafi

Andikithira

Saria

Lindos

Scarpanto

Casos

Crete

Lipso

Mandeliyeh
Gulf

Kulluk

Leros

Gumusluk

KEY TO ANCHORAGES

Calymnos

Cos

Gulf of Kos

Port Deremen

1 - Turk Buku
2 - Yedi Atala
3 - Penzik
4 - Kiervasili
5 - Portolago Bay

Cardamena

Cos

C.Krio

Gulf of
Doris

Fethieh

Niseros

Simi

Elesa

Sirna

Seskli

Ipsera

Piskopi

Rhodes

Alimnia

Maritsa

Khalki

Rhodes

Castelorizzo

0   50   100
MILES

0   50 MILES

Admiral Cunningham, naval Commander-in-Chief, Mediterranean, was against it; and he was backed up by the Chiefs of Staff, who persuaded Churchill to drop the idea – at least for the time being. Accordingly, as has been said, Courtney's Special Boat Section was then earmarked for the Rhodes expedition. When this, too, was aborted the Section was attached for training to the First Submarine Flotilla at Alexandria. Conveyed by sea to their targets, the unit and its canoes could be used for reconnaissance, sabotage, landing agents, etc., on enemy-held coasts.

From February to August 1941 many such operations were undertaken, the majority of which were an unqualified success, the unit being based in the Middle East Combined Training Centre at Kabrit, which had been set up in 1940 in the Suez Canal Zone. In 1942 Courtney returned home to form a second section which, after undergoing similar training to the first – which included a submarine course and instruction in the use of DSEA – was also sent out to the Mediterranean. Thereafter the two sections, known as 'Z Group', worked with the First and Tenth Submarine Flotillas from Malta and Alexandria.

A typical operation carried out by the SBS, code-named 'Anglo', was a daring raid against the two large airfields of Maritza and Calato in Rhodes, one of the principal bases from which enemy bombers were mauling our convoys.

The raiding party consisted of two British army officers, three army other ranks and three Royal Marines, accompanied by two Greek officers and two Greek guides. After being landed from a Greek submarine, hiding their rubber boats and stores and trekking into the hills, the party split up, one section heading for the airfield at Maritza overlooking the north-west coast, and the other making for Calato in the east. Both parties were to rendezvous at an agreed point before returning together to the embarkation beach where a submarine would pick them up.

Unfortunately, after successfully carrying out their attack, the northern party was taken prisoner. The Calato raiders also destroyed a large number of enemy aircraft, but after a hot pursuit only two, the leader of the expedition and a marine, managed to elude the vengeful Italians. Since the party's boats had been discovered and towed away by the enemy, the pair made their escape by swimming out to the British submarine which was waiting to evacuate the raiders. Nevertheless Operation 'Anglo' had been a success. As well as the aircraft destroyed, both airfields had been severely damaged, with the result that no convoy attacks could be mounted from Rhodes for many weeks.

*

Another 'irregular' unit which came into being in 1941 with the blessing of Middle East Command, into which the SBS was eventually to be absorbed, was at first known simply as 'L' Detachment, Special Air Service Brigade.* Its originator was Lieutenant-Colonel (then Second Lieutenant) David Stirling, DSO, Scots Guards, a former Commando officer, with the idea of carrying out sabotage and the destruction of enemy equipment behind the enemy lines, such raids being staged in conjunction with some major Navy, Army or RAF operation in the Mediterranean area.

Methods of reaching targets were to be by land, sea and air, which would necessitate the employment of carefully selected and highly trained personnel, officers and men being chosen from units already in the Middle East. In its early stages, and up to late in 1942, the total strength of the unit did not exceed 100.

The training they were required to undergo was almost unheard of at the time and the hardest ever undertaken in the Middle East. It included parachute dropping, navigation, demolition, languages, the use of British specialised and foreign weapons, boatwork, motor transport and wireless. Full scale operational exercises and extensive schemes were carried out on foot in the desert, some of the exercises consisting of forced marches over difficult terrain with full operational load for distances starting from eleven miles and working up to 100, the only water available being that carried by the men themselves. During training one man walked forty miles across the desert in stockinged feet with a 75 lb load rather than fall out after his boots gave way!

The Detachment pioneered parachuting in the Middle East, and their first drop can only be described as hair-raising. The embryo parachutists consisted of Stirling himself, Lieutenant Lewes of the Welsh Guards, Sergeant Stone of the Scots Guards, Guardsmen Davies and Evans of the Welsh Guards, and Guardsman D'Arcy of the Irish Guards. None had ever jumped before, while the four soldiers had never even been up in an aeroplane!

There was no record of the last periodical examination of the

---

* There was, of course, no brigade; the term was used to fox the enemy.

parachutes they used, and the jump – made from an ageing Vickers Valentia troop-carrier over the desert at dusk one evening – was preceded by throwing out a dummy made from sandbags and tentpoles to see what would happen. As its parachute opened successfully, although the tentpoles were smashed to pieces on hitting the ground, the jump was duly made, the men hatless and wearing only khaki shirts and shorts.

Stirling landed badly, injuring his spine and temporarily losing his sight; the others were considerably shaken, bruised and scratched, but otherwise unhurt. Subsequent parachute training on the ground for the detachment involved diving out of trucks travelling at thirty-five miles an hour which, commented the Director of Military Operations, 'caused a great number of injuries'.

The Detachment operated with the Eighth Army continuously from 1941 up to the entry of the latter into Tunisia, their first parachute jump against an enemy being made in that year. This was to attack enemy aerodromes at Gazala and Tmimi, west of Tobruk, prior to the launching of General Auchinleck's offensive, code-named Operation 'Crusader' on 18 November 1941, being picked up afterwerwards by the LRDG. Unhappily the jump was unsuccessful because of heavy rain and a high wind which swept away the containers. Thirty-two of a total of fifty-three raiders who took part were lost in the operation, many of these having been taken prisoner. An unconfirmed report nevertheless claimed that nineteen enemy aircraft had been destroyed.

As a result it was considered inadvisable to carry out any more parachute operations in the western desert because of the difficulties caused by changeable weather, accurate navigation owing to the absence of landmarks, and casualties sustained on landing in rough country. Thereafter SAS raiding parties were transported by the LRDG for offensive operations on land, and by the Navy for attacks on enemy-held islands in the Mediterranean.

While the principal aim of the Detachment was the destruction of enemy aircraft in order to relieve the pressure on Malta convoys, other targets included shipping, ammunition and bomb dumps, vehicle parks, tanks and armoured vehicles, and petrol and water points. On one occasion, in conjunction with the SBS, to enable a convoy to be fought through to Malta, a number of enemy airfields were simultaneously attacked over a wide area, ranging from Crete to Cyrenaica.

Small parties only were usually employed in such raids, and their carefully planned and skilfully executed attacks on enemy aircraft played a considerable part in enabling Malta convoys to reach their destination. Destruction of enemy equipment was extensive, and because of the care taken in planning attacks and switching tactics, the enemy never knew where the raiders would strike next or how an operation would be carried out. Casualties in relation to successes achieved were extremely low, testifying to the excellence of the Detachment's training.

Later on they acquired their own transport in the form of heavily armed and specially modified long-range jeeps. Fitted with four high-speed light machine-guns, a 50-calibre heavy machine-gun, a mortar and smoke dischargers – even in some cases a high-powered searchlight – these vehicles frequently penetrated as much as 500-600 miles into enemy-held territory, destroying aircraft, mining roads, blowing up supply trains, cutting signal and telephone communications, strafing enemy road convoys, and attacking camps, leaguers and isolated enemy posts at night. At all times the raiders kept in touch with their headquarters by wireless, and were thus able to relay back much valuable information, enabling the RAF to bomb successfully a number of important targets, and ambush and shoot down enemy transport planes.

The Detachment's jeeps frequently traversed parts of the desert hitherto unknown and through areas marked as impassable. Because of the mobility of these raiding parties and the strength of their fire-power, the enemy concentrated his counter-measures on attacks by fighters and bombers. On many occasions individual units located while lying up during daylight were shot up and bombed by enemy aircraft. Their casualties were comparatively light, and in every case they succeeded in shaking off their attackers and got away to rejoin the main body.

During the time that Rommel and his forces were being held up by General Montgomery at El Alamein, the Detachment was busily employed carrying out carefully planned raids in the enemy's rear, some as far west as the Gulf of Sirte. The first such raid, carried out in full strength, was an attack on the vital enemy supply port of Benghazi at night. This resulted in Rommel having to withdraw considerable forces from those facing Montgomery to protect his flanks and lines of communication from further attacks.

Like the LRDG, operational parties of the SAS usually remained in the desert behind the enemy lines for lengthy periods, during which a number of offensive operations would be carried out, personnel being relieved or reinforced as the situation required. Rendezvous for such purposes frequently had to be altered, but good wireless communication between patrols reduced the possibility of error. On one occasion the RAF landed a transport aircraft at night at a rendezvous deep in enemy territory, bringing much-needed ammunition, petrol, water and food. On its return flight the aircraft took with it a number of SAS sick and wounded and escapers from enemy prisoner-of-war camps who had been picked up in the desert.

Some remarkable feats of endurance were performed by individuals and parties of the Detachment who found themselves cut off in enemy territory. Returning to base – always attempted as a matter of pride no matter what the difficulties – sometimes involved trudging a hundred or more miles on foot across the desert without food or water, when the slightest error in navigation could mean starvation and certain death through lack of water. In one instance an SAS officer led his party on foot from Tobruk to Alamein without a single casualty.

For the purpose of carrying out attacks on enemy-held islands, raiding parties were usually conveyed to and re-embarked from the target beaches by submarine. These forays, usually undertaken in the most arduous conditions, resulted not only in the destruction of a great deal of enemy equipment, but played havoc with the morale of enemy garrisons. Making their way back to the re-embarkation beach was often hazardous in the extreme, since the raiders had also to evade hotly pursuing enemy forces while struggling over difficult and unfamiliar terrain.

Raids on enemy airfields by these highly trained saboteurs took the form of placing time bombs in and around parked aircraft, or by armed jeeps attacking in formation and firing incendiary ammunition from their high-speed machine-guns. In such hit and run attacks the ground defences had to be dealt with before the dispersed aircraft could be tackled.

Throughout the whole of the North African campaign from 1941 onwards as the tides of fortune ebbed and flowed, the SAS Detachment was itself responsible for the total destruction of no fewer than 350 confirmed enemy aircraft, in addition to many petrol, ammunition, bomb and torpedo dumps, store depots, and countless vehicles of all types. In some cases enemy outposts were successfully attacked and mopped up. Enemy rail transport was also badly disrupted and supply trains blown up.

By the date of the enemy surrender in Tunisia the personnel of the Detachment included British and Fighting French elements from almost every military unit in the Middle East, and they were later to be joined by the re-formed Greek Sacred Squadron.* Their role in contributing to the final defeat of the Axis forces in North Africa was thereafter to be repeated in a different zone of operations, to the enhancement of their already fearsome reputation and the continued discomfort of the enemy. But before that 'L' Detachment, 1 SAS Brigade had been formed into the 1 SAS Regiment, absorbing the 1 SS Regiment and the SBS, the object being to bring these raiding units under a single command.

Thus the newly formed regiment was to be organised and trained to attack objectives such as landing grounds and aircraft thereon; locomotives and rolling stock; railways and road communications including bridges; supply dumps and other administrative installations; enemy tanks and other troops in leaguer; water transport in leaguer or on the move in back areas; headquarters and important officers; landline communications; base ports and shipping. Depending on the type and locality of the objective, approach would be made by land, sea or air.

*

After the German takeover in the Aegean their island garrisons and those of the Italians were by no means to be left in peace, although it was not possible to mount a major counter-offensive due to the pressure of more urgent events elsewhere in the Middle East.

Meanwhile, towards the end of 1941, Auchinleck, commanding the newly designated Eighth Army, struck back at Rommel and forced him to retreat to Agheila. Then came Pearl Harbour and the disasters in the Far East following the Japanese entry into the war. Early in 1942 Rommel, by now considerably reinforced, launched a new offensive which compelled the Eighth Army to fall back to a line west of Tobruk.

After a brief lull in the fighting, Rommel led off again, and in a fierce armoured battle at a point known as 'Knightsbridge' the British suffered severely from the enemy's powerful anti-tank artillery. Auchinleck was again forced to retire. Then, covered by

* The Sacred Squadron of Royalist officers was a revival of the squadron killed to a man at Thebes resisting the Spartans in 370 BC.

bombers operating from captured airfields, Rommel smashed his way into Tobruk. The moral effect of the fall of this outpost after its garrison had been sustained by the Navy at no little cost during months of siege was considerable. More important, the Eighth Army was now compelled to retreat into Egypt, where it finally halted and prepared to make a stand at El Alamein. This was both the last and best defensive position from which to deny Alexandria and the Nile Delta to the enemy. To the north was the sea, in the centre ridges and sand-covered hillocks, and to the south the reputedly impassable Qattara Depression.

A new army commander was now appointed in the person of Lieutenant-General Bernard Montgomery, and reinforcements of men and material began to reach the scene. By October Montgomery was ready to open a fresh offensive, and soon afterwards Anglo-American forces landed in Morocco and Algeria, to become in due course the northern claw of the pincers which were eventually to crush the Axis forces in North Africa.

*

The Navy had suffered grievously in the battle for Crete, and subsequently in support of the Eighth Army and the efforts to run convoys to Malta. Attacks against Rommel's supply lines, which ran from the Adriatic to Sicily, to the Aegean Islands from the Greek ports of Piraeus, Kalamata and Salonica, and enemy shipping in the Aegean were therefore mainly carried on by submarines operating from Malta and Alexandria. Hence the mission of the submarine *Perseus*, already related. Nevertheless, whenever possible, the Navy and the RAF continued to land and drop agents and saboteurs in Crete and elsewhere, bring off survivors and evaders, and land arms and supplies to local resistance groups.

Along with the LRDG, SBS and SAS, certain other undercover organisations were conducting their own clandestine activities in the area. Thus MO4, the Middle East section of SOE with its headquarters in Cairo, insinuated agents and liaison officers into various key posts from the Balkans to Turkey, trained Libyan Arabs in sabotage to be carried out against the enemy in the desert campaigns, and prepared the way for guerilla operations in the Aegean by establishing contact with patriot elements, laying the foundations for future armed risings and a fifth column to assist our armed forces, and undermining the morale of enemy garrisons. It had its own sabotage school set up on Mount Carmel, near Haifa. Using Greek fishing caiques as transports, this agency also planted secret dumps of arms and stores on various Aegean islands for use in later operations against the enemy. In due course representatives of the American OSS arrived to conduct similar activities.

Another clandestine set-up was known as 'A' Force, a deception and escape organisation, headquartered in Cairo and commanded by Brigadier Dudley Clarke, which, during the fighting in Libya, established a successful western desert escape line with the aid of Libyan Arab agents, who were paid for the men they brought back. Thus RAF aircrews, SAS, SBS and LRDG personnel all carried 'blood chits' encashable in Cairo in case they should be shot down or cut off behind enemy lines.

One of 'A' Force's most active agents, who operated in neutral Turkey, was the British Consul at Izmir, a retired naval officer named Rees. With the connivance of local Turkish authorities, Rees established a clandestine base on the Turkish coast opposite the island of Chios, and set up a caique route through the Northern Sporades by which evaders and escapers from Greece and Crete could be got away. As Admiral Willis, one-time naval Commander-in-Chief in the Levant, was later to record: 'The assistance given by Turkey was entirely in keeping with her position as an ally, and behaviour throughout satisfyingly un-neutral.' 'A' Force was to become even more active in the Aegean as well as elsewhere in the Mediterranean.

Two other agencies conducting undercover operations in the Middle East, also directed from London, were the Political Warfare Executive (PWE), concerned with the dissemination of propaganda to contribute to specific military operations, and to attack the overall morale of the enemy; and the Inter-Services Liaison Department (ISLD) under Captain Cuthbert Bowlby, RN, for the general collection of intelligence.

Throughout the ebb and flow of the desert campaigns, these organisations had been steadily pursuing their respective aims, for which they recruited their own personnel and, where necessary, chartered their own vessels. The Royal Navy also from time to time staged special operations on their behalf by submarine or minor surface craft. Thus by early 1943 these clandestine operations had increased to a very considerable extent. In addition to their specialised secret activities, each organisation fulfilled a useful general intelligence function, but overall their efforts were uneconomical. That situation was now about to be changed.

At a meeting of the Commanders-in-Chief Committee early in 1943, the Joint Operational Staff reported that as the value of raiding forces of a purely overland character had diminished, they were being reorganised, to include the 100 officers of the Greek Sacred Squadron attached to the Eighth Army. The Commander-in-Chief, Levant was raising a force of armed caiques to be manned by naval personnel which, with MTBs and MLs of the Coastal Forces, would form a striking force for raids against enemy commerce and isolated garrisons in the Aegean, to disrupt enemy communications to the maximum possible extent, and divert the maximum number of enemy troops to garrison the islands. The Commander-in-Chief, Middle East Forces was training a military force of Commando type to work with them. The whole organisation would be designated 'Raiding Forces, Middle East'.

Because of their inter-Service character a small joint executive headed by a naval captain would be set up to plan raids, co-ordinate organisation and training, allocate forces for special operations, and help commanders with the detailed planning and preparation of their raids. It would be known as 'Small Raids Incorporated' (SRI), with headquarters in Cairo, all offensive action to conform to strategy agreed by the Commanders-in-Chief. ISLD, PWE, MO4 and 'A' Force would keep in close touch with SRI, and the Commander-in-Chief, Levant would co-ordinate all special operations carried out across the sea on the Levant station.

Accordingly Admiral Sir John Cunningham, then Commander-in-Chief, Levant, took appropriate action, the result of which was that MO4's flotilla of caiques was divided into two groups, one retained by them and based on Haifa, the other transferred to the Commander, Coastal Forces, Mediterranean and based on Beirut. The function of the latter would be the transport of raiding forces and intelligence collecting. Designated the 'Levant Schooner Flotilla', it was officially commissioned on 29 May 1943. MO4's flotilla was given the title of 'Levant Fishing Patrol, to be employed on purely MO4 operations. It was also known as 'Force 133'.

Vessels owned and employed by the various secret service organisations for their own operations, based and operating in neutral or enemy-controlled waters were not permitted to fly the White Ensign; but all other vessels, including those detailed to work with clandestine organisations, were considered to be HM Ships, however small. The former were manned by members of those organisations and other Service personnel attached to them;

the latter solely by naval personnel who volunteered for special service.

The military elements of the newly formed Raiding Forces, Middle East, totalled more than 500 all ranks, and included members of the SBS under Major the Earl Jellicoe, SAS under Lieutenant-Colonel Cater (Stirling had been taken prisoner in Tunisia) and LRDG, all of whom jealously retained their own unit identities, so that no one was quite sure which was which. They were being assembled at Kabrit and in special camps at Athlit and Azzib, north and south respectively of Haifa, for training or re-training. The former was necessary to indoctrinate newly joined personnel, and included vigorous physical training, unarmed combat, navigation by map and compass, swimming, expert (sniper) weapon training, the operation of special devices, demolition, reconnaissance, parachuting, cliff-climbing, camou-flage and signals – even ski-ing in the snows of Lebanon. Not the least important part of their training was in boatwork, using a variety of small craft. These included folding infantry assault boats, rigid and collapsible canoes, small black rubber dinghies, large and small US-type rubber dinghies, and captured enemy rubber dinghies.

In overall command of Raiding Forces was Brigadier Douglas Turnbull. A regular gunner officer, 'Bull' Turnbull was a veteran of the Western Desert fighting, during which he had been wounded and awarded the DSO. His second in command was Lieutenant-Colonel 'Jock' Neilson Lapraik, MC, of the Queen's Own Cameron Highlanders. Appointed as Naval Liaison Officer to the Raiding Forces was Lieutenant-Commander Leslie Ramseyer, RNVR.

A batch of SBS men was detached to work up in the caiques transferred from MO4 to the Levant Schooner Flotilla. The latter had been placed under the operational charge of Lieutenant-Commander Adrian Seligman, RNR, who was empowered to 'raise, equip and train a force of armed caiques manned by naval personnel'. A fitting-out base was established at Paphos, in Cyprus, and in nearby Yeronisis Cove newly commissioned vessels could work up in secret and under similar conditions to those in the islands. For operational purposes the flotilla was based on Beirut under the ship name HMS *Mosquito II*, the parent establishment, *Mosquito*, being the Coastal Force base at Alexandria. Added to the flotilla was HMS *Hedgehog*, a 60-ton fishing trawler from Haifa.

Two army officers, Captains W.E. Benyon-Tinker and Adrian Gardner, were initially seconded to the flotilla, and Lieutenant-

Commander Andre Londos of the Royal Hellenic Navy lent by the Greek naval commander-in-chief to recruit Greek naval personnel to form a second caique flotilla in due course. Subsequently more volunteer army officers, and even one from the RAF joined up.

Seligman was one of a number of Service officers in the eastern Mediterranean at this time who shared a common love of adventure. In the late 1930s he had sailed a 350-ton barquentine round the world with a scratch crew recruited through the 'Personal' columns of *The Times* when such an expedition was rather less commonplace than it would be considered today, and afterwards recorded his experiences in a book entitled *The Voyage of the Cap Pilar*. A tricky wartime job that earned him an early Mention in Despatches for 'skill and seamanship' was to pilot a 10,000-ton Russian tanker through Turkish waters under enemy blockade to Famagusta. Later he commanded the Flower Class corvette *Erica* until she was sunk by a mine off Cyrenaica in February 1943 while escorting a convoy from Benghazi to Alexandria. At the time, however, Seligman had temporarily relinquished command to attend a conference in Cairo. Ramseyer, who had escaped from the Italians after being taken prisoner when his ship was sunk off Tobruk, was another seeker after adventure.

Benyon-Tinker, an army signals officer, and at that time a staff captain (Intelligence) attached to the Spears Mission to Syria and the Lebanon, met Seligman in Beirut and needed little persuasion to join the latter's new 'cloak and dagger' organisation as gunnery and intelligence officer. Gardner, similarly recruited, became responsible for maintenance and supplies.

In due course more caiques were procured by the Principal Sea Transport Officer, Middle East and turned over to Seligman; others were 'enticed' into British service, and several were captured from the Germans. But until sufficient volunteers from naval sources could be found, some retained part of their Greek civilian crews. As the vessels' own Greek names lacked originality – names such as *Taxiarchis, Agios Joannis* and *Evangelestria* cropping up with monotonous regularity although they hailed from different islands – they were given official Navy numbers, commencing at LS1 (Levant Schooner No 1). Early in 1944, however, the flotilla was renamed the 'Anglo-Hellenic Schooner Flotilla' (AHSF), the Admiralty having pointed out that the abbreviation 'LSF' referred to Fighter Direction Ships. Thus LS1 became AHSF1, and so on. But among themselves the crews continued to stick to the original designation – even today their annual reunion get-togethers are held under the title of 'Levant Schooner Flotilla'.

Normally engaged in such peacetime pursuits as fishing, sponge fishing and inter-island trading, the caiques varied in size from about five to as much as 250 tons, with one or two masts depending on tonnage and rig. Of wooden construction, their design varied although remaining basically that of the small caique, with a raked stem, transom stern, and considerable sheer fore and aft, and one mast with a lateen sail similar to a felucca. The larger vessels had a counter stern and bowsprit, two masts and schooner type, or lugger, rig. A few of the latter were taken over to become headquarters ships, fuel, store and repair ships; the smaller ones were converted for operational use, which also involved stepping their masts in tabernacles so that they could be lowered to enable the vessel to be camouflaged when lying up close inshore.

Good sea boats, they were, however, very wet in a seaway due to their low freeboard, and a canvas dodger had to be rigged along the gunwales in rough weather to render them somewhat less wet and uncomfortable inboard. On conversion to naval use, a messdeck was fitted where possible under the foredeck with just enough headroom for two-tier bunks, the customary small cabin aft being used as a chartroom and radio compartment. Steering was done with a tiller from the raised afterdeck. Two anchors were carried forward, using a 5-inch hemp rope as cable, and two lighter ones aft on 4-inch coir ropes to act as a drogue during landings.

Comparatively slow under sail, most of the caiques had boasted an ageing and asthmatic diesel or petrol engine as the principal means of propulsion. The army replaced these with specially converted Matilda tank engines, to give a speed of about 8 knots and an endurance range of some 2,000 miles. Thus in some of the vessels it was not uncommon to find a Tank Corps NCO instead of a naval stoker doing duty as engineer. On operations they carried some 400 gallons of fuel, 80 gallons of fresh water, and provisions for two or three months, mostly tinned. These were supplemented by eggs and chickens obtained from shore were possible, payment frequently being made in the universal currency of cigarettes. Cooking was by Calor gas or paraffin pressure stoves, the latter occasionally proving to be something of a hazrd.

Although lemon powder and anti-scorbutic pills were supplied, it was not uncommon for the crews to suffer from sea boils, brought on by a combination of poor diet, days and nights of tension, little sleep, and the lack of adequate washing and sanitary facilities. There was, however, no shortage of rum; as with money and provisions, it did not have to be accounted for because of the constantly changing crowd of passengers, being written off as soon as supplied. Commanding officers were also issued with a sum of money in gold sovereigns as a contingency fund to pay for fresh food, repairs, and for use as 'sweeteners' in case local officials should turn awkward in the many anchorages used in Turkish waters.

As basic armament for the caiques the most suitable weapon was found to be the Swiss 20mm Solothurn anti-tank gun, one of these being mounted forward, backed up by two 50-calibre mounted aft on collapsible stands. In addition, holes were bored along the gunwales at strategic points and a brass bush let in to take two .303-inch machine-guns. They also carried mortars for assisting in landing operations; limpet charges; demolition equipment, and smoke canisters. All these items, together with ammunition lockers and other necessary gear, were sited in such a way that they could not be seen from outboard. Personal arms for the crews included tommy guns and revolvers, and any other weapons they fancied. In the early days VHF suitcase-type wireless sets designed to work through ISLD were supplied, being later superseded by special light-weight army sets.

The crews, all of whom had a working knowledge of navigation, signalling, gunnery and camouflage – instruction in the latter art being given by an expert from the Ninth Army in Syria – were naval ratings, Royal Marines, army other ranks and Greeks. The commanding officers were usually young RNVR lieutenants or sub-lieutenants. Morale and team spirit were high, but formal naval discipline tended to be very relaxed. As one commanding officer recorded:

> The crews were volunteers, all, I think, motivated by a sense of adventure and the relative freedom of this kind of naval service. My ship's company consisted of a leading seaman as coxswain, a stoker, wireless operator and myself. The coxswain, who was twenty-two or twenty-three, was the oldest, and our average age must have been about twenty-one.

The crews of the Levant Fishing Patrol, which was based at Haifa, were even more polyglot. Thus the commanding officer was often an army captain, or even a major, with a corporal as wireless operator and boatswain, another soldier as engineer/gunner, and a Greek civilian as seaman cook. The captain of one LFP caique which bore the unlikely name of *Santa Claus* was a regimental sergeant-major of the Queen's Own Hussars, and the ship's mate was a staff sergeant-major. The rest of the crew was a mixture of British soldiers and Greek fishermen. In an official report Admiral Sir John Cunningham, then Commander-in-Chief, Levant, wrote: 'Their operations in the area will long remain a fine example of seamanship, fortitude and initiative.'

At sea the LSF/AHSF vessels flew their own special 'house flag'. This was one of Seligman's ideas, who decreed that it could be of any shape or colour so long as it bore the design of a schooner between the letters 'L' and 'F'. He also dreamed up the unofficial motto 'Stand Boldly On' for the flotilla, a sentiment of which Nelson would surely have approved.

Since the caiques were operating in enemy-controlled waters, camouflage when lying up en route to or from an expedition, or while waiting to re-embark a raiding party, was of the greatest importance, particularly as enemy aircraft dominated the Aegean skies. Netting was chiefly used for the purpose, distributed so as to cover the whole ship, and supported on bamboo poles with spreaders to form an irregular shape and break up the outline of the hull. It proved so effective that a caique lying quietly anchored a few hundred yards away from the enemy, even in broad daylight, could be made indistinguishable. Nothing was allowed to be thrown overboard while lying up, because the clarity of the water would have shown up such tell-tale debris. Empty food tins had therefore to be retained until at sea, when they were punctured before being jettisoned. Landings on enemy-held islands were invariably made at night with all gear down to present a low profile and with the engine running quietly at slow speed.

The flotilla early met with misfortune. *LS4*, in peacetime the 10-ton *Natalie*, disappeared at sea on her first voyage as a minor British war vessel. In company with *LS3* she had sailed on a trial trip from Haifa to Cyprus with a crew of six. All went well until the vessels were within forty miles of the Cyprus coast. Then in falling darkness and poor visibility they lost touch. Sub-Lieutenant Bradbeer in command of *LS3* reduced speed thinking that his consort was experiencing engine trouble. When she failed to appear he searched the area for some time, then, deciding that she had probably passed him unseen, continued on to Paphos. But *LS4* never turned up, and as a subsequent air search failed to find any trace of her, it was considered that she had fallen victim to a U-boat.

Not long after this *LS1*, the 7-ton former *Tinos*, commanded by

Londos, while returning from a reconnaissance trip into the Cyclades, struck a submerged reef off the island of Sirina and became a total loss. Fortunately no lives were lost on this occasion.

These, then, were the vessels which, with motor torpedo boats and Fairmile motor launches provided by Coastal Forces, Mediterranean, and a number of RAF air/sea rescue vessels, were for many months to come to transport to and from their objectives the men of Raiding Forces, Middle East who, in the colourful words of one war correspondent, conducted 'a small but murderous campaign fought chiefly at close quarters with grappling hook and bayonet, tommy gun and revolver'. Waxing even more melodramatic, although not very far from the truth, since when the Germans got to know the names of prominent personalities in the organisation* and their methods they threatened the direst penalties against them and any of their associates who might be captured, he went on:

> Hardened by months of fighting in which no quarter is given, every one of them is a killer. They lack only a cutlass apiece to appear the very image of the pirates they emulate. The little ships thread their way through the maze of islands in the Aegean to land these men on German-held territory. Then in small patrols they proceed to stalk the enemy garrison. Nine times out of ten the latter are taken completely by surprise, and the raiders have struck and are away before the Germans know what is happening. In this way wireless stations are destroyed, petrol and ammunition dumps blown up, Greek hostages released and prisoners taken. Frequently a whole German garrison is killed or captured with not one left to tell the tale when the next enemy supply ship calls at the island.

Appropriately enough, the code name for these operations was 'Fire Eater'.

Throughout the spring and summer months of 1943 the various units of Raiding Forces, Middle East operated over a wide area which extended beyond the Aegean – even as far afield as northern Italy – usually being transported by submarine. Thus in March a

---

* One of the most ruthless of these was Major 'Andy' Lassen of the SBS who led many epic missions to enemy-held Aegean islands. 24-year old Anders Frederick Lassen was a Dane who, after serving in the British merchant navy, joined the British Army when his country was occupied by the Germans in 1940, and was later commissioned in the Commandos. He won the MC and Bar for his exploits in the Aegean, but was later killed when leading a raiding patrol while attached to the Eighth Army in Italy and posthumously awarded the Victoria Cross.

new leader of the Corsican Patriot movement and his staff were secretly landed in that island, and his predecessor and henchmen subsequently taken off. Agents were put ashore in Italy, Crete and Rhodes, deception parties in Sardinia, the island of Lampedusa and airfields in Crete raided, and a reconnaissance made of the Salerno beaches in preparation for Allied landings being planned in that area.

Not all the operations were successful. Towards the end of June a number of parties of SAS and SBS, comprising in all six officers and eighteen other ranks, were landed from submarine and dropped by parachute to attack enemy aerodromes in Sardinia. Unhappily everything went wrong. Almost at the outset one party lost its guide, several men were struck down by malaria, from which three subsequently died due to lack of adequate treatment, and three others were killed in action. The survivors were eventually rounded up by the Italians, by whom they were very badly treated. One NCO was kept in solitary confinement for days in an attempt to break his morale; other prisoners were threatened with thumbscrews, and some kept in chains in the most degrading surroundings.

Subsequently all but one were removed to the mainland to be sent to prisoner-of-war camps. The man left behind, Sergeant Scully of the Sherwood Foresters, who had been seriously ill with malaria at the time, was finally liberated by the Americans after the Italian armistice. Not one of the parties had managed to reach its objective.

A hazardous operation with a happier ending was the rescue of Stoker Capes of the submarine *Perseus*.

By May 1942 the islanders in Cephalonia who had been looking after Capes and hiding him from the Italians for months – although he narrowly escaped capture on more than one occasion – had managed to contact an agent of 'A' Force and inform them of his existence.

Among the patriotic Greeks who were working for that organisation was Miltoniades Houmas, master of the caique *Evangelestria*. A native of the island of Chios, Houmas, known as 'Captain Milton', had joined up with the British in 1941. He soon became the most outstanding figure among the caique skippers working for 'A' Force, and was awarded the OBE for his exploits. 'He was always the first to volunteer for any expedition of an unusually hazardous nature, and because of his skill as a sailor, iron nerve, great resource, and commonsense in emergency, was always selected.' Since January 1943 he had already made forty journeys to enemy-occupied territory. The rescue of Capes was considered to be a mission requiring more than normal courage and ability, and Houmas was accordingly chosen for the task.

The *Evangelestria*'s trip across the Aegean to Cephalonia involved a voyage of hundreds of miles through water constantly patrolled by enemy ships and aircraft. Accomplishing the first part of the journey without incident, Houmas sailed boldly into the small Cephalonian harbour of Poros where he was subjected by the Italian harbour police to a long and detailed interrogation regarding the irregularities of his arrival and lack of necessary permits. But he had plenty of experience of dealing with bullying officials and managed to lull their suspicions. Meanwhile the agent he had brought, whose duty was to contact Capes, was quietly slipped ashore. The Italians then ordered Houmas to go to another port.

On arrival there his caique was again boarded by Italian police, but by adroit replies to their questioning and judicious bribery he managed to retain comparative freedom. He now decided that it was necessary to meet Capes himself, despite the fact that this entailed a long journey overland, since the stoker was being frequently moved from one 'safe house' to another. Finally, having evolved a workable plan of escape, Houmas sailed his caique back to Poros, to which Capes was to be taken by his Greek helpers and hidden in an empty house overlooking the quay.

Then, early one morning, the stoker was taken to a small bay about three miles away. Sentries had been posted on a hill behind the bay and at either end of it to warn the escaping party if the Italians came. In fact an Italian *MAS* boat did suddenly appear and came close inshore at slow speed before moving off again northwards. Capes and his companions hid in the rocks and were not seen.

Half an hour later a caique appeared, hove to in the bay and lowered a boat. It was the *Evangelestria*, Houmas having earlier left harbour as if on a normal fishing trip. Capes and the Greek agent were swiftly embarked, and the *Evangelestria* sailed off to Turkey, where she duly arrived safely, having completed a round trip of more than a thousand miles.

In December 1943, after his return to the United Kingdom, Stoker John Capes was awarded the British Empire Medal, not only for his courage, perserverance and calm judgement in extricating himself from the wrecked *Perseus*, but also for his skill and tenacity in escaping from enemy clutches in Cephalonia.

As for 'Captain Milton', he continued to serve 'A' Force with such gallantry that he was eventually awarded the DSO, the decoration being presented by the Commander-in-Chief, Mediterranean in 1945. One of the exploits which contributed to this high award being made took place only ten days after his return from Cephalonia. Sent out to search for Allied escapers from the Dodecanese island of Samos, Houmas left his caique lying up in a nearby inlet and set off alone in a dinghy..

On his way to the shore he was surprised by an enemy patrol boat, which he proceeded to engage with his tommy gun. 'Although his frail craft afforded no cover or protection, he closed with the patrol boat, succeeded in killing four of the Italians on board, and escaped in the subsequent confusion.' Unhappily his caique crew had become alarmed by the sound of firing and sailed away, leaving him behind. Houmas then spent the next fifteen days dodging the enemy in Samos while he searched unsuccessfully for evaders. Finally he stole a boat and calmly rowed back to Turkey where he arrived still carrying his tommy gun!

*

In January 1943 a conference between President Roosevelt and Winston Churchill, accompanied by their advisers, was held at Casablanca to establish strategic military objectives for the coming year. One of the decisions taken was to capture Sicily at the earliest possible date after the conclusion of the North African campaign. Planning was accordingly begun by Middle East Command and went on throughout the closing stages of the fighting in Tunisia.

As the Allied forces closed in, the enemy was driven into the Cape Bon area, and finally capitulated on 12 May. Next the strongly defended islands of Pantelleria and Lampedusa were taken in mid-June, both of which surrendered after heavy bombing and naval bombardment before the Allied assault forces could land. A month later the invasion of Sicily was launched.

By now the Italians had little heart for further fighting, even on their own soil, and the principal resistance was put up by the Germans. The campaign lasted little more than a month, the climax being reached in mid-August when the Germans retreated to the mainland. A fortnight later British troops landed north of

Reggio virtually unopposed.

The collapse of Italy was complete. Mussolini had been arrested on 26 July, and Marshal Badoglio had formed a new government with the object of seeking peace. Even while secret negotiations to this end were taking place, a fresh Allied landing was about to be made at Salerno with the object of capturing the port of Naples. Announcement of the signing of the armistice with Italy was made while the Allied expeditionary force was en route, but the Germans had already made their plans, and the landings were to be strongly opposed. Next day the Italian fleet sailed to Malta and surrendered.

At the Casablanca conference General Maitland Wilson, British Commander-in-Chief, Middle East had also been ordered to plan when required for land operations elsewhere in the eastern Mediterranean, including the Aegean islands. In particular Churchill wanted the Dodecanese to be seized. Possession of these would bring important strategic advantages: Turkey might be encouraged to enter the war on the side of the Allies, and Russia could be supplied through the Dardanelles, thus obviating the need for the hazardous Arctic convoys.

Rhodes was the key island of the Dodecanese, then Leros and Cos, the latter of which possessed an airfield from which fighters could operate. Unfortunately, in order to accomplish these aims, Maitland Wilson's forces would need to be reinforced, particularly as regards shipping and air cover. Accordingly Operation 'Accolade', the capture of Rhodes, was planned and troops allocated in readiness. On four occasions a force was assembled and partially prepared for the operation, on the last of which a division was actually embarked. But the Americans would not agree to any diversion from the campaign in Italy, where fierce fighting was in progress. 'Accolade' had therefore to be abandoned.

Yet had we known it, the Germans were worried about our intentions in the Aegean, the Commander-in-Chief, South-East considering that his forces were insufficient for land, sea or air defences in the area, since it was no longer supplied via the Adriatic.

But their plans to cope with events after the Italian armistice had been well laid, and when the code word *Achse* (Axis) was given, were speedily implemented. This ordered that Italian positions in France and throughout the Balkans were to be taken over; important installations and positions in Italy to be seized; the

Italian fleet to be captured, and German forces to take up new defensive positions.

Aided by the Italian Eleventh Army commander, headquartered at Athens, who refused to co-operate with the Allies (in fact he had little choice since his command had already been taken over by the German Commander-in-Chief, South-East) the Germans were able to acquire in Greek ports some 32 Italian naval vessels, including destroyers and torpedo boats, and six merchantmen, including two tankers. Cephalonia, Corfu and Crete were taken over, the pro-Allied commandant of Corfu being shot, and in Rhodes General von Kleeman, despite his *Sturm Division* being heavily outnumbered by their former Italian allies, forced the capitulation of that island by its vacillating Italian Governor, Admiral Campioni. He then proceeded to strengthen the garrisons on Scarpanto and the neighbouring islands of Casos and Saria where there were radar stations. Subsequently substantial reinforcements of Luftwaffe fighters and dive-bombers arrived in the island.

Since 'Accolade' could not be proceeded with, the best that could be done by Middle East Command was to slip small garrisons into the more important islands where there were few or no Germans, and patrols into other outlying ones to encourage Italian resistance, and take over and hold strategic strongpoints until the arrival of regular troops. And for this the Raiding Forces were to spearhead the expeditions. Fairmile motor launches and caiques crammed with men of the SBS, LRDG and SAS accordingly set forth from Beirut to carry out their assigned tasks, hugging the Turkish coast and flying the Turkish flag.

The majority of the Italian-controlled islands of the Dodecanese were garrisoned only by Italian troops, whose attitude was nevertheless doubtful because of truculent Fascist elements among them. In Leros, for example, a large percentage of the Italian officers were strongly Fascist. Most of their men, however, were war-weary and homesick, and had only one thought in mind – to return alive to Italy as soon as possible, an attitude strengthened by the shortage of supplies, dread of imprisonment and death at the hands of the Germans for betrayal, and the fear of slaughter by the Greek population in revenge for past crimes. Contrary to our belief, the garrisons were poorly equipped for either air or ground defence.

The first capture by the Raiding Forces was the tiny island of Casteloriso, situated close to the Turkish coast and about eighty miles south-east of Rhodes. First seized from the Italians by a small force of British Commandos in 1941, it had been recaptured soon afterwards by the enemy with the aid of dive-bombers from Rhodes, and its garrison considerably strengthened. On 10 September the island fell to some fifty men of the SBS after slight opposition and, code-named 'Trombone', became an advanced base and staging post for further operations in the Aegean.

On the previous day a small mission headed by Majors Lord Jellicoe and Dalby had tried to parachute into Rhodes to contact Admiral Campioni and persuade him to throw in his lot with the Allies and disarm the outnumbered Germans, but were prevented by bad weather. By the time they arrived on the 10th via Casteloriso, von Kleeman had had an extra day in which to organise and undermine Italian morale; thus Campioni lost heart and refused to deal with us. Ninety of his officers were subsequently shot by the Germans.

Other islands with no German garrisons fell to the Raiding Forces. Cos and Samos were secured by the SBS detachment which had captured Casteloriso, along with the Greek Sacred Squadron. Then followed Leros, Symi, Stampalia and Icaria on 18 September, and Calymnos a few days later. In Symi an advanced raiding base was speedily established under Lapraik, and Andy Lassen was sent to take over and strengthen the defences of Calchi, a few miles north-west of Rhodes, which was garrisoned by a dozen Carabinieri.

From Leros, which became our principal advanced operational base under a naval captain, designated Senior British Naval Officer, Aegean (SBNO), where Turnbull himself had arrived, Raiding Force caiques set out across waters patrolled by hostile surface craft and under constant threat of air attack, to collect intelligence and land patrols with wireless sets on outlying islands as far west as the Cyclades. The task of the patrols was to acquire information about German strengths and dispositions, and to keep watch on enemy shipping and air movements, being later withdrawn and replaced with fresh troops.

In several of the islands on which they landed Germans were present in varying strengths who soon became aware of the arrival of the British patrols, and a deadly game of hide and seek frequently ensued. Thus on Kithnos, 100 miles west of Leros in the Cyclades where a seven-man patrol was put ashore, the Germans maintained a wireless D/F station. Fortunately for the patrol, the enemy did not have sufficient men to search for them, and by frequently changing their locality they were able to remain on Kithnos for a month sending back valuable reports.

Another seven-man patrol was landed on Naxos, largest island in the Cyclades, which had a German garrison of 650 men. Aided by patriotic islanders, the patrol dodged enemy search parties for seventeen days, during which they managed to report considerable enemy shipping movements. As will be seen, one of their reports led to the almost total destruction of a German invasion convoy.

On Seriphos a six-man patrol set up their lookout post in an abandoned goatshed on the summit of a high cliff. The enemy garrison was quartered in the town a few miles away, but the local Greeks organised an efficient warning system which went into operation whenever German troops appeared likely to approach the patrol's hideout. Not least of the latter's worries was the persistent attentions of low-flying German aircraft, whose aim was to prevent the transmission of vital information. Nevertheless the Raiding Force men remained on the island for three weeks without discovery, and were duly relieved by a fresh patrol at the end of that time.

Meanwhile motor torpedo boats and Fairmile motor launches of Coastal Forces were employed on coastal patrols around the captured islands, helping to augment the AA defences, landing operations and the transport of troops, in rescue work, off-loading stores brought by the destroyers of Levant Command, and running supplies to other islands. By 28 September 2,700 men had been landed, 21 guns, 7 vehicles and 450 tons of stores and ammunition. Acting on air reconnaissance and reports from agents in the Piraeus area, destroyers carried out sweeps against enemy merchant shipping in the Aegean at night, returning to Samos or lying up in Leros during the day.

But all these efforts were doomed to end in humiliating defeat because insufficient forces were available, lack of adequate shipping and landing craft to transport heavier weapons and vehicles, the dire need for efficient anti-aircraft defences, and the fact that the nearest Allied air cover was based in Cyprus, 350 miles away, while enemy airfields were in close proximity.

German reaction to reports of the British landings was swift. Orders came from Berlin that the entire Aegean area was to be reinforced and defended. Troops were accordingly withdrawn from the Balkans, aircraft from France and the Russian front, barges and lighters wherever they could be obtained, and transport planes to operate between Greece, Crete and Rhodes. By mid-September the Germans had sent raiding forces to the Cyclades to evacuate Italian garrisons and such food and war materials as they could lay their hands on. They did not garrison all the islands in force, but established observation positions on the strategically placed.

The arrival of heavy enemy reinforcements in the area soon made their presence felt. In bombing attacks on Leros two Allied destroyers were sunk, and the activities of our surface forces were restricted to sweeps in the dark hours. Subsequently these bombing attacks were stepped up by large numbers of Ju88s, no alarm being given and little or no AA fire opened by the Italian gunners. On 1 October the available fleet destroyers of the Levant Command were ordered to Malta for escort duty, and this left only the smaller Hunt class whose speed and endurance made it difficult for them to operate far into the Aegean and get clear by daylight.

Then came the first enemy success in his campaign to recapture the islands we had taken. Resulting from information received that enemy shipping and landing craft were being assembled at the Piraeus and in Cretan harbours and embarking troops and equipment, three Levant Command destroyers, two of them Greek, were ordered to patrol to the east of Crete. By the night of the 2 October they were running short of fuel and in no position to take action on a report from one of our reconnaissance aircraft of an enemy convoy sighted off Naxos believed to be bound for Rhodes. Since this was well to the north, however, the destroyers were ordered to Alexandria to fuel.

Unhappily the convoy was in fact bound for Cos, and at 0500 on the 3rd enemy invasion forces landed on that island, the seaborne assault being reinforced by paratroops. Since no surface forces were available to interfere with the landing, submarines on patrol were ordered to the area to attack enemy invasion shipping. The British battalion on Cos received little assistance from the Italian garrison, and although they resisted stubbornly, they were speedily overwhelmed, and all resistance had ceased by the 4th. In consequence nearby Calymnos had to be evacuated, and advanced Raiding Force headquarters, which had been transferred to that island, was withdrawn to Leros. The loss of Cos brought about an almost total collapse of Italian morale.

An attempt by the Germans to capture Symi, however, was repulsed with considerable loss to the enemy by the SBS-stiffened garrison headed by Lapraik and Lassen. The island was then subjected to heavy bombing, and Lapraik was finally ordered to withdraw. The Germans now began to prepare for the eventual invasion of Leros, and daily bombing raids against that island and Samos became continuous, the enemy airmen selecting their targets and systematically destroying them one by one.

Meanwhile, supplemented by air drops from Cairo, destroyers from Alexandria, submarines from Beirut, Coastal Force craft and Raiding Force caiques continued to run the gauntlet of enemy air attacks to bring supplies and reinforcements to those hard-pressed islands. By arrangement with the Turkish government, supplies had been moved to that country for the purpose, and some forty anchorages along the coast made available.

Following the fall of Cos some of the caiques were diverted to evacuate survivors from that island. Conspicious among these rescue missions were those carried out by *LS2* under the command of Lieutenant Alex McLeod, RNVR, and the efforts of an SBS detachment under the leadership of Captain Walter Milner-Barry. The latter's experiences are worth relating in some detail.

On the night of 3 October he, along with another SBS officer and twelve men, were landed from *LS2* on Cos to do, in his own words, 'A bit of sabotage of planes, vehicles, etc., if fighting was still going on.' If resistance had ended, however, Milner-Barry had been told to get out as soon as he could, and warned that he might become involved with evacuation work. McLeod arranged to return for them at the same or a nearby beach on the night of the 7th.

Disembarking just before dawn, the party had only time to hole up in an inlet because the LRDG wireless set they had brought, which Milner-Barry had been told could be handled by three men, was found to need seven to carry it about. They spent the whole of that day in their place of concealment watching German dive-bombers strafe the auxiliary airfield being constructed at Antimachina, then proceed systematically to flatten the principal aerodrome at Cardamenas. During the day a few escaping RAF personnel were contacted; then Italians began to filter in from Cardamenas.

Late that afternoon German lorried infantry appeared and began driving across the plain from the bombed aerodrome towards the party's hiding place. The panic-stricken Italians fleeing before them swarmed into the inlet from both ends and ran screaming about the beaches. When the Germans started to bring down mortar fire on them, Milner-Barry decided that the time had come to get out.

In any event he had intended to 'whistle up a boat' to take his party and the RAF evaders off that night if possible, 'but my bloody wireless set would receive but not transmit'.

The party then moved off down the coast for about two miles where they discovered some rafts the Italians had built and 'very sensibly abandoned'. Milner-Barry offered all hands the chance to leave the island by this means, and everyone volunteered except two RAF men who said they could not swim. It seemed obvious that with the Germans holding the hills and apparently intending to drive along the coast and comb all the coves and inlets the Britons would otherwise be bound to be caught. 'Left to ourselves we should have stood a fair chance,' he wrote in his subsequent report, 'but with the wadis full of hysterial Italians who wouldn't leave us, we should not have been able to conceal ourselves.'

In the end more than a dozen men put to sea on the rafts. The one that Milner-Barry clung to rode so low that he was up to his neck in water. Good progress was made for a couple of miles, but then they got into a current which carried them eastwards. During this time Milner-Barry's raft became more and more waterlogged. After paddling desperately for about three hours it was evident that they were making no headway, so they all turned round and tried to paddle back to the shore. 'But the bloody raft wouldn't move that way either,' recorded Milner-Barry, 'so there was nothing for it but to swim, jettisoning binoculars, revolvers, torches, and anything heavy.' Fortunately for him as it turned out, Milner-Barry kept his boots on.

The swim took about two hours, and the exhausted men landed on a beach close to a waterhole, and found a cave in which to bed down for the night. With the captain were three other ranks of his original SBS party. Next day he collected more of his men and some of the RAF ground staff, and made contact with some Greek shepherds from whom they obtained food and information. But when they searched the beach for the packs they had brought with them and hidden, these had disappeared, having presumably been discovered and taken by the Italians.

On the 6th with the aid of the Greeks more RAF personnel were found, and next day some men of the Durham Light Infantry who had formed part of the island's British garrison. By now the party's movements were restricted as they only had three pairs of boots between them, and some of the SBS were suffering from exhaustion due to their long swim and lack of food.

When darkness fell on the evening of the 7th they made their way along to another beach where they found the second raiding party officer who also had a party of escapers with him, and it was into this beach that Milner-Barry was able to signal *LS2* which, true to the promise made by McLeod, had returned to make the pickup. She took off twenty-three escapers at about midnight, then came in again some three and a half hours later for the other nineteen. All were landed at a deserted point on the Turkish mainland. Milner-Barry with two of his men, Lance-Corporal Watson and Gunner Geddes, remained behind however to search for further parties of evaders who might be hiding in the hills or trying to find their way to the shore. Arrangements had been made with McLeod that he would return to collect the SBS men around midnight in four days' time.

The three set off inland, and the next night made contact with a party of one Durham Light Infantry officer and sixteen of his men. Security among the Greek islanders was so good, however, that it took a further two days to discover another party of British evaders hiding in the hills, whom the SBS men led down to the beach. The whole party, totalling more than fifty officers and men, was duly taken off by McLeod on the night of the 12th.

Soon afterwards an important until of the flotilla was lost in circumstances which illustrate the peculiar hazards of this phase of the inter-island war.

Apart from the provision of some temporary air support for a few days, General Eisenhower, Supreme Allied Commander in the Mediterranean, continued to refuse to divert forces and equipment to the Aegean operations, being backed up in his stand by President Roosevelt despite Churchill's personal appeals. Following the fall of Cos the Admiralty, however, did order the cruisers *Aurora, Penelope, Sirius* and *Dido* and two fleet destroyers from Malta to proceed with all despatch to the area, but because of enemy air mastery the ships could operate only by night to avoid crippling loss.

On 6 October the LRDG patrol on Naxos sighted and reported an enemy convoy consisting of an ammunition ship and six ferry barges crammed with troops en route to swell the German invasion forces assembling at Cos. During the hours of darkness on the 7th the cruisers *Penelope* and *Sirius*, accompanied by their two fleet destroyers, duly fell upon the convoy and practically annihilated it, only one ferry barge managing to escape. Caught in daylight by enemy bombers, however, while they were withdrawing from the area, the *Penelope* was severely damaged.

Some eighty survivors from the convoy eventually reached Stampalia, where they were rounded up by Raiding Force troops on the island. When news of the affair reached Leros the trawler *Hedgehog*, commanded by Sub-Lieutenant Harding, RNVR, which was about to sail with provisions and stores for the LRDG men, was ordered to bring back the German wounded and a maximum of ten unwounded for interrogation. Two soldiers were embarked as guards for the enemy prisoners.

The trawler accomplished the first part of her mission without mishap, but on her way back to Leros she developed engine trouble. To effect repairs, Harding decided to put in to the small island of Levitha, some twenty miles south-west of Leros, which was thought to be unoccupied by the enemy. Unfortunately the island was in the hands of the Germans. The trawler was attacked and set on fire, and Harding and his crew taken prisoner, their former captives having managed to overpower them. It was not until two days later when a motor launch became available to go in search of the missing vessel that the wreck of the trawler was spotted still smouldering in the harbour, and the launch itself was fired on when trying to approach the island.

An operation to retake Levitha was then staged by the Raiding Forces in Leros, one important reason for recapturing the island being that it could be used as an observation post and warning station against a German attack on Leros. Although hastily conceived, the attack went according to plan. Unhappily not only were the Germans present in considerable strength but, aided by bombers from Cos, they compelled the invaders to surrender before they could establish themselves ashore. This failure demonstrated the effectiveness of air support.

Throughout the rest of the month efforts continued to supply and reinforce Leros and Samos, while available cruisers and destroyers made occasional forays against enemy shipping in the Aegean, covered by such air strength as could be provided. But losses were heavy, not only from air bombing but also enemy minelaying. By the end of the month our naval forces were so reduced that they could hardly continue to reinforce Leros, much less carry out offensive sweeps.

In that badly battered island the local population was reduced to living in caves, while the caique crews were forced to quit their vessels at night and come ashore to seek shelter in the open or behind the walls of wrecked buildings in order to snatch a few hours much-needed sleep. The constant threat of air attack not only denied them adequate rest, but also the proper maintenance of their vessels. Destroyers and other craft bringing supplies had to creep in after dark and get away before dawn to escape the attentions of the Stukas. Such military stores as could be got ashore were looted by the civilian population since they could only be insufficiently guarded. It was also obvious that Fascist elements among the Italians were aiding the Germans, since our every move seemed to be known to the latter.

Up to the end of October military operations in the Aegean had been controlled by Middle East Command through 3 Corps Headquarters – known as 'Force 292' – and 234 Brigade under the command of Major-General Francis Brittorous, headquartered on Leros. On 1 November Major-General H.R. Hall was appointed GOC Aegean with orders to hold Leros and Samos, and he duly set up his headquarters in the latter island. The SBNO remained on Leros, and was fated later to be taken prisoner.

The occupation of Levitha, coupled with the steady German build-up in Cos and Calymnos, and the intensifying air attacks on Leros and Samos pointed to an imminent attack on the former island, and an atmosphere of foreboding pervaded the place. It was difficult for our few surface warships to interfere with the stealthy approach of enemy invasion craft moving east with troops from Greece and Crete since they laid up during daylight hours in various island harbours under strong air cover and moved only by night.

Then, early in the morning of 12 November, the blow fell. Leros was invaded from the sea at a number of points, while paratroops were dropped on the narrow waist of the island, thus cutting the defences in two. Wave after wave of dive-bombers pinned down the defenders. The three available British destroyers which had retired to an anchorage off the Turkish coast, came in to bombard enemy shore targets after dark, but they were too late, and efforts to reinforce the defenders from Samos were hampered by bad weather. Although the British put up 'a tenacious resistance', according to the German report on the operation, the garrison – the Italians being less than enthusiastic – was gradually overwhelmed, and finally forced to capitulate on the 16th. Four days later Samos was evacuated as being indefensible, the withdrawal being carried out at night and, towards the end of the month, Casteloriso also abandoned except for a token force.

Since success or failure to hold the islands we had occupied depended more on air power than any other single factor, the outcome was inevitable. Yet the Germans themselves had been doubtful if they could take Leros, Lieutenant-General Mueller who commanded the operation, being subsequently commended by Hitler himself for making the capture 'with limited means and in the face of various setbacks'. German losses had been heavy, a great many of their troops being drowned before they could reach the beaches.

Orders were now given for all caiques and schooners in the forward area to be withdrawn to Beirut to refit and reorganise, but along with a number of Coastal Force motor launches some remained behind for almost a fortnight to carry out evacuation schemes previously prepared. Operating from anchorages along the Turkish coast, they made repeated trips to the islands to rescue isolated parties of British troops, including several senior officers. Seligman himself got back to Beirut from Samos via Turkey.

Prominent in these operations was Lieutenant-Commander Ramseyer. He had commanded the coastal forces which landed the first Allied troops in the Aegean islands after the Italian armistice, and subsequently became the SBNO's right-hand man at Leros, working ashore as his senior staff officer. During the period from mid-September until Leros capitulated Ramseyer had been responsible for the naval side of Raiding Force operations. At the height of the battle for the island he collected scattered groups of men and stimulated them to further resistance.

In the words of General Maitland Wilson, who personally recommended him for an immediate decoration:

> Although he had many other tasks in connection with naval activities in the Aegean which involved continuous days and nights with little or no sleep, Ramseyer was tireless in his efforts to achieve all possible co-operation with the Raiding Forces, and such successful operations as were conducted by them were largely due to his able and efficient organisation. After the capitulation Ramseyer arranged the escape of a considerable number of officers and men, and having reached the Turkish mainland himself, continued to arrange methods of escape although desperately in need of sleep. He acted as commanding officer of various craft involved on several successive nights, refusing to consider his own safety in the dangerous sea journeys between Turkey and Leros. Many of the escapes that were made were due to Ramseyer's efficient organisation.

He was awarded a well deserved DSC.

Apart from some civilian vessels the Raiding Force caiques which took part in these hazardous missions were *LS3, LS7* and *LS8*, while *LS9*, a 130-ton schooner, successfully got away from Samos laden with troops. Most of the men rescued were initially landed at Budrum, in Turkey, some fifty miles from Leros by sea, the only casualty being *LS7*, which was damaged and beached at that place. She was later salvaged and sailed to Beirut. Coastal Force motor launches closed the island beaches after dark and sent in folbots to pick up stragglers and escapers.

Another prominent figure in this work of rescue was 'Captain Milton' of 'A' Force, whose brush with an enemy *MAS* boat off Samos has already been described. This courageous Greek made twenty-five trips to the enemy-occupied islands, during which he brought away forty-eight Imperial personnel, 100 Italian soldiers and many Greek refugees. On one occasion the engine of his caique broke down while en route to Cos. Undaunted, he carried on,' picked up a number of British escapers, then completed the return trip to Turkey by rowing the whole distance, 'a feat difficult to surpass for determination and courage', wrote the commander of the Force, 'not only on account of the mileage involved, but the danger of enemy interception'.

This was very real, for the Germans were concentrating every effort to prevent British escapers; the waters between Turkey and the islands were keenly patrolled from land, sea and air, and were also heavily mined.

*LS2* made a hazardous journey as far as Seriphos, in the Cyclades, to pick up a patrol which, because of the momentous events described, had become long overdue for relief. Returning safely, she brought back not only the patrol, but also six RAF airmen rescued from shot-down aircraft. Another patrol which unexpectedly found itself out on a limb, whose experiences typify the difficulties which had to be faced, was LRDG's *Y1*.

Comprised of five other ranks under the leadership of Captain Moir Stormonth-Darling, the patrol left Alinda Bay, Leros, in *LS8* at dusk on 3 November. Their mission was to establish an observation post on the island of Mykonos, which lies almost in the very centre of the Aegean, keep a 24-hour watch on the harbours in Naxos and Siros and the channel between them along which ran the enemy's principal sea route to Cos. All convoys were to be reported at once.

After lying up during daylight on the 4th at the tiny island of

Stapodia, *LS8* arrived at Mykonos in the early hours of the 5th. The patrol disembarked, all stores were landed and hidden, and they had established themselves in a nearby goatshed by dawn. Local Greek patriots were then contacted, who brought ponies to transport the patrol's personal kit, wireless set and battery over the rugged terrain which led up to the crest of a hill. The observation post was set up in a small chapel which, although in a somewhat exposed position, provided an excellent all-round view.

The leader of the local patriots was a priest, and from him Stormonth-Darling learned that Germans had landed on Mykonos on 27 October and installed themselves in a house on a hill, which they surrounded with barbed wire. They had also taken over the lighthouse, in which they later installed a machine-gun to cover the harbour entrance. At first the Germans had kept aloof from the islanders, but as time went on they made many friends among the Greeks, who were impressed by their manners and smartness, and the fact that their officer spoke Greek and English. Although they were unaware of the presence of the patrol, it was obviously only a matter of time before they found out from their Greek friends.

With the aid of the priest, his helpers and their ponies, the charging engine for the patrol's wireless set, spare batteries and rations, were brought up to the OP, and the rest of the stores buried. Unfortunately they had trouble with the charging engine, and life in the batteries was reduced to five hours. This meant that the frequency of reports had to be drastically curtailed.

The patrol observed and reported a great deal of enemy air traffic, and heard the sounds of distant bombing. On the 11th they learned of the imminent threat to Leros, and next day that the island had been invaded. That night Stormonth-Darling met the priest and discussed with him an escape plan for the islanders, 150 of whom the priest had earlier helped to get away to Samos and the Middle East. It was decided to keep a special watch on the Germans in Mykonos, and volunteers who wished to leave the island evacuated to Samos.

A gale raged all next day, and the patrol was unable to contact either Advanced Headquarters or Cairo on the wireless set. On the 14th the patrol's hiding place was discovered by a crowd of women, and they had to move to a barn and goatshed some distance away. By now there was little life left in the batteries, and even after linking them together they were still too weak to enable Advanced Headquarters to hear their calls. Stormonth-Darling then decided to listen to the BBC until the batteries were flat.

On the 16th the patrol moved to another location and hid up in the house in which they had concealed themselves on their first arrival. All the wireless gear and rations were buried in the sand, and a watch kept on the bay. A great many aircraft were seen, mostly Ju87s, and the sound of bombing now became almost continuous. Then on the 18th Stormonth-Darling learnt from a BBC broadcast that Leros had fallen.

The patriotic Greeks were becoming worried about the number of their fellow-islanders who knew of the presence of the patrol: thus the latter was forced to keep on the move. But as each new hiding place was discovered they attracted an embarrassing number of curious visitors. At any moment the enemy might appear among them. Finally, because of the danger of betrayal which would bring down the wrath of the enemy on the islanders, Stormonth-Darling asked the priest if he could arrange for a caique to take them off.

Fortunately one of the local caique owners who possessed two of these craft, had previously worked for the British. He got together a crew of reliable fishermen who knew the islands well, and on the night of the 24th the patrol got safely away. They were only just in time, for that same day the Germans had declared a ban on all caique movements in the Cyclades, none being allowed to leave harbour without permission.

*

Before the fall of Leros it had been intended, as already mentioned, to form a second caique flotilla with Greek personnel. The First Flotilla under Seligman would have its main base at Beirut and an advanced base in the Samos-Leros area under the operational control of the SBNO Aegean. The Second Flotilla under Londos with predominantly Greek crews was to be based at Alexandria, with an advanced base at Casteloriso, to work under the orders of the Naval Officer in Charge in that island. But now the situation was changed.

Since normal military activities were no longer possible, the Commanders-in-Chief, Middle East decided that operations in the Aegean should continue with the object of disrupting enemy communications to the maximum possible extent by means of Coastal Forces and Raiding Forces, using bases inside Turkish territorial waters. It was also hoped to divert the maximum number of enemy troops in the area to garrison the islands against raids. Outlying garrisons would also be attacked in what one participant felicitously dubbed a '*Nervenkrieg*', while Beaufighters from Cyprus and blockading Allied submarines would strike at enemy shipping and whittle it down until the island garrisons 'withered on the vine'. In short, Operation 'Fire Eater' was to be re-launched with increased fury.

The work of refitting the newly formed First Levant Schooner Flotilla and the formation of the Second was hastened. Londos, now designated Senior Officer, Second LSF, selected a number of caiques in Cyprus and these were sailed to Alexandria for conversion. They were then numbered *LS21* to *28* inclusive. Conversion took longer than anticipated, but the first three were able to join the Raiding Forces in February 1944.

To function as advanced army and naval headquarters ships, anchored in Turkish coastal water, four large schooners were taken up. They were the *Tewfik*, 120 tons; *Agios Georgios*, 100 tons; *Sevasti*, 150 tons, and *Thalia*, 130 tons, which were given the numbers *LS31* to *34*. Two more subsequently joined up to become separate headquarters and store ships for the Greek Sacred Squadron. With a planned increase in Coastal Force operations, there was also a need for fuel caiques.

Difficulties arose, however, in finding suitable Greek crews for these vessels, as the Greek naval commander-in-chief was unable to meet his commitments. The situation was further aggravated by mutinies in the Greek armed forces in April 1944. But by conscripting a number of the original Greek merchant navy sailors, and the provision of certain selected Greek army officers, the operational craft were satisfactorily manned. Unhappily the fact that the Greek merchant navy crews received higher rates of pay under Greek law than either Royal Navy or Royal Hellenic Navy personnel gave rise to a certain amount of friction.

Because of the growing need for more craft to supply forward bases and transport reinforcement and for operational duties, additional caiques were taken over and given AHSF numbers. Most of them were captained by young RNVR sub-lieutenants from the Middle East Combined Operations Base, HMS *Saunders*. By the time operations ceased against the enemy in the Aegean, the AHSF totalled forty-six such vessels of just under 4,000 tons. In addition the Levant Fishing Patrol comprised thirteen caiques ranging from five to eighty tons, for which a 280-ton steam yacht was taken over to act as floating base and workship. With their maintenance and repair base in Cyprus, the number of private caiques in the pay of 'A' Force grew to thirty-two.

In January 1944 the *Tewfik*, along with several operational caiques, was taken forward to be anchored off Turk Buku, in the Gulf of Mandeliyeh, as military headquarters ship. A second Raiding Force anchorage was established in an inlet in the Gulf of Doris off the village of Kiervasili, and a third haven at Port Deremen, in the Gulf of Cos. Many more anchorages along the Anatolian coast were examined as opportunity offered and earmarked for use when required. All were beautiful natural harbours and conveniently situated for mounting Raiding Force operations. Subsequently Seligman was given the title of 'Comaro I' (Commander, Aegean Raiding Operations) with his headquarters in one of the forward base ships, being relieved in the post by other officers at monthly to six-week intervals.

Following their capture of Leros German policy was to strengthen the defences of the more important Aegean islands under their control, and reduce supply problems by evacuating all unwanted persons, who included prisoners, to the mainland. The less important were occupied by small companies for brief periods. To this end German Naval Group Command South requisitioned and repaired every ship it could lay hands on, and began to hasten the despatch of reinforcements and equipment to the garrisoned islands.

At first large vessels, some of which had been brought down from the Black Sea, were used, but when these proved too vulnerable, smaller steamers, caiques and naval auxiliaries were substituted. Despite the fact that we too were disregarding their neutrality, we protested to the Turkish government about German transports and naval auxiliaries being passed through the Dardanelles, a score of which came through in January, claiming that their official inspection was too perfunctory. Eventually, however, these were stopped. The Germans also protested to Ankara, and while Turkish attitudes stiffened somewhat, they showed little desire to check our operations.

Allied aircraft from Middle East bases periodically bombed the Piraeus and carried out offensive sweeps over the Aegean, but although they sank a number of large vessels they lacked the necessary range, and their attacks were not heavy enough to worry the Germans, who were thus afforded a valuable breathing space in which to reinforce their island garrisons. Within a week of the resumption of Raiding Force activities, however, caiques of the Levant Schooner Flotillas began landing detachments on half a dozen islands.

Andy Lassen led a raid on Calchi, a few miles west of Rhodes, and captured a German motor launch which was towed to Turkey with stores and prisoners. Another party landed on Stampalia in bad weather and fought their way through the German defenders to destroy all the shipping in the harbour. On Piscopi the enemy garrison was successfully attacked without loss. On Archi the crew of an RAF Beaufighter which had crashed in the harbour while attacking an enemy caique was rescued by raiders, and in Calymnos a store of oil fuel was blown up and part of the German garrison wiped out.

In one island harbour, used by the Germans as a staging post, a large enemy caique en route from the Piraeus to Rhodes with a supply of troop comforts was captured. The vessel's cargo of champagne, beer, casks of wine, radios, etc., included also a considerable quantity of perfumed toilet rolls. This valuable prize was despatched to Yedi Atala, another of the Raiding Force's Turkish bases, with a solitary Royal Marine as armed guard. He had orders to see that the vessel was scuttled if it should be stopped by the enemy. It duly arrived safely at its destination, where the local villagers were presented with some of the toilet rolls. Apparently unacquainted with their real purpose, the Turks used them instead to decorate the trees around the anchorage!

A detachment which raided Piscopi for the second time learned that two German armed auxiliaries laden with food, wine and reinforcements intended for Cos were due to stage en route at Niseros, one of the islands which was only periodically garrisoned by the enemy. This was reported to base, and a specially assembled raiding party rushed to Niseros to prepare an ambush for the lighters. When the latter arrived, they were attacked and captured after a brief battle which resulted in five enemy killed and seventeen taken prisoner. Both vessels with their cargoes were sailed in triumph to Turkey.

Not the least important and hazardous aspect of Raiding Force operations was reconnaissance. One of the caiques engaged in this work was commanded, not entirely unusually, by a petty officer who, after working with a naval mine disposal unit which accompanied the Eighth Army during its advance from Alamein, had volunteered to transfer to the Levant Schooner Flotilla.

Ordered to take a Royal Marine patrol on a reconnaissance of the island of Milos, in the western Cyclades, he wrote in a report remarkable for its understatement:

> Milos was not a nice place to approach because of enemy D/F gear, searchlights and shore batteries. We therefore decided to land the marines on Kimolos, a neighbouring island, and let them paddle across to Milos in folbots.
>
> While we were lying up at Polygandros waiting to effect the pickup in due course, a gentleman informed us that on another nearby island there were thirteen Germans desirous of surrendering. I said we'd take them, and later that day they entered harbour in their own boat and secured alongside. They were dirty and hungry and had had enough of the war.
>
> The Milos reconnaissance having been successfully completed, we made a round trip of Naxos, Ios, Siphanos and Siphos. But on our way back to base the engine seized up and refused to budge. We had to sail, and once used our two sweeps manned by twelve men on each side. One night with the wind gale force we logged twelve knots for two hours. Finally, however, the wind failed altogether, and we had to be towed the last 40 miles along the gulf of Cos to base.

This cheerfully laconic Lower Deck skipper, who spent twelve months in the flotilla, was eventually awarded the DSM and BEM.

While the caiques of the LSF were thus engaged, Coastal Force craft prowled among the islands, attacking any enemy shipping they could find. Working long hours in narrow and dangerous waters, they took on everything they came across and inflicted damage and loss to the enemy out of all proportion to their size and numbers. The Germans retaliated with heavily armed schooners and other naval auxiliaries. They also employed 'Q-ships', and their minelayers were continually at work mining the channels.

In an assessment of Raiding Force operations from January to the end of July, the Flag Officer, Levant and Eastern Mediterranean (FOLEM) – the appointment having been downgraded from that of a commander-in-chief – reported that as a result the enemy had been forced to increase the strength of his garrisons, withdraw those from isolated positions and concentrate at strategic points, and take special defensive measures, which included mining and wiring all important objectives. In addition a Brandenburg Battalion had been brought in as a counter-measure.

Enemy vessels captured included one 40-ton, one 25-ton, and six smaller caiques; one 100-ton caique 'enticed', and two EMS barges; while 99 vessels totalling more than 2,700 tons, and a Ju52 floatplane had been destroyed. Most of the vessels were carrying arms, ammunition, wheat, olive oil, comforts and other general cargoes. Telecommunications between Niseros, Cos, Leros and Patmos had been cut; telephone lines on Stampalia destroyed; a cable station on Calino damaged and the cable head cut; a wireless station on Santorini destroyed; a wireless set and valuable documents captured on Amorgos together with arms and equipment; a cable hut and submarine cable, slipways and a motor hut on Chios destroyed; a wireless station, telephone exchange and twelve telephones, baggage room, caique yard, shipbuilding facilities and fortifications destroyed on Symi and a cable to Piscopi and Niseros cut; and an olive oil warehouse fired on Mitylene.

Stores destroyed included 2,000 gallons of petrol on Piscopi; a ton of explosives on Amorgos and six tons of ammunition on Cos; a 15-ton diesel fuel dump, two large ammunition dumps, and a 5-ton store of explosives on Symi; and seven petrol dumps totalling between 500-600 tons in Crete. Local resistance was especially active in the latter island, and, aided by Raiding Force parties and officers from Force 133, the German garrison was continually harassed. Agents and supplies of arms and stores were landed in the face of such hazards as a network of enemy radar stations, coastal defences, and offshore schooner patrols. Helped by local *Andartes*, one Force 133 party even ambushed and kidnapped the German garrison commander of the island.

Arms, equipment and vehicles destroyed by the Raiding Forces in their depredations included guns, mortars, rifles, pistols, grenades, trucks, staff cars and searchlights. 370 casualties, sixty per cent of them German, had been inflicted, prisoners, both German and Italian, had been taken, from whom much valuable information had been obtained; also Quislings and Axis collaborators. The crew of a Beaufighter had been rescued, more than 100 Greek refugees taken off along with any who might have been threatened by the enemy through giving help to the Allies. Wherever possible food had been landed for the Greek islanders.

The cost in Allied casualties and craft had been comparatively light. Four officers and twenty-one other ranks of the Raiding Forces had been killed, wounded or taken prisoner; and seven officers and nineteen ratings of the RN and Royal Hellenic Navy killed, wounded or missing. A motor launch had been lost by stranding, and a caique crew with a raiding party killed or captured, but they had managed to destroy their ship. Another motor launch had foundered, and a motor launch and motor torpedo boat damaged. More than thirty islands had been raided, some as far west as the southern Cyclades.

Levant Fishing Patrol caiques had been equally active about their own clandestine business. Typical was Operation 'Noah's Ark', carried out by *LF8*, a 50-ton schooner-rigged caique armed with concealed Breda guns and commanded by Sub-Lieutenant Spanos of the Royal Hellenic Naval Reserve. Her mission was to carry as many tons of stores as possible from Famagusta to Egrilar, near Izmir. Also taking part in the operation was *LF9* commanded by Captain Pagniez of the Essex Regiment.

The passage from Haifa to Cyprus was uneventful, apart from a U-boat scare which caused a delay of several days. But from then on the weather turned sour, bringing heavy gales accompanied by hail and rain. The two caique captains decided to take different routes to their destination, *LF8* going north around Cyprus and *LF9* going southabout. But both experienced identical weather conditions on their 600-mile voyage. As these grew worse all canvas had eventually to be taken down, and in terrifyingly giant waves crews and passengers were tossed about along with unsecured items of cargo and badly bruised. Not the least unpleasant of their experiences was to be fired on by Turkish soldiers while subsequently surveying possible future anchorages.

Operation 'Expedite' was fraught with additional hazards. For this mission the caique *St Nicholas*, recently acquired and commanded by Sub-Lieutenant Powers, RNVR, had to take a Greek officer and two Greek NCOs and land them with a wireless set and other equipment on the mainland of Greece. Not only was the chosen pinpoint well inside the Gulf of Thessalonika, it was close to a base from which German patrol caiques operated. Nevertheless the mission was successfully accomplished.

Intelligence-collecting missions were also undertaken on behalf of ISLD. In April a 10-man patrol including a folbot team was landed on Piscopi for this purpose from a motor launch. Although the canoeists were unable to get into the harbour, the main force contacted local Greek patriots from whom they garnered useful information, and while they were about it, killed four Germans in ambush.

A small reconnaissance party was landed by caique on Niseros.

Helped by local Greeks who included a town mayor, they evaded German counter-espionage patrols, and obtained valuable information about the distribution of the enemy garrison, food supplies, morale, shipping, and reprisals after previous raids.

One particular aspect of this work came in for special mention by FOLEM, who reported that:

> In addition to more normal operations carried out by Coastal Forces, certain motor launches were regularly engaged in secret and often hazardous missions in conjunction with ISLD and Force 133 on the south-west coast of Crete. Under the enemy's nose motor launches landed stores and personnel, and took off German and Italian prisoners of war as well as Allied personnel escaping from the enemy or carrying valuable information. The weather was sometimes so bad that craft were forced back, but they always carried out specific operations in the end.

In mid-March the senior officers of the Coastal Forces and AHSF were informed that the Raiding Forces had been given a new directive by GHQ Middle East with a view to co-ordinating activities with other organisations such as the ISLD and Force 133 operating in the Aegean, and dealing with shore targets in accordance with priorities decided between the Royal Navy, RAF and GHQ Middle East. All semi-independent flotillas were put under AHSF, and in future senior naval officers would be informed by periodic signals of priority tasks to be undertaken in the succeeding period, and the areas where unrestricted operations could take place.

One of Turnbull's more ambitious plans for the Raiding Forces, which had been under consideration for some time, was a full-scale assault on Symi to liquidate the garrison, destroy military installations and capture or destroy enemy shipping and leave within twenty-four hours, while at the same time airfields on Rhodes and Cos were being bombed. But because of the presence in the Aegean of several former Italian destroyers which had been taken over and manned by the Germans, this had had to be held in abeyance.

Based in the United Kingdom was a small elite body of Royal Marine canoeists with the cover name of 'Royal Marine Boom Patrol Detachment' (RMBPD). It was a section from this detachment that carried out the famous attack on German blockade-runners at Bordeaux in December 1942, which earned them the title of 'Cockleshell Heroes'. The existence of the RMBPD and its functions had been made known to various overseas commands, to which it could be temporarily attached if required. Allied Force Headquarters in the Mediterranean asked for two sections of the Detachment to be sent to the Middle East for operations in the Aegean. Early in 1944 they arrived at Raiding Force headquarters in Palestine and began acclimatisation training.

One night in mid-June, when an enemy supply convoy bound for Rhodes with a two-destroyer escort was known to be staging en route in Leros, Operation 'Sunbeam'* was put into effect. Its purpose was the destruction of the major escorts, considered by FOLEM to be of paramount importance. 'They are irreplaceable and their removal would make easier the task of our submarines in their offensive against enemy shipping.' Conveyed from Turk Buku in a Fairmile motor launch, and subsequently safely picked up by the same craft, the RMBPD canoeists duly entered starlit Portolago Bay, in Leros, severely damaged the destroyers with limpet charges and sank three smaller escort vessels. The destroyers took no further part in the war. The RMBPD Detachment also distinguished itself in subsequent operations in the Aegean.

The way was now clear for Operation 'Tenement' – the planned attack on Symi.

Accordingly on the night of 13 July the raiding force totalling more than 200, including the Greek Sacred Squadron, under Turnbull himself, embarked in motor launches and large caiques from Penzik Bay in the Gulf of Doris, at the entrance to which lay their target. Landing unseen at three points on the island, the attack was a complete success, although unhappily two Greek officers were accidentally drowned while climbing down into their boats. Twenty-seven Germans were killed and 160 taken prisoner along with a number of quislings. Gun emplacements were demolished, ammunition and fuel dumps blown up, and a wireless station, telephone exchange and cable heads, and nineteen caiques in various stages of construction destroyed. Two EMS barges were also captured. After leaving food for the islanders, the raiding force was then evacuated, their only casualties apart from the two Greek officers being six Greek and British personnel wounded.

* See *The Secret Navies*, A. Cecil Hampshire, Wm Kimber, 1978.

Next day the Germans savagely bombed the island, and later reoccupied it.

But by now it became apparent that it was only a matter of time before the enemy's position in Greece and the Aegean islands became untenable. It was even possible to see the end of the war in Europe, although that was still relatively far off.

In June the Second Front had been opened, and the subsequent Allied breakthrough in Normandy had set the Germans reeling back. In the East the Russians launched a fresh offensive, and by early May they recaptured Sebastopol, and the Germans evacuated the whole Crimea. Shipping was sent from the Black Sea down to the Aegean, which threatened to undo much of the good work performed by the Raiding Forces. Losses we had inflicted were made good, and the enemy was again running supplies to Cos and Leros. But after one of their most important convoys to Crete had been destroyed by the combined efforts of Allied aircraft and submarines, they were forced to revert to small craft.

Early in August the Turks broke off diplomatic relations with Germany. Following this rupture the Aegean situation entered a new phase. Hitherto, sure of Turkish neutrality, the enemy had been able to concentrate on the southern bastion islands, being able to count on the Black Sea to make up shipping losses. Now with the Aegean likely to remain a closed area the Germans had to rely on depleted shipping resources. In addition they were experiencing trouble with the crews of Bulgarian ships in the northern Aegean. Fourteen Axis caiques totalling 620 tons were sunk during the month and one 30-ton vessel captured, almost all by our submarines. Nevertheless they were determined to keep supplies going.

Then when the Russian armies began sweeping across the eastern frontiers of Rumania and Bulgaria, both those countries hastily sought armistice terms. On 27 August Hitler authorised a gradual withdrawal of German forces to the central Balkans. Accordingly they began to reduce their garrisons in southern Greece, Crete and the Aegean islands.

The task of Coastal and Raiding Forces was now to harass the enemy withdrawal and obtain information as to his intentions. In particular the Dodecanese islands of Mitylene, Chios, Lemnos, Samos, Cos and Leros were kept under close observation by raiding parties and reconnaissance patrols.

After Operation 'Tenement', which marked the official end of

'Fire Eater', a proportion of the Raiding Forces, including SBS and LRDG units, was ordered by the Supreme Allied Commander, Mediterranean to be withdrawn from the Aegean to operate in the Adriatic against targets in Jugoslavia and Albania. The Greek Sacred Squadron now began to figure more prominently in the operational activities of the Raiding Forces.

During August patrols from the squadron, transported in Coastal Force craft and caiques of the AHSF, carried out reconnaissances of a score of islands, some as far west as the northern Sporades, much valuable information being obtained, and casualties inflicted on the enemy wherever possible.

Early in September a British naval striking force was formed to stop enemy movements by sea in the Aegean. Known as 'Force A', it was composed of escort carriers, cruisers and destroyers. While Allied bombers from Italian bases attacked airfields and ports, Force A made repeated sweeps into the northern Aegean, during which they sank enemy convoys, bombarded shore bases or attacked them with carrier-borne aircraft.

There was thus less for the Raiding Forces to do, although they continued their active reconnaissance work. As many of the islands became free, they as well as the caiques of the LFP were first on the scene, where they frequently took control and acted as guardships. On 12 September, the island of Chios having been evacuated by the enemy, orders were given for the advanced base of the Coastal Forces and AHSF to move to that island, and on the 16th Comaro set up his headquarters there.

At the end of October Raiding Force HQ was informed that they were to undertake no further offensive action in the Aegean. By then the Germans had withdrawn entirely from Greece. Despite our efforts they succeeded in removing nearly 40,000 troops, mostly by air, from Crete and the Aegean to the mainland, along with substantial quantities of stores and equipment. But in Crete, Rhodes and a few smaller islands there were still substantial garrisons, and on 8 November Berlin defiantly declared Rhodes, Crete and Leros to be 'fortresses to be defended to the last'. Since they could now do little harm it was decided to leave them to 'wither on the vine'.

In his final report on Raiding Force operations FOLEM recorded that one 1,500-ton tanker, one 200-ton lighter, one 10-ton EMS barge, and a landing craft had been sunk, the tanker with all hands; one 300-ton tanker, one 200-ton caique and six smaller caiques had been captured, and seven others enticed from the enemy. We had lost one motor launch captured after engaging a superior enemy force, one motor fishing vessel mined, and one AHSF caique grounded and sunk. German killed and wounded numbered 114, and 391 taken prisoner; Italian 8 wounded and 1,415 captured, 1,000 of whom had surrendered to a Raiding Force patrol on Samos. Our own casualties, both Coastal and Raiding Forces, totalled 84 killed and wounded.

The Second AHSF was now allocated to Operation 'Manna' – bringing supplies to Greece – and they played an important part in the Allied entry into the Piraeus. Having been among the first arrivals, accompanied by four large 'Aid to Greece' caiques, they assisted with the disembarkation of troops and vehicles. Later they took part in operations leading to the occupation of Salonika, and were the first Allied ships to arrive there carrying reconnaissance parties and Commandos. With the outbreak of internal political trouble in Greece they were re-organised into anti-piracy patrols and operations against ELAN caiques.

The deterioration of the weather, and the relatively stabilised conditions in the Cyclades and other islands of the archipelago, led to the decision in January 1945 to transfer the First AHSF to the Greek mainland and turn it over to the Royal Hellenic Navy for manning.

During the closing weeks of the Aegean campaign the caiques of Force 133 continued their own operations, landing tons of Red Cross supplies for the starving Greek islanders, as well as supplying their own stations and collaborators in the Cyclades with food, etc., and picking up prisoners and ISLD agents. By sheer nerve and with the aid of the skipper's whisky one Force 133 caique, the 20-ton *Santa Claus* mentioned earlier on, even brought about the surrender of the German-occupied island of Santorini, sixty miles north of Crete.

In command of the *Santa Claus* was Regimental Sergeant-Major John Medley, DCM of the 4th Queen's Own Hussars. The ship's mate was Staff Sergeant John Clayton, the engineer Lance-Corporal Memear of REME, the wireless operator Corporal Boyes of the Royal Signals, the boatswain Andania Chrondroukakis, Greek patriot, and the gunners Bombardier Coleman and Lance-Corporal Roberts. The eighth member of her company was the ship's cat, a Cypriot animal answering to the name of 'Symi-Symi'.

On the caique's arrival at Santorini the German commandant

came on board, and after plying him with drinks Medley demanded the garrison's surrender. A long heated discussion followed, at the end of which, having emptied Medley's last bottle of whisky, the commandant agreed to surrender to a larger Allied vessel. This news was immediately reported to headquarters, who at once informed 'Force A'. The *Santa Claus* then received the following signal:

> Cruiser *Ajax* due off Cape Akrotirion dawn tomorrow. You will hang out any washing you have got and use caique recognition signal. You will then take landing party of marines ashore. After evacuating prisoners you will look after the island and distribute food until further notice.

Medley's subsequent log entries read:

> 18 Oct 1944. Wet tea 0500. Slipped mooring and proceeded towards Cape Akrotirion. 0600 sighted *Ajax* before it was light. Flashed caique recognition signal, also made our number by Aldis. We were glad it was not necessary to hang out washing. Signalled to come alongside, when the humble went alongside the mighty.

The *Santa Claus* then ferried the cruiser's Royal Marine landing party ashore, and afterwards Medley landed every tin of food he had.

Proudly added to the caique's log was the following signal:

> From *Ajax* to *Santa Claus* Force 133. Congratulations. I am sorry *Santa Claus* did not have the fun of surrender yourself, but we knew very well that it was due entirely to the good work of all your team over many months. John Cuthbert, Captain.

The same sentiment of course applied to all units of the combined forces who took part in this least publicised of campaigns of World War II.

# II

## The Surfboard Commandos

Under a bright Californian moon a detachment of men from the United States Marine Corps Raider Battalion was guarding a railway bridge over the San Mateo canyon on the Pacific Coast of America. Becoming bored with inactivity, the keen edge of their vigilance gradually blunted as the night wore on. After all, the possibility that enemy raiders who would have to be specially transported thousands of miles across the ocean to stage an attack on this unimportant objective, seemed the least likely to become reality.

Although the United States had been at war for some eighteen months, ever since the treacherous Japanese attack on Pearl Harbour in December 1941, the latter had made no attempt to carry hostilities to the American mainland. Only the officer in charge of the Raider detachment appeared irritatingly alert. Cursing his 'no smoking' order, the bridge sentries squatted with their rifles between their knees, chewed gum and gazed unseeingly into the night.

The sea which flowed into the shallow lagoon over which the bridge carried the railway line running from Los Angeles to San Diego, was dappled with silver under the moonlight as the ebb tide surf waned in strength and the waves gradually receded from the foreshore. The war seemed very far away indeed. Yet, unknown and unseen by even the most alert watcher, menace was slowly and steadily approaching.

Some three miles away from San Mateo ten men had launched themselves into the sea and were heading towards the guarded bridge. But they were not swimming. Each man lay flat on a specially shaped wooden board. Clad only in swimming trunks, their faces and bodies darkened with a special pigment, the men propelled themselves along by means of small rounded wooden paddles strapped to their hands and swim fins on their feet. In front of each man, in a light waterproof haversack secured to the board,

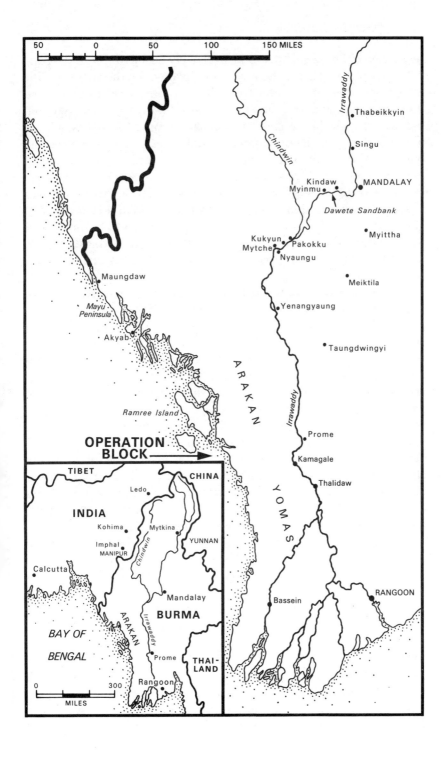

50   0   50   100   150 MILES

*Irrawaddy*

Thabeikkyin

*Chindwin*

Singu

Kindaw
Myinmu
MANDALAY

*Dawete Sandbank*

Myittha

Kukyun
Mytche  Pakokku
Nyaungu

Meiktila

Maungdaw

*Mayu
Peninsula*

Yenangyaung

Akyab

A R A K A N

Taungdwingyi

Ramree Island

*Irrawaddy*

**OPERATION
BLOCK** ➡

Prome

Kamagale

Thalidaw

Y
O
M
A
S

TIBET

Ledo

CHINA

INDIA

Kohima   Mytkina

Imphal
MANIPUR

YUNNAN

*Chindwin*

Calcutta

Mandalay

BURMA

Bassein

RANGOON

ARAKAN

*Irrawaddy*

BAY OF

BENGAL

Prome

THAI-
LAND

0   300

Rangoon

MILES

he carried either limpet demolition charges or a light machine-gun.

Opposite San Mateo the formation headed for the shore. As the men reached shallow water they allowed themselves to be carried through the moderately breaking waves, finally to be left lying on the wet shingle like a shoal of outsize stranded fish. For several minutes they remained completely motionless, their eyes carefully scanning the terrain in front of them. To the north, outlined against the sky, they could make out part of the framework of the bridge which was their objective: the other end of the structure was obscured by scrub and tall rushes. Ahead of them a shallow crest about thirty yards inshore created an area of dead ground. There was no sign of any beach watchers, although the attackers knew that there was a beach patrol and that both ends of the bridge would be guarded.

One by one the swimmers began wriggling cautiously forward, dragging their paddle boards with them over the soft sand. When they had successfully negotiated this part of the approach without challenge from any shore watcher, paddle boards and flippers were swiftly concealed in the brushwood fringing the beach, and charges and weapons removed from the haversacks. Then, creeping noiselessly inland on rubber-soled shoes, they split up into two parties. Two men in each section carried the demolition charges: the other three were armed with sub-machine-guns. While one party made its way towards the northern end of the bridge, the other approached its southern extremity. Then, as the men with the charges flitted forward like ghosts to fix these in position on the bridge structure, the covering trio silently stalked the bored sentries and kept them under close observation. Should the alarm be given, they were ready to spring into instant action.

Within forty-five minutes the sabotage mission had been successfully accomplished, and the swimmers were back on the beach. Charges had been placed along the whole 600-foot length of the bridge, thus ensuring its total destruction since it was almost entirely of wooden construction. Throughout the whole operation the sentries and the beach patrol had seen and heard nothing.

Paddle boards were quickly and noiselessly disinterred from their temporary hiding places and, dragging these with them, the saboteurs crabbed their way flat on their bellies down to the water's edge. They knew that before dawn broke the incoming tide would have obliterated from the sand all traces of their clandestine visit. Pushing their boards into the gently breaking surf, they clambered on to them and, as stealthily as they had arrived, paddled away into the light sea mist.

But the bridge was never blown, although the officer in charge of the marine defenders, who alone had known what was to be attempted and that it was only a dummy exercise, had to endure a mild roasting from his commandant next morning when the charges were discovered. For the 'attackers' were British, and by their exploit successfully demonstrated the deadly skills of a new seaborne offensive unit, which could be added to the armed forces of both our countries.

\*

Some two years before this mock attack took place a young sub-lieutenant of the Royal Canadian Naval Volunteer Reserve was standing watch in a small ageing motor launch patrolling the seaward side of the anti-submarine boom which barred entrance to the harbour of St John's, Newfoundland. It was not his normal job. He was in fact awaiting appointment to one of the Canadian naval corvettes on Atlantic escort duties, and had been detailed to take over as temporary relief for the boom patrol vessel's proper commanding officer, who had reported sick.

Crewed by Newfoundland naval reservists, and armed with one depth charge of ancient vintage and uncertain performance, the launch's duty was to patrol up and down the boom and keep an eye open for any U-boat which might come nosing around. If one was spotted, the alarm was to be raised and the launch speedily to quit the area while the shore defences took over.

As the little vessel pitched and rolled in the short choppy swells, the sub-lieutenant, whose name was Bruce Wright, passed the time by idly pondering how we would set about beating the net defences of a protected harbour such as St John's. A strongly built athlete of near Olympic standard himself, Wright came to the conclusion that this could best be done by underwater swimmers.

He recalled a magazine article he had recently read about the abalone divers of California who hunted this edible and tasty shellfish, with its fascinating descriptions of the paddle boards, dive masks and swim fins they used, about which he had never previously heard. It now occurred to him that just such a diver could be put overboard from a submarine outside the boom defence to tow a cigar-shaped plastic mine through a hole cut in the net. Having attached the device to the hull of a warship or merchantman, he could return to his parent vessel by the same route. At that time Wright had never heard of such a method of attack being used before, and was excited by the notion. Yet, like so many bright ideas, it was not new.

In 1918 Sub-Lieutenant Raffaele Paolucci, a young surgeon in the Italian navy, dreamed up the idea of single-handedly attacking the Austro-Hungarian fleet anchored in its base at Pola, on the Adriatic coast. Conveyed in a motorboat to a gap in the harbour breakwater, he would enter the water and swim with a special mine of his own invention to one of the enemy battleships. The mine was some five feet long, two feet in diameter, and shaped like a cigar, with two air tanks, one forward and one aft. The centre compartment of the body contained a charge of some 200 lbs of TNT primed by an externally controlled time fuse.

On arrival beneath the selected target, the after air tank would be opened, causing the device to change position from the horizontal to the vertical. With a rope carried round his waist Paolucci would then secure the mine to any protuberance on the warship's hull, or, if this was impossible, to the lower point of a davit or accommodation ladder. The fuse would then be set for one hour, and the foremost air tank opened. This would leave the mine hanging by the rope at a depth of about four metres. Paolucci would then swim back to the breakwater beyond which the motorboat would be waiting, and with a watertight torch signal for it to come and pick him up.

But after some months of training the scheme was abandoned, and Paolucci was ordered to join forces with Naval Engineer Major Raffaele Rossetti on the production of a new weapon. This was a special compressed-air torpedo. Controlled by an external lever, the torpedo was fitted with a magnetic device by means of which it could be attached to the hull of a ship; the charge, or warhead, being detached from the body. On the last day of October 1918, a few days before the Austro-Hungarian surrender, Paolucci and Rossetti entered the sea from a torpedo-boat with their weapon off Pola harbour. After a hazardous swim towing their weapon, the men successfully blew up the battleship *Viribus Unitus*.

These were not the only novel forms of seaborne attack dreamed up by the Italian navy against the Austo-Hungarian fleet in the war of 1914-18. One which was to be further developed, but in somewhat different form during the second world conflict, was a boom-climbing craft. The invention of a Commander Pellegrini, the *grille* (cricket) was an explosive motorboat fitted with caterpillar tracks which in theory would enable it to surmount the protective harbour boom at Pola naval base. Unfortunately for Pellegrini the *grille* got stuck halfway across the obstruction, the noise he made alerted the enemy, and he was captured.

Curiously enough, the contemporary issue of *Janes' Fighting Ships* credited Pellegrini with sinking the *Viribus Unitus*, although that authority seemed doubtful if the vessel actually existed!

In 1935, fearing attack by the British fleet during the Abyssinian crisis which brought our two countries close to war, two sub-lieutenants of the Italian La Spezia flotilla produced a 'human torpedo' which did not require the operator to come to the surface. Along with other Italian naval officers, they formed the nucleus of the Tenth Light Flotilla which, under the command of Count Valerio Borghese, was reconstituted at La Spezia in 1940. After Italy's entry into the war, the first human torpedo attack by the flotilla was designed to be carried out from the submarine *Iride* against the British fleet in Alexandria.

The planned attack, unknown to us at the time, was unwittingly foiled by a Royal Marine captain serving in the Fleet Air Arm. Piloting a Swordfish torpedo-bomber from the carrier HMS *Eagle*, at that time undergoing repairs in Alexandria, Captain Oliver Patch was leading a sub-flight of three Swordfish from Sidi Barrani in an attack on an Italian submarine depot ship with a submarine alongside reported to be anchored in Bomba harbour. When the Swordfish arrived over the harbour, the depot ship was found to be anchored close inshore with a destroyer and another vessel alongside, while the submarine was lying surfaced some distance away charging her batteries.

Pointing his aircraft directly at the submarine, Patch launched his torpedo from a range of a hundred yards, turned and headed out to sea. The torpedo struck the submarine squarely beneath the conning tower and sent her to the bottom. After the war Patch met two of her survivors, who told him that the submarine was the *Iride* and that she was carrying a small band of specialists in underwater sabotage. One of their targets was to have been the *Eagle* herself.

In October 1940 the Italians tried again, this time against British warships at Gibraltar. Their human torpedoes were to have been launched from the submarine *Scire* commanded by Borghese himself. But when the submarine was within fifty miles of Gibraltar, the attempt was ordered to be cancelled, information having been received that the British fleet had sailed. Subsequently Italian frogmen and human torpedoes operated against the British Mediterranean Fleet from time to time with varying results, but they never became a serious threat.

Another novel idea of the Italians was the formation of the 'Gamma Group', a detachment of underwater 'assault infantry'. Wearing close-fitting rubber suits, dive masks and a small breathing set, they were literally to march along the sea bed. On exercises the unit was said to have covered distances up to 2,000 metres in full 'war kit'. Their principal weapon, known as the 'bug', was a circular metal charge consisting of three kilogrammes of explosive which could be attached to the hull of a ship by means of an inflatable rubber ring. Later on the 'bug' was superseded by a limpet charge. There is no record, however, of these 'underwater soldiers' ever being used in an actual operation.

Rumours became current after the entry of Japan into the war that the Japanese had used assault swimmers in their attacks on Hongkong, the Philippines and Malaya, but these appear to have been based on one episode only. On the night of 15 December 1941 several companies of Japanese soldiers pushing small rubber boats and rafts made of petrol tins carrying their arms and equipment did in fact attempt to swim across to Hongkong from Kowloon and Stonecutters Island. All, however, were shot in the water by the British defenders.

It was also believed that Japanese assault swimmers succeeded in putting out of action our minefields between Hongkong and the mainland. This, however, seems unlikely to have happened, for the first question that Commodore Collinson was asked by the Japanese senior naval officer who took his formal surrender of the dockyard and naval installations was the whereabouts of our minefields. No mention of Japanese assault swimmers appears in the official reports of the campaign in Malaya; but later on in the war the Japanese were reported to have formed military swimming units.

The Germans also created a 17,000-strong unit called the *Kleinboote Verbande*, or small boat command, which included human torpedoes and two-men midget submarines. But, rather than swimmers, the majority of these 'small battle units' consisted of mechanical devices, some of them radio-controlled.

As has been said, however, Wright knew nothing of any such early natatorial notions and thought his idea to be original. Soon after completing his stint in the boom patrol motor launch at St John's, he was duly appointed to a corvette and spent the next few months on escort duty in the North Atlantic. In odd leisure moments, however, he continued to think about his idea, becoming more and more convinced of its novelty and practicality, and finally discussed it with his captain.

The latter was sceptical at first, but eventually advised him to put the whole thing on paper which he promised to forward to higher authority. Wright duly set to work, and produced a dissertation which he entitled 'The Use of Natatorial Assault and Reconnaissance Units in Combined Operations'. Later he learned that his paper had reached the desk of the Flag Officer, Halifax, from whom it had been forwarded to the Director of Naval Intelligence in Ottawa.

From thence the document was sent on to the Director of Naval Intelligence at the Admiralty in London. Thereafter no further word came from official quarters. But Wright's suggestion had by no means been overlooked. It had reached Combined Operations headquarters, whose Director at the time was Commodore Lord Louis Mountbatten, who had taken over that post from Admiral of the Fleet Sir Roger Keyes. It was one of a number of suggestions for all manner of unorthodox offensive operations against the enemy and methods of accomplishing these which came flooding in around this time.

What probably brought Wright's paper to more immediate attention was the fact that Italian human torpedoes and limpet swimmers had been used in attacks on Malta, Gibraltar and, with conspicuous success, against the British fleet in Alexandria, where two of our battleships were put out of action. The raiders had also intended to set the harbour at that port ablaze by firing escaping oil fuel from a tanker they also hoped to sink. This last had brought forth a stinging rebuke from the Prime Minister to the Chiefs of Staff asking why we were not imitating the Italians, or, better still, ahead of them.

The result was the issue of a summons for Lieutenant Wright to report to Combined Operations headquarters in London to develop his proposal, bringing with him a surfboard, dive mask and swim fins; also an underwater spring gun complete with 'arrows'.

This was easier said than done, for Wright possessed none of this gear, nor had he ever personally used any of it. Before the war he had been employed by the Dominion Forest Service, and it was to his old department that he applied for money to purchase the equipment. The fact that he had now been attached to the Naval Intelligence Department for 'top secret special duty' helped in this respect for, somewhat surprisingly, the money was duly made available. Not only that, the Forest Department promised to take this peculiar-sounding gear on their charge and hold it for Wright.

Unhappily he failed to obtain a specimen of the special type of underwater spring gun he wanted from its inventor, and had to be content with a set of photographs of the weapon. Next he travelled on to Los Angeles to find out what skin-diving equipment was available. There he discovered a small firm specialising in the manufacture of such gear and, along with one of the firm's partners and a retired lifeguard-turned abalone diver, tried out various types of equipment along the coast, and learned to use mask, fins and paddle board.

Then, having despatched specimens of the best types of gear to the Ottawa headquarters of the Dominion Forest Service, he sat down and wrote another paper which he entitled 'The Organisation and Equipment of a Natatorial Unit'. After that he was ready to fly to London, but a snag cropped up: his equipment was too bulky to be carried by air, and it had to be sent on by sea.

After reporting to Combined Operations headquarters early in 1943, he was interviewed by Mountbatten, who asked him to stage a demonstration. When he confessed that all he had been able to bring with him was a dive mask and some photographs of the rest of the gear, Mountbatten sent him down to Portsmouth to train a special party of Royal Marines in the new technique.

The unit to which Wright was to be temporarily attached was officially known as the 'Royal Marine Boom Patrol Detachment (RMBPD), whose commanding officer had already read Wright's paper and asked for him to be attached to the unit. Expert canoeists, these were the men whom the press was later to dub 'Cockleshell Heroes' for their canoe attack on German blockade-runners in the River Gironde in 1942. Their commanding officer, Major 'Blondie' Hasler, and his fellow canoeist, Corporal Sparks, were the only two survivors of that raid. Hasler was later to play an important part in the creation of the formation Wright was eventually to command.

At this stage of the world conflict considerable time and efforts were being devoted to the investigation of all aspects of underwater offensive operations, and the development of the necessary 'hardware' and equipment for waging this form of warfare, ranging from the midget submarine to the British version of the Italian human torpedo, known as the 'chariot'.* Thus as well as straightforward canoeing, the Boom Patrol men were also experimenting with an explosive motorboat copied from the Italian version but to be dropped from the air, and a motorised form of one-man submersible canoe. Various types of shallow-water diving dress were also under trial and development. Today scuba, or skin diving, with self-contained breathing apparatus has become a commonplace, but at that time such equipment had not been dreamed of.

During the weeks he spent with the marines, Wright was able to teach them a good deal about swimming, and prevailed upon the firm of Dunlop to manufacture American-type swim fins and dive masks, which were enthusiastically adopted by the Detachment. By then he had learned that all his own gear had been lost when the ship bringing it over from America was torpedoed and sunk in convoy. After the marines in turn taught him their canoe techniques and the use of the Davis Submered Escape Apparatus (DSEA), and introduced him to the type of diving dress they were using, he made the rounds of various specialised training establishments, and also underwent a Commando course in Scotland.

Not least important of the unpublicised establishments he visited was the Inter-Service Research and Devices Section of Special Operations Executive, whose boffins were concerned with the invention and development of all manner of devices ranging from the simple and practical to the complicated and fiendish for use by their own personnel. Waterproofing arms and limpet mines were two of the subjects under trial that particularly interested Wright.

The role of the unit he had in mind was

> to make special reconnaissances of landing beaches; to attack shipping and shore objectives in defended harbours; and to act as amphibious scouts and raiders in inland waters. Thirty feet was considered to be the limit of our interest in diving, as anything below this was of no importance to amphibious assaults.†

---

* Stress was laid on the tremendous effect of the destruction or neutralisation of ships on the course of the war.
† *The Frogmen of Burma*, William Kimber 1970.

After staging a successful personal demonstration equipped with British-made fins, dive mask and paddle board for Mountbatten, aided by Blondie Hasler, events at last began to move. Combined Operations headquarters put up a scheme to the Chiefs of Staff Committee for 100 volunteers from the Navy, Army and Air Force to be trained as swimmers, capable of penetrating and carrying out offensive operations in places inaccessible to folbots and other surface craft. Thus they would be distinct from other specialist units such as the RMBPD and Combined Operations Pilotage Party (COPP) because of their different approach to the target.

Naval operations would include reconnaissance of beach and harbour defences, attacks on shipping by limpet charges, and cutting-out expeditions. Military operations would consist of small-scale raids, reconnaissance, demolition, sniping and guerilla warfare. For these purposes the men were to be equipped with special underwater swimming gear and aids to surface swimming, and would be known as the 'Swimming Unit'.

By now, on assuming the post of Chief of Combined Operations (CCO), Mountbatten had been promoted to the acting ranks of Vice-Admiral, Lieutenant-General and Air Marshal, and as such had been admitted as a full member of the Chiefs of Staff Committee. Nevertheless, as he told Wright, 'Some of them treat me like a schoolboy.' Thus, despite his eloquence in support of the scheme, the Committee decided that as the Services were short of manpower, and the operations of such a unit were unlikely to make any large contribution to the defeat of the enemy, the proposal should be deferred.

Such, however, were Mountbatten's personal charm and persistence, that at another meeting only a week later the Committee agreed to the initiation of the scheme 'on a small scale to explore and develop techniques'. Approval was therefore given to obtain ten volunteers with good swimming qualifications from each of the three Services and from Combined Operations, a total of forty. Since it was considered that the waters around our coasts were too cold and underwater visibility not clear enough, they were, at Wright's suggestion, to undergo their training in California. He was officially appointed to command the unit and given the acting rank of lieutenant-commander.

Accordingly a telegram was sent to the head of the British Admiralty Delegation in Washington requesting that arrangements be made with the Americans for accommodation and facilities to be provided. For security reasons the name 'Swimming Unit' was considered to be unsuitable. Instead they were to be known as the 'Amphibious Reconnaissance Party'. This title was eventually changed to 'Sea Reconnaissance Unit' (SRU).

When, in July 1943, the US Navy Department agreed to train the unit with the US Marine Corps at San Diego, Wright was sent back to Canada with a letter from Mountbatten to Vice-Admiral Nelles, Chief of the Canadian Naval Staff, authorising him to get the scheme under way. Meanwhile a call was put out to the Admiralty, War Office and Air Ministry asking for volunteers to join the new unit. The proposed syllabus drawn up by CCO included training in the use of swim fins, paddle boards and surfboards of all types; underwater swimming and equipment; devices for protection against dangerous fish; explosives for underwater attacks on shipping; net-cutting and boom-destruction devices, and the use of a light portable machine-gun. The men would also be taught elementary pilotage, fieldcraft, cliff-climbing and unarmed combat. All volunteers were to be vetted by Hasler at HMS *Northney*, a Combined Operations training base in Hayling Island.

Wright's own more detailed programme envisaged at least twelve weeks' intensive training* in the use of fins, mask and paddle board, to include body surfing proper with the over-passing of heavy breakers while swimming to seaward; riding and returning through heavy breakers on a board; night paddle-boarding and swimming. At least three weeks to be spent on oxygen breathing gear, culminating in the ability to dive and work at thirty feet. Standard infantry training in scouting and patrolling; stalking and cliff-climbing; exercising in wet and dry jungle and scrub cactus; attacks on shipping; limpet attacks and boarding attacks to familiarise all with the general layout of a ship's wheelhouse, wheel and engine-room telegraphs, anchoring arrangements, officers' and crew's quarters, and armament. Lectures on dangerous marine fauna, such as shark, barracuda, moray eel, octopus and sting ray, and instruction in spear-fishing; weapon training and unarmed combat, to include rifle, pistol, sub machine-gun and grenades and knife fighting; demolition, using all types of military explosives against wood, concrete and steel; underwater demolition; booby traps, mines and cratering; speed marching and runs over standard infantry assault course; and finally a general resumé of all subjects.

* The Italians had to undergo a minimum of ten months training before being permitted to take part in an operation.

The first requirement, however, was to obtain a team of instructors. Wright's own choice fell upon Lieutenant Albert Bruton Strange, RCNVR, a former professional footballer and athlete, and an old classmate of his during initial officer training. At a sports meeting in the training establishment both had competed in a 100-yards free-style swimming race, in which Wright had only just managed to beat his rival. Strange was also a member of Yale University swimming team, and had considerable experience in sailing vessels, having sailed a small schooner across the Atlantic in peace-time. Much to his surprise, 'Brute' Strange, who was serving in the Canadian escort destroyer *Chambly*, found himself relieved of his appointment and ordered to report to Wright in Ottawa.

Captain Humphrey Tollemache, RN, Combined Operations representative with the British Admiralty Delegation in Washington, was ordered to take Wright's unit under his wing and iron out any difficulties they might encounter with the Americans.

The establishment of the unit was to comprise four sections, each of two officers and eight men. Non-operational personnel were to consist of three Special Branch lieutenants as instructors, to be recruited in California and entered in the Royal Canadian Naval Volunteer Reserve; one DSEA instructor from HMS *Dolphin*, the principal submarine base in the United Kingdom; and one storeman, also from Britain. A medical officer was later added.

The list of gear approved to be provided for the unit was impressive. It included 30 paddle boards; 45 pairs of swim fins, sea diving masks and swimming trunks; 30 light-weight diving dresses as designed by the Admiralty Diving Committee for Combined Operations with open-mouth type helmets; 50 rubber bathing caps, also as designed by the Committee; 50 pairs of swim shoes; 30 sets of back breathing gear manufactured by the firm of Sieve Gorman to Diving Committee specifications; 30 sets of DSEA gear for training purposes; bath towels, knives and sheaths, fish spears, spearheads, water-glasses, and underwater compasses and watches. The bulk of this gear was obtainable in the United States.

While these requirements were put in train for fulfilment, candidates were arriving at HMS *Northney* for vetting by Blondie Hasler. The qualifications laid down for acceptance were (a) to be a volunteer for hazardous service; (b) to be between the ages of twenty and twenty-five; (c) to be of a high degree of physical fitness; (d) to be a first-class swimmer; and (e) not subject to seasickness. Preference was given to those possessing mechanical or engineering experience and an elementary knowledge of navigation.

For his other two instructors Wright recruited Hal Messenger, the diving equipment manufacturing executive, and Frank Rodecker, the former abalone diver, who had worked with him earlier on. Both men were ideally qualified. Messenger was President of the Professional Beach Guards' Association of America, who for some years had been active in the commercial diving field in design and production of equipment, and was an outstanding authority on the Pacific coast on shallow-water diving. Rodecker was the lifeguard champion of the Pacific coast. Although American citizens, they were specially entered in the Canadian Naval Volunteer Reserve in the ranks of lieutenant and sub-lieutenant respectively on the authority of the Chief of the Canadian Naval Staff in Ottawa, backed by Mountbatten.

By the end of August 1943 a sufficient number of volunteers had been obtained in the United Kingdom. They included four naval officers – two of them midshipmen – eleven naval ratings, among them a stoker and a telegraphist, and four Royal Marines; three army officers and eight other ranks, six of them NCOs; and a flying officer and nine airmen.

Of these, Captain 'Mick' Muldoon, MC, had served with the British West African forces throughout the East African campaign against the Italians, where he won his decoration. Captain 'Jock' Elder of the Black Watch won an MC during the Dunkirk evacuation, immediately after which he volunteered for hazardous service. Second Lieutenant James 'Dick' Turpin was a former ranker who had served for five years in the Guards and had spent his childhood in British Guiana before coming to England for his schooling. Lieutenant John Junor, RNVR, a superb athlete with considerable experience in tropical sea, came from Jamaica, and had played cricket for the Royal Navy in England. Sub-Lieutenant Barry Kimmins and Midshipmen J.R. Docherty and C.C. 'Bonzo' Booth were fresh from their officer training in HMS *King Alfred*. Flying Officer Harry Avery, RCAFVR, was a Canadian from Ottawa and former inter-collegiate swimmer, who had been serving at an isolated radar station in Britain when he answered the call for volunteers.

In due course Muldoon was appointed executive officer of the unit. Elder was given command of No 1 Section, with Kimmins as his second in command; Strange command of No 2 Section, with Docherty as his deputy; Junor No 3 Section, with Midshipman Booth as second in command; and Avery charge of No 4 Section, with Turpin as his deputy. Among the naval ratings and army and Air Force other ranks were men with knowledge of diesel engines, infantry weapons, experience of driving trucks and armoured vehicles, physical training, signals, and dinghy sailing – all useful skills.

Subsequently Surgeon Lieutenant Douglas Robertson, RNVR joined the unit as medical officer. A gynaecologist in civil life, he was neither able to swim nor had he any knowledge of diving equipment or the ills to which divers can be subject. These shortcomings, which shocked Wright, were to be remedied in due course.

The first batch of volunteers arrived at Camp Pendleton, on Oceanside in southern California, on 7 September. Training base for the US Marine Corps, the camp was little more than an extensive stretch of arid scrub along the coast, fronting the endless breakers of the Pacific Ocean. Quarters for Wright's unit consisted of a cluster of bell tents in a former rubber camp known as San Onofre within the perimeter of the main camp.

The party had endured a miserable journey from New York. Not only had they been separated from their kit, which did not arrive until a day later: they had been crammed into one railcar fitted with makeshift bunks, and confined to this vehicle for the entire journey. Captain Muldoon, who was in charge of the party, managed however to retain all their stores and ammunition in the teeth of opposition from the railroad authorities.

As soon as they had been settled in, the party was assembled as the camp swimming pool, clad in swimming trunks, or 'jocks', to demonstrate their capabilities. Wright was dismayed when he compared their poor physique with the splendidly muscled and bronzed bodies of the American marines. Although he tried to comfort himself with the knowledge that Hasler had picked the best material available and that only brave men would have volunteered for hazardous service, he knew that courage alone was not enough.

The colonel in charge of the training centre had given permission for the unit to use the pool for four hours a day for one week in which to undergo preliminary instruction. Thereafter all training would have to be carried out at San Onofre.

Captain 'Dutch' Smith of the US Marine Corps Reserve had

been attached as liaison officer to the unit. Olympic high-diving champion of 1936, he suggested to Wright that as an initial test each man should jump from a height of thirty feet into the pool. They could thus be instructed in the correct technique of abandoning ship from, say, an aircraft carrier, and the feat would require nerve. Only one man failed this test of courage; later on he had to be discharged from the unit as unsuitable.

After Wright had lectured the party on the nature of the training that lay ahead, although telling them little more than that they would be required to cross heavy surf by day or night while under fire, they were issued with masks and fins. But before they could learn to use the latter efficiently, they had to be taught the 'flutter kick'. This was followed by instruction in the correct use of the dive mask. By the end of the week progress with these important items of equipment had been so satisfactory that from them on there was no problem in transferring training to San Onofre. Yet in Wright's own words:

> The great rollers pounding in on the beach in this area with the full force of the Pacific behind them was an awe-inspiring sight, even to those who had grown up with them. What they must have meant to these raw recruits from England can only be imagined.* .

All hands now embarked on a course of 'body surfing' in the breakers. Within a week they had mastered the technique and, using swim fins and masks, had become so proficient that they could tackle ten-foot breakers with a degree of confidence that alarmed their instructors. Unhappily not all proved to be such adventurous spirits. But as the original number of volunteers selected by Hasler had been increased to more than fifty, the target force of forty remained after those who were unable to face the risks involved had been returned to the United Kingdom.

The next step was to train the unit in the use of paddle boards. The latter differed from the normal surfboard in a number of respects. The paddle board was about twelve feet long and 42 inches across at the widest part, with a pointed stern; whereas the average surfboard has a square stern. Hollow and made of a light material, the paddle board was faster and more manoeuvrable. It was also strong enough to carry in addition to a swimmer either explosive charges or a light machine-gun. It thus made an ideal

* *The Frogmen of Burma,* op cit.

vehicle to convey a scout or military assault swimmer, showing a minimum of silhouette, through surf and over lakes, rivers and swamps.

To learn to use the boards efficiently took time and practice. For those who lacked it, a sense of balance had to be acquired and, since the boards had to be propelled entirely by hands and feet, the muscles of shoulders and arms developed. Practice runs on the boards were gradually lengthened to increase the unit's range of operations. Camouflage was another important requirement. Dark green and dark blue paint, non-soluble and in stick form, was used for the body, and a white cellophane headdress for swimming through a breaker line.

As the marines were also training their war dogs at Camp Pendleton, a series of trials of mutual interest to both sides were arranged. For Wright's unit it was important to determine the ability of a dog to detect a man on a paddle board and swimming, while the marines needed realistic experience for their animals. The latter were Dobermann Pinschers and Huskies, fierce and dangerous to approach, even when accompanied by their handlers. Accordingly the swimmers who took part in these exercises carried a diving knife in case an animal should slip its leash!

> We soon learned a curious fact that was most valuable to the dog masters [recorded Wright]! A swimmer coming in from the sea gave off almost no scent, and often a dog and its master passed within ten yards of one of our men lying on the beach without detecting him. This scentlessness could be reinforced by simply rolling in the dry sand. Using this method we beat the dogs time and again.

Thus they obtained proof that there was no more reason to fear a dog than an alert sentry. Nevertheless, arrangements were put in hand for the development of a blow-gun so that if necessary a canine guard could be silently disposed of.

Wright next obtained permission to carry out mock attacks on railway bridges along the ocean front. Starting from a point about three miles away to simulate an approach from a submarine, sections were required to paddle along at some distance to seaward from the beach, then come ashore, go through the motions of blowing up the bridge, regain their boards and paddle back to the start point. Concealment of the boards was the most difficult part, although they were invisible from the shore, and even from the top of a 70-foot cliff.

(*right*) A Greek schooner
minesweeping

(*below*) A caique of the
Levant Schooner Flotilla

Submarine *Perseus* and (inset) Stoker John Capes

As soon as proficiency was achieved, the next step was to attack defended objectives, hence the exercise at San Mateo related earlier. Thereafter, however, the marines were always informed when an attack was to be attempted. Although this gave the defenders an unfair advantage, the unit nevertheless managed to achieve a fifty per cent success rate. 'It was a bit dicey at times,' recorded Wright, 'as our chaps were dying to carry out some of the methods they had been taught for silently disposing of a sentry – and the marines were fully armed.' But there were no serious accidents.

Thus far little attention had been paid to the problem of dangerous fish, nor was there much information available on the subject. A Dutch army officer interested in paddle boards and designing collapsible rafts to fit into a submarine or flying boat who visited the unit, suggested that cyanide balls were used throughout the East Indies for fishing and that these might prove a highly effective shark repellent. Wright noted that there were great white sharks – the most dangerous kind – off the beach where they were swimming every day and night. 'But so far there had been no incidents. I had my fingers crossed.'

Not far away, however, were some colonies of sea lions, and Wright and certain picked members of the unit deliberately swam close to them to observe their reactions. Although some of the older bulls became agitated and roared their protests during the breeding season, bachelor bulls and females merely showed a mild curiosity towards their visitors. Other dangerous sea creatures which could be encountered off the California coast were octopuses and sharks. Of the former, those seen were undersized and harmless, and of the latter a few leopard sharks, too small to be dangerous. Nevertheless Wright considered that the shark question needed more closely investigating, and arranged with Captain Tollemache to visit Nassau, in the Bahamas, the home of all the dangerous species of sharks.

But before that, Tollemache had inspected the unit at Camp Pendleton. Considerable interest was, he said, being taken in the unit. At the Quebec conferences Major-General 'Wild Bill' Donovan, Chief of the Office of Strategic Services (OSS), had after discussion with Mountbatten decided to create a similar American formation. It was designated the 'OSS Maritime Unit', and Captain 'Dutch' Smith was appointed to take charge of their training. The unit was to be of equal strength to the SRU, but 150 of the finest watermen in the country were to be recruited, from whom forty would be selected. British methods of training were to be copied in every respect. The unit would be sent to the Far Eastern theatre.

Tollemache's report to CCO of his visit to Camp Pendleton emphasised how much he had been impressed with the men's general appearance and keenness and that, although much of the training was novel to them, they were shaping well. Teamwork formed the background of the training, which was entirely offensive in character. The unit was organised in sections with an officer in command of each, and taught to work and operate together singly, or in groups depending on the type of operation.

He expected that it would take three months from the date of receipt of diving suits from the United Kingdom before the men could be regarded as sufficiently trained and possessing the necessary skill and confidence to carry out the extremely arduous and hazardous duties they would be required to perform. He hoped the unit would remain as a team and not be broken up to act as instructors to other formations. He also suggested that two more officers and eight other ranks should be recruited as a reserve.

Meanwhile back in England the future of the unit had been under consideration at the highest level. Various authorities were told by CCO that a SRU of approximately forty strong would complete training in the United States in March 1944. Totalling four sections, each of two officers and eight other ranks, they would be qualified in surf landings, able to swim under water, and navigate fairly accurately for about a mile. They were trained in the use of paddle boards, elementary navigation, the use of limpets, and had an elementary knowledge of explosives. It was felt that climatic conditions in the Eastern and Mediterranean theatres would suit the unit better than northern European waters, although there might be isolated occasions when the unit might be useful in home waters.

COSSAC (Chief of Staff to Supreme Allied Commander – the planning organisation for the future Allied invasion of Europe) indicated that he had no requirement. Allied Force Headquarters in Algiers said there was no requirement in the western Mediterranean, but the Commander-in-Chief, Middle East considered that a section would be useful to assist in the destruction of enemy shipping in the Aegean, Black Sea, Adriatic, and on the Danube. South-East Asia Command asked for the entire unit.

The Chiefs of Staff, however, deferred their final decision as to the latter's allocation until training was completed. No personnel were available to form additional teams, so the unit would probably be allocated partly to South-East Asia and partly to the Middle East, to be available for operations or as instructors for training locally raised teams.

When Wright was informed of this he strongly objected to splitting up the formation. It would, he said, be disastrous to use a unit of less than forty. Some men were always likely to be on the sick list, and out of each section two or three would have to be left behind in the transporting submarine or surface craft to act as communications numbers and to guard the tethered boards. CCO backed Wright and recommended that the entire unit should go to South-East Asia Command, and that training should be concentrated on anti-Japanese warfare.

In the meantime Wright had visited Nassau and decided that the area would provide conditions closest to the unit's needs. Underwater visibility was better than almost anywhere, and as the Bahamas were a British colony, there would be no difficulty about the allocation of a suitable training area and accommodation. In November a second progress report from Tollemache to CCO noted that sea and air temperatures on the Californian coast were becoming too cold for the unit to continue night training at Oceanside. Approval was therefore given for the unit to be transferred to Salt Cay, in the Bahamas. Wright would have preferred them to go to Hawaii, but was informed that that area was too congested.

The next three weeks were taken up with moving the unit from Camp Pendleton to the new training area in the Bahamas. On completion of the first part of the course at Oceanside, eight other ranks who had failed to attain the required standard were returned to unit (RTU). These, together with one man who was rejected for disciplinary reasons, resulted in the unit proceeding to the advanced training base fifteen per cent under strength. Replacements to make up these deficiencies were subsequently received from the United Kingdom. As before, they included naval ratings and NCOs from the army and RAF.

In mid-November before the Britons left, the OSS Maritime Unit, totalling seventy men drawn from the US Coastguard, Naval Combat Demolition Unit, US Navy, US Marine Corps and US Army, arrived at Camp Pendleton. In the spring of 1944 they, too, were transferred to Nassau, still faithfully following the course of training initiated by Wright and his unit.

Salt Cay, more romantically known locally as Treasure Island, which had been leased as the training area for the unit, is a coral island some two miles long and 300 yards wide, situated about $2\frac{1}{2}$ miles north-east of New Providence, location of the group capital of Nassau. This strip of coral rock, with a small lagoon at its eastern end, was clothed in a tangle of sea grape, and dotted with Caribbean pines and palm trees. At that time it also accommodated a beach bungalow, a small stone tower, and a concrete tennis court, the latter of which the unit converted for basketball. The islet was just far enough off shore to be secluded although, Wright noted, everyone in Nassau soon got to hear of the 'Commandos' training there.

The officers were billeted in a private house in Nassau called Ballycrystal, leased from a Canadian millionaire. Ratings and other ranks were accommodated in the RAF barracks at Oakes Field, headquarters of No 111 Operational Training Unit. By mid-December all hands were duly installed and ready to begin the next phase of their training.

This had two main objectives: to teach the use of underwater breathing apparatus, and to familiarise the unit with dangerous marine animals. Wright decided that those most likely to be encountered world-wide were the killer whale, larger species of sharks, barracuda, and the estuarine crocodile. These he called the 'Big Four', and in due course the unit was to meet them all.

Soon after the move from Camp Pendleton, Petty Officer Frank Cooke joined the unit from England with the DSEA gear. A former submariner, Cooke was also a diver and boom defence rigger, and thus brought with him several useful skills. Since a technical flaw had been discovered in the special back-breathing apparatus being developed for the unit, they had to use the DSEA gear for training.

But, developed between the wars, DSEA was a form of self-contained breathing apparatus designed, not for working under water, but to bring a man up from a sunken submarine. It consisted of a breathing bag made of reinforced rubber worn on the chest, inside which was a metal canister containing soda lime, known as 'protosorb'. A moulded rubber mouthpiece was connected to the canister by a corrugated rubber breathing tube, a noseclip sealed the nostrils, and goggles protected the eyes. Flasks in a pocket below the breathing bag contained 56 litres of oxygen.

In use the oxygen passed from flask to breathing bag, an exhaust valve at the bottom of the latter – open under water – allowing excess oxygen to escape. Pure oxygen was admitted to the breathing bag, and all oxygen to and from the lungs passed through the 'protosorb' to remove the carbon dioxide. The gear also included a buoyancy bag to bring an unconscious man to the surface. The apparatus could, however, be used for shallow-water diving to a maximum depth of $5\frac{1}{2}$ fathoms for half an hour.

For the purpose of underwater training the buoyancy bag and goggles were discarded. Unhappily oxygen was difficult to obtain in the Bahamas, and the tropical sun and sand quickly ruined the DSEA sets. But not before several full-scale exercises had been successfully carried out, one with the unit carrying sten guns, ammunition and grenades on their paddle boards through known shark-infested waters at night.

Soon after their arrival on Salt Cay the unit suffered an epidemic of minor injuries, mostly small cuts which became infected by coral sand. One man was stung by a jellyfish, which could have proved fatal had he been alone and swimming off shore at the time. Wright himself suffered a ruptured eardrum caused by chasing after a grouper fish at 20 feet. Sharks, barracuda and sting ray were frequently encountered, but so far no shark repellent had been received for the unit.

Wright studied all the available literature concerning sharks. From what he had read and heard, the latter were supposed to be most avid if there was blood in the water. Accordingly he carried out a number of tests with turtle blood, sheep's blood and offal, but he found that the sharks paid no attention whatever. Some other attraction was needed, and Wright suspected this might be movement.

He therefore tried using live and wounded fish as bait on the end of a line to see if sharks would attack.

> The wounds produced the blood, and their struggles on the hook provided the movement. In two hours I had taken 9 barracuda and one shark, and on subsequent occasions I had hooked and lost five other large sharks. Movement was therefore the catalyst that released the attack.

A little later on an incident occurred which demonstrated the accuracy of this theory somewhat alarmingly.

Wright and two other members of the unit were fishing one hot day, but as the fish were not biting they decided to go for a swim.

The first man over the side of the boat was treading water while he donned his mask when he spotted an 8-foot shark curving away from his legs. He yelled a warning just as Wright and the third man had taken off in their dive. The shark was now head-on with tail quivering ready to charge. But as two more bodies splashed into the water, it saw that there were now three targets to tackle instead of one, and made off. How one man would have fared could only be guessed at, but there was no prize for the answer.

It was also found that, far from scaring them away, explosions under water actually attracted sharks. An old wreck off Salt Cay was used by the unit for practising cutting steel under water. Wright himself had a fright when, after setting off a number of charges of TNT in an exercise, he entered the water to pick up some dead fish. As he was reaching for a fair-sized specimen, a ten-foot shark slid past and snatched the fish from his grasp. He beat a hasty retreat to the boat, from which half a dozen sharks could now be seen circling the wreck. Yet the unit had been working round it under water for half an hour with no sign of any!

On one occasion the unit was swimming in formation around the eastern end of Salt Cay a quarter of a mile off shore when Captain 'Jock' Elder was suddenly seized by cramp and had to fall out. He told his second in command, Sub-Lieutenant Kimmins, that he felt capable of reaching the shore unaided, and duly set off. When about 200 yards from the beach, however, his cramp became very severe and he could barely remain afloat. As soon as he started to flounder he saw a barracuda coming for him. Passing within a foot of his head, it circled for another run. The fish now made several more runs past him and was obviously becoming more excited and working itself up to attack, behaviour characteristic of the barracuda.

Elder now began to yell for help, and fortunately his shouts were heard by Wright, who by now was nearly a quarter of a mile away. Several men from No 1 Section turned back to the rescue of their commanding officer, but they were recalled as No 2 Section had responded in a body. Elder was about to go down for the last time when they reached him, the barracuda 'flashing about in a most alarming manner'. The section formed a circle round the stricken captain and towed him ashore, the barracuda following closely and being most reluctant to leave. It was significant, recorded Wright, that the barracuda paid no attention to the men swimming past in a group, but immediately attacked the man in difficulty.

He kept a careful account of all their encounters with dangerous fish: sharks – including one of the great white variety – barracuda, sting ray, moray eels – some of the latter 12 feet long which could, and did, attack one man – jellyfish, coral and sea urchins. The sting rays, some of which measured six feet across, were not aggressive, but as they bury themselves in the sand, can inflict a fatal wound with their poison-spiked tail if trodden on. Jellyfish stings were very painful, although not severe.

Since, however, the incidence of attacks was relatively low, Wright decided that they did not constitute an element to worry military swimmers. All could be accepted as normal hazards, against which it was not necessary to wear special protective clothing.

Before leaving Nassau he wrote a study of the distribution and habitat of dangerous fish in Bahamian coastal waters, with operational recommendations. One of the latter was that everything worn in the water should be dark; bright-coloured or shining objects attracted all fish, especially the dangerous ones. Not the results of carefully planned and controlled experiments, but the day-to-day experiences of men who had spent thousands of hours in the water, his paper constituted, said Wright, the largest accumulation of experience available at that time.

Training was now chiefly concentrated on exercises and the completion of a demolition course. Through the good offices of the Combined Operations' liaison officer with OSS, a demolition expert in the person of First Lieutenant Chester Pomeroy of the US Army Corps of Engineers, was temporarily attached to the unit, and gave an extensive series of lectures and demonstrations in the use of all modern military explosives.

Specialists in the US Naval Research Laboratory in Washington had been working on the production of an effective shark repellent, and tests had shown that the chemical, copper acetate, answered the purpose satisfactorily. Two of their number, Professor Stuart Springer and Lieutenant Fogelberg, visited Salt Cay to see the unit in action and decide on some form of container. In due course they came up with a special belt to be worn by military swimmers.

Night exercises for the unit consisted of limpet attacks on ships, using the old wreck off the island as a target; cutting-out operations against local cargo vessels and one of the motor torpedo boats loaned from the West Indies Command; speed marches through jungle country on New Providence island by day and night; sabotaging aircraft, and demolition.

When Captain Tollemache paid his final visit to the unit, accompanied by a number of senior officers, Wright laid on their most ambitious exercises. For the first time in many weeks a fresh wind of between 15 and 25 miles an hour whipped up a choppy sea with three to four-foot waves, but in the exercises all objectives were achieved. In each of these a section had to proceed on the surface for some three miles from the intermediate carrier (which was the unit's diving tender) to reach their targets.

Following in a boat, Tollemache reported, somewhat ambiguously, that

> Although there was a bright moon, it was astonishing how invisible were these men with their darkened faces and bodies, and thrilling to see ten men propelling themselves at about four knots and carrying gear and explosives on their paddle boards in close formation behind their leader, who was steering by compass.

In a second exercise the men with their equipment disembarked from the intermediate carrier on to their paddle boards and proceeded to a point just outside visibility distance from a local convoy. There, two men broke off to attach limpets to the hulls of the merchant ships successfully. The remaining eight, armed with hand grenades and pistols, approached the motor torpedo boat in which Tollemache and his fellow officers were observers, boarded and took over the vessel, started the engines, and placed a plastic charge for blowing up an important underwater cable, all within four minutes. 'The whole operation was carried out with impressive stealth and in complete silence, each man knowing precisely the task he had to perform.'

The next night a section disembarked from the intermediate carrier two and half miles from the point on shore where they were to land, their passage being made in a beam sea, with the section leader steering by compass. The coast consisted of jagged limestone rocks with a certain amount of surf breaking over them. The section landed successfully at the given point, carried their boards over rocks inshore and hid them beneath branches and foliage. From thence they had to travel half a mile to the rendezvous position, then a further 600 yards carrying explosives through dense jungle to an old building representing a radar station which was their objective.

They blew gaps in the protective wire which had been placed around the approaches to the building with Bangalore torpedoes, and demolished the 'station'. The entire mission was accomplished and the men back on the beach within fifteen minutes. Although the section was not large, they were, noted Tollemache, men of impressive fitness – a far cry from the days when they first arrived at Camp Pendleton. They carried M.13 sub machine-guns, had grenades, limpet charges, .45″ automatics, 2 lb plastic charges and a fighting knife. For shore attacks such as this, sections also carried boots, socks, shirts and trousers in a waterproof container on their paddle boards.

Tollemache and his party of senior officers were not the only VIPs for whom the SRU staged an impressive exercise. Governor and Commander-in-Chief of the Bahamas was HRH the Duke of Windsor, who had been appointed to that post in July 1940. He, of course, was well aware of the presence of the unit, and in February 1944 Wright and his officers were officially invited to dinner at Government House.

Over brandy and cigars HRH asked when he could see the unit exercising, and a date was duly fixed. Unhappily every lady present who had entertained the unit clamoured to come along, but after Wright had pleaded the necessity for secrecy, the Duke ruled that only he and his staff would attend the demonstration. For this Wright decided to pull out all the stops and use live ammunition at every stage.

First item on the programme on the appointed day was beach infiltration. Although Wright had a man lying in plain sight on the beach with a sten gun, neither HRH nor anyone else in the royal party was aware of him. 'Well, where are the men?' asked the Duke after a few moments. 'Right here, sir,' replied Wright, ordering the man to stand up. The latter promptly rose from his position a few yards away and fired a burst to seaward from his sten gun. He had earlier swum ashore, having previously oiled his body, then simply rolled on and burrowed into the sand, this rendering him almost completely invisible.

The next phase in the demonstration was a simulated night attack on a strongpoint which had previously been prepared along the beach, complete with sandbags and barbed wire. A section was to paddle ashore from the intermediate carrier and attack and capture the strongpoint, using live grenades and ammunition. The attackers duly came in from the sea almost undetected on their paddle boards, assembled their weapons, and within minutes had demolished their objective with deadly efficiency. A fragment from one of their grenades ploughed up the sand within a few feet of the Duke who at that moment was incautiously peering out from behind a palm tree.

After demonstrating the art of stalking a sentry, and an exhibition of underwater swimming with DSEA, the final stage of the display involved a limpet mine attack on a submerged boiler. For this the Duke and his staff embarked in the diving tender with Wright, while Sub-Lieutenant Rodecker placed the underwater charges and set the time fuses. The latter functioned perfectly and, after witnessing the subsequent explosion and viewing its results, HRH returned to Government House after thanking Wright for a vastly interesting day, and wishing him and his unit good luck in their forthcoming operations. He subsequently wrote to the Chief of Combined Operations expressing his admiration for the unit, whose behaviour during their stay in Nassau, he added, had been a credit to the Service.

At home the final disposal of the unit had again come up for consideration. In March Middle East Command indicated that they no longer had any requirement for them, a section of the RMBPD having been sent out to work with the Raiding Forces in the Aegean. Accordingly the Chiefs of Staff Committee agreed that the entire unit should go to South-East Asia Command, who now remained the only bidder for their services. Tollemache in Washington was so informed by CCO and told that the unit should return to the United Kingdom as soon as practicable.

Arrangements were therefore made for them to sail from New York on board the troopship *Highland Chieftain* which was leaving with some 4000 American troops in a fast convoy early in May. Wright was to fly to London independently to be briefed on the next move. Before the unit bade farewell to their glamorous tropical island, the OSS Maritime Unit arrived from California to take their place. By June the Americans, too, were trained and ready. One section was sent to the United Kingdom for possible operations in the European theatre, and three went to Pearl Harbour to work with the Pacific Fleet.

On their departure from Salt Cay the SRU totalled forty-six officers and men, none of the former having changed. Thus, besides Wright, they consisted of Captains Muldoon and Elder and Lieutenant Turpin; Surgeon Lieutenant Robertson, now as fully qualified as the rest of them; Lieutenant Messenger, the chief training officer, and Sub-Lieutenant Rodecker, his assistant;

Lieutenants Strange and Junor, and Sub-Lieutenants Kimmins, Docherty and Booth, and Flying Officer Avery.

In addition to Petty Officer Cooke, the diving instructor, the naval ratings included Leading Seaman D. Hollinghurst, Able Seamen C.F. Robson, W. Long, A. Taberer and D. Richmond, RCN; Signalmen J.O. Bye and R. Newman; Telegraphist S. Sellers; Stoker A.S. Bailey; Ordinary Seamen E.R. Bedder, D. Redwood, J. McKellar, R.S. Morrell and A. Skead, RCN; and Ordinary Telegraphist E.C. Leyland; Marines J. White, R. Gilchrist and G. Pettit, who was the unit's storeman.

Army other ranks were Sergeant G. Whitlock, Corporal P.S.V. Smith, Lance-Corporals E. Harrison and G. Cotton, and Gunner W.H. Gridland. The RAF was represented by Flight-Sergeant E. Shand, the unit's CSM; Flight-Sergeants A.V. Cave and F. Davies; Sergeants L.R. Bretton, P. Colgan and N. Cochrane; Leading Aircraftmen W.R. Pennell and F. Gill; and Aircraftmen H.A. Cobb and J. Stewart.

The *Highland Chieftain* duly docked at Liverpool on May 23, and two days later the SRU with its arms and equipment found itself in HMS *Robertson*, a hutted encampment near Richborough, in Kent. A holding base for trained landing craft personnel, the depot provided accommodation for 1200 Royal Marines and 100 officers. The whole of southern England at that time was an armed camp. Final preparations had been made for Operation 'Overlord', the Allied invasion of Europe, and D-Day was less than a fortnight away. Officers and men of the SRU felt sure that they were destined for a role in the forthcoming landings.

But they were to be disappointed. When Wright reported to Combined Operations headquarters in London he found few people who had the time to talk to him. Worse still, many of the officers who had known of and taken an interest in the unit had gone. Mountbatten himself had been appointed Supreme Allied Commander, South-East Asia, his place as Chief of Combined Operations having been taken by Major-General Robert Laycock. Blondie Hasler, too, had gone to south-east Asia. 'After a week of poking my unwanted nose into every doorway of COHQ, the best I received was a vague "There will be a role for you. Be patient!"' commented Wright gloomily.

In due course D-Day came and went, and thereafter supplies of men and material began pouring endlessly across the Channel as Allied strength was built up around the beachheads. Allied fighters and bombers droned overhead by day and night, and the landing craft teams in HMS *Robertson* were engaged in ceaseless activity. The disconsolate SRU could only occupy its time with exercises, physical training and route marches. Some of the officers went out on nightly forays in Coastal Force craft. Possibly in order to get Wright and his importunities out of their hair, the top brass at COHQ approved of his suggestion that the unit should qualify as parachutists, so that if necessary they could be dropped from the air as near to surf as possible.

Accordingly they were sent off to the Airborne Training School at Ringway, near Manchester, and, such was their enthusiasm, that in five days they had completed the ground training, which usually took two weeks. All hands duly qualified in this new skill, and on their return to HMS *Robertson* proudly put up their parachutist's wings. It was now that Hal Messenger and Frank Rodecker left them, having been ordered to return to America. These two experts had imparted all they knowledge they could, and their job was at an end.

The waiting period which lasted for so long and had begun to undermine the unit's morale was due, of course, to the fact – although they could not be told this – that nothing and nobody could be spared for any other theatre of war until every possibility of employment in the great enterprise in Europe had been exhausted. With all hope of an operational role abandoned, Wright sent on leave anyone whose home was within reach, and various drop-outs for medical reasons were replaced. There were very few of these, however, and no officers were involved. Wright himself was finally given permission to take some leave in Canada, with instructions to rejoin by the beginning of October.

Orders now came from COHQ that the unit was to leave as soon as possible for Ceylon. Wright was to follow a few days later by air. Before they left HMS *Robertson* for the last time they received this signal from CCO:

> On your departure for South-East Asia Command good luck and best wishes from all at COHQ. We are confident that your fine unit will make a great name for itself in the war against Japan.

On 8 October Wright left England at the start of his long flight to Colombo, in Ceylon. Reporting to SEAC Headquarters in Kandy, where he spotted a number of remembered faces from COHQ, he learned that the unit was to come under the control of the 'Small Operations Group' based at Camp Hammanheil on Kayts Island, in the Jaffna peninsula at the northern tip of Ceylon. Colonel Humphrey Tollemache, Royal Marines, a relation of his namesake in Washington, commanded the Group, and Wright was cheered to learn that Blondie Hasler was the depot's second-in-command.

At this point it is necessary to glance at the course of the war in south-east Asia in order to provide a background to the operations in which the unit was to become engaged.

Following the Japanese attack on Pearl Harbour in December 1941, the new enemy turned his attention to Hongkong and swiftly brought about its surrender. Malaya was then speedily overrun, and the victorious Japanese advanced upon Burma with the object of securing their western flank and cutting the Allied supply line to China. By May 1942 our small and weak defending forces had been driven from that country and over the border into India, whose frontier with Burma was now threatened. In northern Burma Chinese forces led by the American Lieutenant-General Stilwell had also been compelled to retreat, and had disintegrated. Then the monsoon came down, putting a stop to a further Japanese follow-up and a temporary end to the fighting. By then Britain and America, her new ally, were fully preoccupied with further misfortunes occurring elsewhere.

Extending for some 700 miles, the front in Burma comprised three principal sectors: the Northern, for the defence of which fresh Chinese troops were being hurriedly trained in India; the Central, concentrated in and around the hilly State of Manipur, in Assam, just inside the Indian border; and the southern land route to India, a coastal strip of swamp and jungle-covered hills some 200 miles long in the Arakan, where a Japanese thrust towards Calcutta had been held with difficulty.

Two small-scale offensives were launched by the Allies towards the end of 1942: the first to retake the Mayu Peninsula and Akyab Island in the Arakan; and the second, a daring raid by a special force of 'Chindits' formed and led by Brigadier Orde Wingate, to cut the Japanese lines of communication in the centre, and to co-operate with a Chinese offensive to be launched from Yunnan. Although the latter did not eventuate, Wingate persuaded the authorities to allow the Chindit operation to go ahead.

Unfortunately our first Arakan campaign petered out due chiefly to lack of air superiority and transport planes to drop supplies to our hard-pressed forces. Although Wingate's raiders blew up bridges and cut railway lines to the enemy's rear, these were speedily repaired, so that on the whole their efforts, too, amounted to a military failure. But they had proved that a considerable British force could penetrate and operate in the jungle hundreds of miles behind the Japanese lines and return. Wingate's foray thus provided a welcome morale-booster.

Meanwhile the Allies continued to strengthen their forces, re-building combat units and increasing the flow of supplies, while also constructing roads, railways and airstrips in preparation for an offensive designed to recapture Burma. Then came the setting up of a separate South-East Asia Command to prosecute the war against Japan, and the appointment of Mountbatten as Supreme Allied Commander, bringing a new drive, new resources and a promise of better times to this seemingly 'forgotten' theatre of war. Lieutenant-General 'Bill' Slim, who had commanded 'Burcorps' during the earlier retreat, was given command of the newly created Fourteenth Army, while Lieutenant-General Stilwell was appointed Deputy Supreme Commander, and assumed command of the combined Chinese and American forces in the north, with orders to recover northern Burma and re-open the land route to China by constructing a highway from Ledo to link up with the old Burma Road at a point beyond Myitkina.

In March 1944, however, the Japanese who had also been reinforced, decided to carry the war into India, break up the bases where Allied armies and fleets were building up for the final assault on Japan, cut off the northern front and disrupt air supplies to China. Thus, while Stilwell was beginning his advance into northern Burma, Slim on the central front was preparing to meet the expected Japanese onslaught in Manipur.

Earlier to derange the enemy's plans, a fresh Allied thrust had been launched in the Arakan with the object of clearing the Mayu peninsula and capturing the small port of Maungdaw through which our forces could be supplied. But the Japanese switched an extra division from the central front to deal with this threat. Our advance was repulsed, and then the enemy went over to a counter-offensive. This was held, and by February 1944 our forces had managed to gain the ascendant. Although the Japanese continued to fight on, they were eventually compelled to retreat. This success marked a vital turning point in the campaign.

The main enemy offensive, which centred around Imphal and

Kohima, was launched in March. But Slim was ready. The Japanese attacks were firmly met, held and finally broken, resulting in massive enemy casualties. At last the tide had been decisively turned against the Japanese in Burma.

Slim's aim – he had now been appointed to command all Allied land forces in Burma – was to advance across the Chindwin river, occupy the area between that river and the Irrawaddy, cross the latter and force battle on the retreating Japanese in the plain above Mandalay before they could re-form. At the same time Stilwell, aided by another long-range penetration by the Chindits to harass the Japanese and disrupt their communications, would continue his advance southwards from Myitkina, which he had captured after a long siege. In the Arakan a renewed thrust was to be made to secure forward bases and airfields to aid the final advance of the Fourteenth Army on Rangoon.

This, then, was how the situation developed while the SRU was en route to Ceylon, leaving the prospect of much hard fighting ahead. Wright was told that his unit would be needed to operate along the eastern shores of the Bay of Bengal, in Burma as required, and possibly in Malaya – a potential sphere of operations stretching from Mandalay to Singapore.

Hammanheil Camp was situated on a beach in Kayts Island amid coral reefs, sandbanks and small offshore islands. After reporting to Colonel Tollemache and arranging for the reception of his unit, Wright decided that he could most usefully fill in his time by touring the coastal areas of Ceylon to find out all he could about the type of coral which could be expected around the coasts of Burma and Malaya, and garner all available information relating to sharks and other dangerous marine fauna.

Although large sharks are commonly to be found in the Bay of Bengal, Wright could discover no recorded case of shark fatality in Ceylonese waters. There were, however, plenty of aggressive swordfish, poisonous sea snakes, sting rays, scorpion fish and stinging jellyfish; also dangerous estuarine crocodiles. Since both Burma and Malaya are jungle countries, with rain forests and coastal mangrove swamps, Wright now became only too well aware that the unit lacked bushcraft and jungle skills, and that these would have to be learnt. There was a Jungle Battle School in India, but it was too far away. There was, however, jungle of a sort in Ceylon containing plenty of wild animals, including elephant, reptiles, leeches and other unpleasant creatures, which could be utilised for training. As there was still time before the unit was due, he set out on a solitary six-day trek to test conditions for himself.

Soon after his return the unit arrived and settled in at Hammanheil Camp. But before their acclimatisation and hardening programme could be got under way, Admiral Mountbatten inspected the base. The unit demonstrated swimming with fins, paddle boards and other equipment, and also carried out an exercise which involved swimming ashore and kidnapping the headman of a local village – fortunately he had been forewarned! 'Supremo' was very well satisfied with their performance and promised Wright that they would soon be required for operations.

The acclimatisation programme for the unit included, in addition to swimming and paddle-boarding, canoe training and canoe towing, paddling long distances, day and night tactical exercises, jungle training and dropping from the air. Jungle training was carried out in the northern area of Ceylon which Wright had explored during his long trek, and included night marching by map and compass. This culminated in a full-scale escape exercise staged in the southern 'wet' jungle, 'an area of huge trees interlaced with climbing vines and parasitic plants – the jungle of the movies'.

The exercise began by off-loading the unit from a truck on a moonless night beside a jungle track and a river they had never seen before, to simulate a parachute descent into enemy-held territory. They were required to bivouac until daylight, then construct individual bamboo rafts and make their way downstream to the sea. Apart from suffering severely from the attentions of leeches, and a close brush with the nest – fortunately temporarily unoccupied – of an estuarine crocodile, the unit came through without accident.

Soon after their return to Hammanheil Camp came news that the Fourteenth Army was approaching the Irrawaddy, and that landings were also planned along the Arakan coast. No 1 Section was to move off first. Commanded by Jock Elder, with Sub-Lieutenant Kimmins as second in command, the Section consisted of Sergeant Cave RAF, Corporal Smith, Aircraftman Cobb, Leading Seaman Hollinghurst, Able Seaman Robson, Marine White, Signalman Bye and Ordinary Seaman Bedder. They were to be attached to the famous 33 Corps which had relieved besieged Kohima, driven the Japanese back and opened the road to Imphal.

Frogman on a paddle board

An SRU patrol crawls ashore in a daylight demonstration

SRU operational team on completion of training

It is necessary however to pause once again and glance at the way General Slim's plans were working out.

Following the decisive Japanese defeat in the central sector, the speed and strength of the British advance in pursuit of the retreating enemy prompted the latter to yield the area of the plain above Mandalay and retire behind the barrier of the Irrawaddy. Slim was bent on bringing the main body to a stand-up battle. He had received orders to destroy all the Japanese forces round Mandalay, and to capture Rangoon before the onset of the monsoon in mid-May. Meanwhile our forces in the Arakan were to seize Akyab and Ramree Island to secure airfields from which the Fourteenth Army could be supplied as it advanced.

In making his overall plan for the recapture of Rangoon, Mountbatten was relying on a promise by the Combined Chiefs of Staff of considerable reinforcements for the Fourteenth Army. Unfortunately events elsewhere intervened. In Europe the German counter-attack in the Ardennes deranged plans, and in China an advance of the Japanese resulted in the withdrawal from the northern front in Burma of two Chinese divisions and several American air squadrons to deal with this threat. Thus Slim had to carry on with existing resources.

In terms of troops the Fourteenth Army comprised two corps, the 4th and 33rd. The 4th consisted of the 7th and 17th Indian Divisions, a tank brigade, the 28th East African Brigade and the Lushai Brigade, veteran native jungle scouts commanded by a British officer. 33 Corps consisted of the 2nd, 19th and 20th Divisions, and two additional brigades, one of them armoured. In reserve were two Indian Divisions, motorised and parachute-trained. 15 Corps, which was conducting the Arakan offensive, consisted of two Indian Divisions, two West African Divisions, and a tank brigade, augmented by 3 Commando Brigade, formed of two army and two Royal Marine Commandos.

The Irrawaddy constituted a formidable obstacle. Its average width varies from 2,000 to 4,000 yards, and in places the river is obstructed by islands and sandbars which change position with every flood. Since a direct assault would be too risky, Slim decided to strike against the enemy rear. Accordingly 4 Corps would be switched from the northern flank above Mandalay and launched in a surprise thrust across the Irrawaddy near the town of Pakokku, 100 miles south-east of Mandalay. From there the Corps would head at top speed for Meiktila, some fifty miles east, which was the main enemy administrative centre, containing supply bases, ammunition dumps, hospitals, depots, airfields, also the nodal point of road and rail routes. The Japanese would thus be caught between the anvil of 4 Corps and the hammer of 33 Corps.

This move was all-important because upon it rested the whole fabric of Slim's battle plan. Since No 2 Section of the SRU, temporarily under the command of Wright himself, was to spearhead the river crossing of 4 Corps upon which so much depended, it will be convenient to follow their fortunes first rather than recount the experiences of the sections in chronological or numerical order.

The Section, consisting of Sub-Lieutenant Docherty ('Brute' Strange, its leader, was in hospital), Sergeant Cochrane, RAF, Lance-Corporal Harrison, Leading Aircraftman Pennell, Aircraftman Stewart, Marine Gilchrist, Able Seamen Skead and Redwood, Rifleman Booth, and Trooper Holding – three of them replacements for men who had fallen out since Salt Cay – flew to Calcutta first. From thence, after a wait of several days, they were air-lifted with their crated paddle boards, weapons and equipment to a dusty airstrip in the Irrawaddy plain at Mytche, near which was the temporary headquarters of 4 Corps. There they were assigned to the 7th Indian Division, whose forward position had been established south of the large Japanese-held town of Pakokku, and some three miles from the village of Kukyun on the west bank of the river.

This area was low-lying and cultivated, with ricefields, but Nyaungu, on the Japanese-held east bank, lay behind a line of rugged cliffs 100 feet high pierced with holes. At night the Japanese often sent patrols across to prowl the area of no-man's-land around Kukyun, while there were known to be spies and enemy agents in the village itself.

On reporting to Divisional headquarters, Wright was told that a reconnaissance of embarkation points along the waterfront was urgently needed that night. The water level had fallen, the river had changed its bed, and new sandbanks had appeared. Since no direct passage was possible, the crossing would have to be made obliquely over a distance of some, 1,500 to 2,000 yards. Information was required about beach approaches, whether the banks were firm enough for tanks, how close boats with a four-foot draught could be brought in, and the depth of water around a sandbank which extended along the whole of the waterfront.

The Division had originally intended to make a daylight crossing with full artillery, tanks and air support. But a reduction in the available airlift brought about by the withdrawal of some of the American air squadrons, and the difficulties of road transport made it impossible to dump a sufficient stockpile of ammunition. A silent moonless crossing had been abandoned as boats would not be able to find the main channel: it would therefore have to take place before dawn.

The assault crossing would be mounted from a number of points on the west bank, upstream of Kukyun, to seize five beaches on the east bank and the cliffs above. There would then be a rapid follow-up in daylight by three battalions and tanks. The rest of the Division would then cross at Nyaungu, and the bridgehead widened to allow the passage of 17 Division to swing northwards against the Japanese at Pakokku.

Wright decided that two swimmers, himself and Marine Gilchrist, would be sufficient to carry out this preliminary reconnaissance. A small group of the SBS (see page 18) was also attached to the Division, and one of their officers had been posted missing the day before. They would send along an officer and a corporal to take beach measurements.

After nightfall the four set off on their mission. The SRU men were clad in jungle battledress, with rubber-soled shoes but no headgear. Each was armed with an automatic pistol and a Commando knife, and carried a spare magazine in a waterproof holder. They also took swim fins but no masks. As a crude method of depth sounding, each man had painted a mark on his chest at a height of four feet from his toes. Cautiously traversing no-man's-land, they passed wraithlike through Kukyun. But despite their stealth they heard the sound of bamboo tapping, which was the usual warning by villagers that strangers were about. It could also mean that a Japanese patrol was at large.

Arriving on the upstream bank of the river, the four split up to carry out their individual tasks. Wright and Gilchrist divested themselves of their battledress, fitted swim fins on their feet, and waded into the black and uninviting water of the Irrawaddy. As Wright afterwards wrote:

> I had thought about crocodiles, but could get no information without giving away too much of our plans. We would have to risk them. There were also regal pythons up to 30 feet long that lie at the water's edge at

night waiting to grasp and coil around anything that comes to drink. Last but not least, there might be Japs swimming like ourselves in the river.

They found that the channel between the embarkation beaches and the sandbank fronting them was too shallow for laden boats, which meant that the only exit was at its downstream end. To reach this, they swam out into the river, judging the depth of water at intervals by lowering their feet to the bottom. No enemy was encountered, but Wright spotted a pinpoint of light on the sandbank as they went past, which meant that Japs must be on it since the villagers' boats had been taken away from them to prevent any communication with the enemy. He hoped that if spotted, he and Gilchrist would be taken for a pair of crocodiles!

Having obtained all the information they could, they then swam back and joined up with the SBS men to wait for daylight. The results of their night's work were given verbally to the Divisional staff officer on their return, which enabled the latter to fill in important blanks on his plans.

The next task on the following night was to chart the channels between the sandbars in the river and examine the landing beaches in detail. For this the whole ten-man Section was to take part, using paddle boards. In order to help in transporting these to the river bank, a military fighting patrol was attached.

Every effort was made to conceal the 12ft paddle boards from prying eyes in the village, but the soldiers dumped the boards in the wrong place in an upstream *chaung*. As they were being brought down next morning, a man was seen to run from the village, clamber into a boat and start to paddle over to the Japanese-held bank. Unfortunately he was too far off for them to take a shot at.

During the day a lookout post was established from which the beaches on both sides of the river could be kept under observation through binoculars until nightfall. Useful information about the depth of water along the beaches was obtained simply by watching the villagers swimming. Several sites which might harbour concealed enemy gun emplacements on the opposite bank were also located for further reconnaissance that night.

After darkness had fallen and all had become quiet, the Section set off in four pairs, or patrols, on their boards. The objectives of the first patrol, consisting of Docherty and Holding, were the upstream sandbar and Nos 1 and 5 beaches. The second patrol of Booth and Stewart was to reconnoitre No 4 beach. Cochrane and Gilchrist, and Pennell and Skead, along with the SBS men, would examine Nos 2 and 3 beaches. Wright and Redwood patrolled all beaches, finally retiring to the sandbank to cover the withdrawal. In case of alarm, they carried phosphorus grenades with which to create a smokescreen.

A practical channel between the sandbars in the main stream was charted; the depths of water and nature of the bottom off the beaches obtained, and their extent and slope measured with the aid of a bamboo pole and a piece of string; the nature of the beach exits, and the positions of any wire defences and sentries carefully noted. The SBS also reconnoitred the banks of *chaungs* leading to the beaches. It was also important to check the depth of water at the downstream end of the large sandbar opposite the landing beaches where all boats would have to turn for their final run-in.

All these difficult, not to say hair-raising, operations were successfully carried out completely undetected by the enemy, although there were one or two heart-stopping moments. Voices were heard at No 5 beach, and at No 4 a Japanese sentry was only located because he struck a match within twenty yards of Booth and Stewart, who had watched the beach for fifteen minutes, decided that there was no one on it and were crawling ashore. On No 2 beach a flashlight was played on Cochrane and Gilchrist from close range, but the sentry apparently did not recognise what he saw, switched off his torch and walked away. Within a minute, however, he was back again playing his light on the same place, but by then the patrol had withdrawn into mid-stream. As there were a lot of dead bodies drifting down from battles farther up river, the Japanese probably thought that what he had seen was merely a pair of bobbing corpses.

Patrolling around the downstream sandbar, Wright and Redwood came across an SBS folbot and one of their own men who had lost their bearings, and re-directed them to the rendezvous. Before dawn all patrols had returned safely to the lying-up point east of Kukyun village without further incident, and a detailed report was despatched to Divisional headquarters in time for the morning conference on the forthcoming crossing.

Z-hour was to be in the early dawn of 14 February, and the SRU and SBS teams were allotted their official roles in the crossing. The SRU were to mark navigational hazards in the stream, make a final reconnaissance of 1 and 4 beaches prior to the landing and mark them for the assault. The SBS team would take similar action in respect of 2 and 3 beaches. Both teams were to carry out a final pre-assault reconnaissance of all beaches, to start at 0100 and be completed by 0300.

A battalion of the South Lancashire Regiment was scheduled to spearhead the assault in what Slim later described as 'the largest opposed river crossing in any theatre of war'. They had been loaned from another brigade, having had previous experience in boatwork and taken part in the capture of Diego Suarez in 1942. After embarking, C Company was to round the upstream point of the principal sandbar at 0345 and paddle their boats to No 4 beach, which would be unlighted. The white sandbank lights were to be put on at 0345, or as soon as the Company's boats came in sight, and extinguished immediately they had passed. The markers at No 1 beach were to show a green light at its upstream point, those at No 2 beach a blue light, and a red at No 3. While Sergeant Cochrane took station on the upper sandbar, Wright would do the same at the downstream end of the one fronting the landing beaches.

The night was pitch black and a strong wind raised an unwelcome lop on the water, but the final reconnaissance went according to plan and without interference from the enemy, although one alarming incident occurred. The crew of the SBS folbot returning from No 2 beach spotted two men swimming away from our embarkation points on the west bank. Major Kealy, the SBS officer, challenged them, expecting them to be members of one of the SRU teams. As their reply was unintelligible, he risked playing a torch on them. Both had shaven heads, wore swimming trunks and were heading for the east bank. They were obviously Japanese, and Kealy immediately killed them with a burst from his tommy gun. The shots alerted both banks, and Rifleman Booth returning from his reconnaissance of No 4 beach, was fired on by a machine-gun and his paddle board hit. He promptly abandoned board and equipment and swam the rest of the way across the river, arriving back at his own bank exhausted but uninjured.

At 0345 Cochrane and Wright heard the first wave of assault boats approaching and exhibited their lights. All went well, and C Company landed unopposed. At 0510 the lights were put on again to guide the main assault, which should be coming down the channel east of Kukyun. But by 0530, when it was almost daylight, there was still no sign of the boats. Unhappily, they were ageing craft of wood and canvas with old-fashioned outboard motors, which had suffered badly during their 100-mile journey along jungle tracks. Because of the noise they made it was not possible to start the motors until the men had embarked. Many refused to start, and some of the boats leaked badly. Eventually the colonel ordered them away regardless of scheduled flights.

Thus it was 0615 before the main body of the assault wave began to arrive off the beaches. The three leading boats which had managed to get their motors going had taken some of their comrades in tow, while others were being paddled along or drifting. To make matters worse, one of the boats in the van in which part of the reserve company was embarked was trying to turn in midstream to take its proper place at the rear, throwing the rest into confusion. It was at this point that the Japanese opened concentrated machine-gun fire from the cliffs on the three leading craft.

All four company commanders, the adjutant, and two air liaison officers in the first boat were at once killed or wounded. Only one man survived. He was the colonel of the South Lancashires, and Wright saw him rise to his feet, hurl his bush hat in defiance towards the enemy, and dive overboard. He eventually reached the west bank and rejoined his command unscathed. Casualties in the other two leading boats were equally heavy, more than sixty being killed and wounded.

At 0625 the main assault force turned back to the sandbank fronting Kukyun, where casualties were disembarked and an attempt made at reorganisation. There were thus several hundred British troops milling about in the open with no cover in broad daylight within easy range of Japanese machine-guns. But for some reason these soon ceased fire.

When the main assault had turned away, the SRU and SBS beach-marchers left their beaches and returned to Kukyun. They had carried out their hazardous part of the operation to the letter, and luckily got away without casualty. While Docherty was lying on his paddle board covering the position of his light on No 1 beach with a machine-pistol, a Burman and two Japanese, one of them an officer, came within twenty feet of him to examine the light. Because the main assault was then approaching, he held his fire but, curiously enough, the enemy made no attempt to interfere with the light.

At the downstream end of the sandbar fronting the landing beaches, Wright's light was required to be in four feet of water.

This necessitated wading 150 yards further down river, from which position when the light was extinguished he could not be seen from the bar. When he returned there to retrieve his paddle board, he found that a Japanese had followed his footprints to the point where he entered the water, written something in the sand and drawn a circle round it. Thinking this to be a trap, Wright took 'appropriate avoiding action'. Then he remembered the two Japanese killed by Major Kealy, and the mystery was solved. The man who had left the marks in the sand must have mistaken Wright's tracks for those of one of his own swimmers and left a message for him.

Following the failure of the attempt by the rest of the South Lancashires to get across the river, a full air strike and artillery barrage was laid on, and the Divisional crossing was accomplished without further opposition.

No 2 Section of the SRU was, however, to be given no breathing space, for immediately afterwards they were transferred to 114 Brigade for interception patrols on the river in the Pakokku area. When the brigade had closed in on that town, the Japanese sent in reinforcements and put up a stubborn fight. At Kokkhala, just below Pakokku, the Section was attached to the leading company of the 1/14th Punjabis.

The Irrawaddy at this point was blocked to some extent by islands and sandbanks, which were obscured at night by fog or mist. The Japanese had dug in on an island opposite the town while their positions on the east bank were strengthened. A reconnaissance was at once carried out to determine the practicability of operations in the southern channel. But the SRU men found the current – running at between three and four knots – and the distance such that operations from the north bank were impossible. The only craft available by means of which these difficulties could be overcome was a solitary Mark VI powered canoe belonging to the SBS.

On the night of 16/17 February, folbot and Mark VI canoe patrols were undertaken to familiarise personnel with the intricate channels in that part of the river, which were found to be quite unlike those shown on the map. Next night, using paddle boards and swimming, a two-man patrol consisting of Marine Gilchrist and Trooper Holding set off to reconnoitre an area between two army map reference points on the Japanese bank, but were unable to reach their objective because of the fierceness of the current. Instead they reconnoitred the much more heavily guarded area separating the villages of Letpanchibaw and Thayetkon.

The former was strongly held by the enemy, and Japanese motor transport with lights on was using the road running south-east to the main highway. The SRU men calmly examined the beach between the two villages, notwithstanding that Japanese were working on it only a short distance away. After spending a total of seven hours in the river, swimming and paddle-boarding, they returned safely to Kokkhala with much valuable information.

Although the Japanese evacuated Pakokku on 18 February as part of their general withdrawal across the Irrawaddy, their departure being closely followed by the entry of the Punjabis, they still held the island opposite the town. On the following night Docherty joined a fighting patrol of Punjabis to find out if it was possible to mount paddle board and canoe operations from Pakokku to intercept Japanese leaving the island. Unfortunately the channel was found to be impassable. The SBS, however, using their Mark VI canoe, managed to get in 'two good shoots' at Japanese motorboats crammed with enemy troops before the island was also evacuated.

The battle for Pakokku, intended only as a feint to divert enemy attention from the 7th Division crossing further down the river, was now over, and Wright decided to withdraw the Section for a brief period of refit and maintenance. Cancelling any further operations for them for the time being, he left to join up with No 4 Section attached to 33 Corps.

The Corps was comprised of 2 British Division, 19 and 20 Indian Divisions, plus two additional brigades, one of them armoured. Slim was anxious to push 2 Division over the Irrawaddy nearer to Mandalay when the Japanese began to realise the threat to Meiktila of his right hook at Nyaungu and started to pull troops back.

Wright found the Section attached to 5 Brigade and accommodated at brigade headquarters. As this was a British Division, living conditions as regards messing, transport and general amenities, including a rum ration, were vastly superior to the conditions experienced by No 2 Section who had been living with the Punjabis. Their morale was high, and the general complimentary about their work. When he learned that the SRU had their own doctor – Robertson at that time having joined up with 2 Section – he told Wright that an extra medical officer would be useful in the Division's forthcoming river crossings. The surgeon lieutenant was accordingly flown up from Pakokku.

Led by Flying Officer Avery, No 4 Section consisted of Lieutenant Turpin, Sergeant Colgan, Stoker Bailey, Gunner Gridland, Able Seaman Richmond, Ordinary Seaman Morrell, Telegraphist Sellars and Signalman Newman.

Just below Mandalay the Irrawaddy turns in an east-to-west direction for several miles. Averaging about 1,000 yards in width, the main stream is broken up by islands. On both sides the land is flat with numerous small villages, and is indented with creeks, or *chaungs*. Farther on, the land on the left bank becomes higher and wooded and the bank steeper.

The Divisional crossing plan was for two bridgeheads to be secured by separate assault forces, the first on an island due south of the village of Kindaw by the Royal Welch Fusiliers, who would embark at Kindaw; and the second near a strategically convenient *chaung* by the Cameron Highlanders, embarking at the village of Myittha. This landing was to be backed up by an assault force of the Worcestershire Regiment, who would launch their boats from a point known as the Dawete sandbank, to establish a bridgehead on the right flank of the Camerons.

The plan had been drawn up in the light of experience gained by 4 Corps, and it was decided that instead of using beach lights to guide in the assault waves, these should be led in by the SRU men on paddle boards who had previously reconnoitred the landing beaches. Lights would be exhibited by the Royal Engineers only after the assault waves had landed and secured their beacheads.

The preliminary reconnaissances had already been carried out by the Section prior to Wright's arrival. Avery and a small patrol examined the beach where the Worcesters were to land, the SRU men on their paddle boards being accompanied by a Royal Engineers officer in a folbot to test the beach for the passage of tanks. It was found to be perfect for the landing, and the party withdrew undetected.

Avery was then asked to make a similar reconnaissance of the other two beaches, and he decided that the SRU should do these on their paddle boards, which would enable them to test the strength of the current, and mark the position of any sandbars. The Camerons' beach was chosen first. On their way across the river a long sandbar was encountered, and Avery detached a two-man patrol to explore this while he and his partner continued on towards the beach. But before they had got very far, several boats crammed with Japanese troops suddenly loomed up.

Submerging themselves until little more than their eyes showed above the surface, they watched the boats pass by. Avery said afterwards that they could have dropped a grenade or so in at least two of them, but this would have betrayed their presence in the river. In a state of helpless frustration, they saw the Japanese portage their boats over the sandbar, re-embark and disappear in the direction of the position held by the Worcesters.

It was obvious that the proposed landing beach could not now be used. Collecting their fellow paddle-boarders from the sandbar, who had hastily concealed themselves when the Japanese appeared, they made their way back to the northern bank. En route they saw the flashes of grenade bursts and heard the sound of rifle and machine-gun fire. Later they learned that the Japanese raiding party had landed undetected, overrun the Worcesters' forward positions and killed or wounded a number of men before withdrawing.

Several nights later, when things had quietened down, Turpin and Colgan reconnoitred the Royal Welch Fusiliers' beach, found it usable, and withdrew without incident. This left a third beach to be found. While Avery and Sellars undertook this mission, Turpin took the rest of the Section a couple of miles upstream to stage a 'jitter party' and thus divert the attention of the Japanese. Using paddle boards and folbots, they took with them in addition to rifles, bren guns and grenades, a number of plastic explosive charges.

Avery and Sellars were therefore able to locate a satisfactory landing beach without difficulty, while the 'jitter party', firing indiscriminately in the direction of the enemy-held bank, drew down on themselves Japanese mortar fire, most of it fortunately wild. In order to continue to annoy the enemy for the rest of the night, they left behind their plastic charges timed to explode every hour!

All of them subsequently returned safely to base with the exception of Turpin, who had set off independently on his paddle board. As time wore on and he failed to appear, the Section became increasingly alarmed. Then, just as daylight was near, he appeared swimming, having lost his board. He had, he said, been paddling along below a cliff on the south bank when he happened to glance up and saw the figure of a man silhouetted against the night sky. Fearing that he had been spotted, he paddled into the shadows cast by the cliff and waited with one foot on the beach and the other on the paddle board.

Then his foot slipped and the board started to drift away. But he made no attempt to retrieve it, for by now he had been able to distinguish that the Japanese was an officer and that he was holding what appeared to be a briefcase. Turpin decided to capture this prize, but as he climbed upwards he dislodged a rock. The sudden noise so startled the Japanese that he promptly turned and fled, dropping the briefcase in his hurry. Turpin picked it up, strapped it to his belt, returned to the bank and set off swimming down the river. But in his excitement he forgot to take his bearings. As he approached what he took to be the Worcesters' position and was about to crawl ashore, he heard Japanese voices. It was the wrong bank and an enemy search party was looking for him. Nevertheless, after rolling himself in the sand, he risked taking a much-needed breather. When he finally set off again he was spotted by an enemy sentry and came under mortar fire, but escaped being hit.

On examination the briefcase was found to contain orders of the day for the Japanese Fifteenth Army. But they were of little help to us, since they merely amounted to the laconic instruction: 'When the British try to land they are to be pushed back into the river.'

Although a satisfactory landing beach for the Cameronians had been found, there was a sandbar across the front of it, which meant that their boats would have to turn in at the downstream end as at Nyaungu. The position of this bar and the depths around it were carefully charted.

Then came a new worry. A sentry in the Worcesters' forward position reported having heard strange noises coming from the direction of their designated landing beach. That night, therefore, Avery swam over to investigate, taking with him one of the Section's replacements who had not had as much swimming training as the others. When they were halfway across, the man fell behind shivering violently and obviously in need of a rest. After the pair had drifted some way downstream, Avery told him that they would go ashore where he could roll himself in the sand and warm up.

But as they were crawling on to the beach, a Japanese guard dog bounded out at them, barking furiously. They backed off into the river and waited, but no one came to investigate, and eventually the dog gave up and disappeared. Again they crawled out, and both rolled themselves in the sand and rested. Presently they became aware of a Japanese soldier standing a short distance away, who might well have been alerted by the dog barking. They could also clearly hear the sound of hammering coming from the landing beach, which could only mean that this was being fortified.

Suddenly they were assailed by shouts from all sides, and they sprang up and hurled themselves into the river. With bullets whining about their ears, they ducked below the surface and swam submerged for about fifty yards. When at last they surfaced and ventured to look back, they could see a group of men with rifles on the beach they had just vacated. After making it safely back to their own bank, Avery reported what they had heard, but headquarters decided that it was too late to alter the crossing plan.

On the night before the assault Avery and Turpin made a final reconnaissance of all three breaches in a four-hour swim without paddle boards. Apart from the hammering on the Worcesters' beach, all appeared to be well.

Conditions for the crossing, which started at 2230 on the night of 24 February, were not ideal, for it was bright moonlight and therefore too much to hope that the landings could be made undetected. The crossing was, however, to be silent and the boats paddled. The latter were six-man collapsibles but, like those at Nyaungu, ageing and in none too good a condition. Fire was not to be opened unless fired on. Turpin and Colgan were to lead the assault wave of the Royal Welch Fusiliers, and the team of Gridland and Bailey to mark the end of the sandbar for the Cameronians with a one-way beacon; Avery would lead their boats round it. Since the Worcesters could see their own landing beach, they would not require to be led.

Unhappily, things were to go very wrong, due chiefly to poor boatwork, aggravated by inadequate and faulty loading trials.

Both the initial assault waves of the Cameronians and the Fusiliers came under enemy fire from rifles and light and heavy machine-guns while they were still 100 yards from their landing beaches; the Japanese also lit a signal fire which illuminated the scene still further. Nevertheless both assault waves succeeded in establishing a bridgehead, although subjected to continuous mortar fire as well as machine-guns and small arms.

As already mentioned, the plan called for the Worcesters to launch their assault boats from the Dawete sandbank and establish a bridgehead to the right of the Cameronians. But their boats failed to reach midstream, and many of them sank due to overloading. The remainder turned back, beached on the sandbank, and the troops started to make their way up towards Myittha.

Boats returning from landing the first wave of the Cameronians also found it impossible to make their way back to Myittha against the current after rounding the midstream sandbar, and landed on Dawete. This left the second wave of the Cameronians up river without boats. The same thing happened at the Fusiliers' beachhead. When their boats failed to make headway, they landed downstream of the embarkation point. Thus it came about that an area of about 800 yards in extent was being held by approximately 200 Cameronians, while the Fusiliers were in similar case on their beachhead.

An attempt was then made to get the second wave of the Cameronians across in a pair of DUKWs, but after rounding the midstream sandbar these thin-skinned craft came under heavy enemy fire and a good many casualties were sustained. When the engine of one of them failed after being hit and it grounded on the sandbar, the SRU markers helped to haul it off and get it started again. Subsequently they were forced to dig in, and spend the rest of the night dodging overs from flank fire directed at the assault wave by the enemy.

At daylight the situation remained unchanged. The Cameronians' beachhead was still held by the first assault wave with a few reinforcements, as also was that of the Fusiliers. The colonel of the Cameronians now asked Avery if he could swim back across the river and inform headquarters that things were not going too well, and that his radio was out of action. Although shot at for most of the way, the SRU man carried out his mission successfully.

The situation on the Fusiliers' beachhead had now become critical, and here, too, their colonel appealed to the SRU for help. Turpin was asked if he could attempt an even more difficult feat: to cross the river to the northern bank and bring back badly needed medical supplies. Without hesitation, Turpin and Colgan set off on the hazardous swim to Kindaw. There, after they had reported on the situation, the necessary medical supplies were assembled and bundled up in groundsheets, to be floated by the SRU men over to the island on Mae Wests.

While they were at Kindaw it was decided to make an attempt to evacuate the more seriously wounded from the beachhead, and machine-guns were set up to cover the operation. On the return of Turpin and Colgan to the island, a number of usable boats were collected and lashed together, and filled with the worst of the casualties. The SRU men then pushed and paddled this makeshift ferry back to Kindaw. Both men were subsequently decorated for their bravery, as also was Avery.

Leaving Surgeon Lieutenant Robertson to continue working at an advanced dressing station, Wright now recalled the rest of the Section back to base. He had every reason to be satisfied with their performance, as was the Divisional general, who specially commended the Section in his despatch to Slim. Later the Corps Commander also reported to the Commander-in-Chief that:

> The work of this small unit and the conduct of its personnel was an example to all ranks. The preliminary reconnaissances, often made in close proximity to enemy positions, proved invaluable, and these crossings could not have been made without the very hard and often hazardous work they put in.

After the partial failure of the initial crossing by 5 Brigade, our forces were reorganised, fresh troops were brought up, and under cover of smoke two brigades were successfully put ashore on the enemy-held bank. As a postscript, the mystery of the hammering heard by the alert Worcesters' sentry and Avery and his companion was explained when it was found that much of the destructive machine-gun fire directed at the British assault boats came from an enemy bunker sited at the foot of a cliff from which the sounds had emanated. Immune to air bombing, it had to be individually winkled out.

While his men were taking a well-earned rest, Wright headed northward to join up with No 1 Section, which was attached to 19 Division at Singu, forty miles above Mandalay.

Headed by 'Mick' Muldoon, the Section consisted of Jock Elder, Sub-Lieutenant Kimmins, Sergeant Cave, Corporal Smith, Aircraftman Cobb, Leading Seaman Hollinghurst, Able Seaman Robson, Signalman Bye, Ordinary Seaman Bedders and Marine White. By the time Wright joined them their operations had virtually been completed, and they were back with the Division alongside whom they had originally worked on their first arrival in Burma.

As early as 9 January, when 19 Division reached the Irrawaddy, a patrol was put across near the ruby mine port of Thabeikkyin, after a preliminary reconnaissance by the SRU men. Five days later the Division had crossed in force and established themselves on the east bank near Singu. Although continuously attacked by the

Japanese, they could not be shifted. During this period the Section was transferred to 20 Division further south and attached to 100 Indian Infantry Brigade, which was to cross the Irrawaddy near the town of Myinmu, down river from the scene of 2 Division's operations which have already been described.

Two crossings in fact were to be made: the main one by 100 Brigade west of Myinmu, and a subsidiary crossing by 32 Brigade seven miles further on. The river in the 100 Brigade area was some 1,500 yards wide and obstructed by partially submerged sandbanks between which ran strong currents. On their paddle boards or swimming the Section reconnoitred long stretches of the river in the neighbourhood of the intended crossing, mapping sandbanks, examining landing beaches, and charting currents, all matters of vital importance since the crossing was to be made at night.

Then, in the afternoon prior to D-Day, the river rose unexpectedly, and new embarkation points and landing beaches had to be selected and surveyed at the last minute. The brigadier later reported that without the work of the Section consequent on the sudden rise in the river, he doubted whether he could have got enough men over in the assault waves to hold the beachhead. For the actual crossing, the SRU men were to mark the new channels with buoys, and guide the assault boats in with shaded torches.

The leading flight of the first assault wave pushed off in silence at 0400 on 13 February — fortunately for the superstitious not a Friday. The night was very dark and the freshening wind put a troublesome lop on the water for the laden boats. Despite the mark buoys, several of them grounded on sandbanks and failed to get off. At first there was no opposition from the enemy, but after the initial landing had been effected, fire was opened. Nevertheless, by 0800 the whole brigade was safely over, as was 32 Brigade lower down.

Following this success the Section rejoined 19 Division, where Wright found them in poor shape. They had been in the field continuously for ten weeks, and the nature of their living conditions had brought about physical deterioration. Both Muldoon and Elder had become medically unfit to enter the water. As Wright pointed out to fiery Major-General 'Pete' Rees, the Divisional Commander, when asking for the Section to be withdrawn to refit, they had had to march with the soldiers during the day and work under arduous conditions in the river throughout the night during the advance.

Despite this, General Rees was reluctant to part with them, and insisted that he should be provided with a replacement unit as he anticipated a further requirement for them between Singu and Mandalay. Accordingly 4 Corps was asked if No 2 Section could be spared, but while negotiations were under way, 19 Division broke out of the Japanese encirclement, and the further requirement lapsed. No 1 Section was therefore sent back to Hammanheil Camp, while Wright thumbed an air passage southward to join No 3 Section in the Arakan.

This Section, led by Lieutenant Junor with Booth as second in command, and composed of Sergeant Britton, Telegraphist Leyland, Lance-Corporal Cotton, Leading Aircraftman Hill, Able Seamen Long and Taberer, and Ordinary Seaman McKellar, he found to be living comfortably and in good physical condition and spirits. If they had any complaint at all, it was that they were not carrying out enough operations, although these had averaged one a week.

They were attached to 26 Division of 15 Corps. As mentioned earlier, 15 Corps under Lieutenant-General A.P.F. Christison, had been charged with the task of capturing Akyab and Ramree Islands, and securing airfields to bring Rangoon within flying range, and to establish a supply base for the invasion of that city.

Separated from the rest of Burma by a mountain range known as the Arakan Yomas, the Arakan is a strip of land lying between the mountains and the sea, covered with thick jungle, which extends in places from the hills down to the high tide mark. The coast is screened by mangrove swamps, and intersected by muddy, shallow *chaungs,* uncharted and unpredictable, with a few beaches of soft sand washed by a noticeable tide. The whole area is malarial and the haunt of some of the largest species of crocodile.

15 Corps, which began its advance in December 1944, comprised two Indian and two West African Divisions plus the 22nd East African Brigade, 50 Tank Brigade, and 3 Commando Brigade. Supporting its seaward flank was Force 'W', a motley collection of warships assembled from the East Indies Fleet, ranging from the battleship *Queen Elizabeth* down to motor launches and landing craft. It was thus an amphibian campaign, with the Navy landing troops, stores, mules and vehicles, and carrying out bombardments, deception raids, sinking enemy vessels, and penetrating into swamps with small craft to shoot up the retreating Japanese.

The Mayu peninsula was captured by Christmas, and the

invasion of Akyab soon followed. Operating under topographical conditions entirely different from those of the Irrawaddy, No 3 Section, along with elements of COPP (Combined Operations Pilotage Parties), had been working in the mangrove-covered *chaungs* behind the island. They had led no major landings, but were used in planning forward movements.

Gradually, with the Japanese fanatically resisting all the way, 15 Corps continued its advance. After the capture of Akyab came the invasion of Ramree Island, the SRU being required to reconnoitre the coastal mangrove swamps between that island and the mainland. As well as flies, mosquitoes and scorpions, they had to contend with the additional hazard of estuarine crocodiles attracted by the bodies of slain Japanese. The enemy garrison was steadily driven southwards, until finally came Operation 'Block', when the survivors trying to escape to the mainland were herded by the army into the swamp where the Navy prevented them from crossing. On paddle boards, in folbots and swimming, the Section with other reconnaissance units was sent into the area to find a passage where the 'blockships' could penetrate. Then the light craft, armed with mortars in addition to their 3-pounders, Oerlikons and Bofors guns, went in to lie in wait. When the Japanese tried to swim through this deadly barrier at night, the whole area was illuminated; thus they had little chance of escape. The SRU Section, two of whom were forced to spend a night in mangrove branches after being chased by a crocodile, with bullets whistling round them as the Japanese shot at the creatures, helped to account for more than 100 enemy killed in this operation. An untold number perished from starvation and disease rather than surrender.

Each *chaung* in the path of our advancing troops had to be checked for any concealed enemy force which might be lurking there and prepared to sell their lives dearly. Some of these creeks were protected with mined booms, around or under which the SRU had to find a way for the naval craft to enter. But the hard-fought third Arakan campaign was at last nearing its end. Further beachheads were established, and by mid-March the way was clear to launch the seaborne invasion of Rangoon. Their work at an end, 3 Section was withdrawn to Hammanheil.

There was, however, a further requirement for the unit. North of the town of Prome the Japanese forces, retreating before the advance of the Fourteenth Army, were still astride both banks of the Irrawaddy. It was the task of 33 Corps to destroy all the enemy in the Irrawaddy valley, open the road and railway from Prome to Rangoon, and capture the port of Bassein at the river mouth. Accordingly No 1 Section, rested and refitted after their spell at Hammanheil, left for Calcutta on 14 April to join up with the Corps. After being kept waiting several days for onward passage, they were air-lifted to Mytche, where Elder reported to Corps headquarters. There he learned that the Section was to join up with 20 Division.

After 33 Corps had overcome the formidable Japanese defences in the oilfields around Yenangyaung, a series of armoured hooks sliced the remaining enemy into fragments. Spearheading one of these, 20 Dvision had distinguished itself by seizing Taungdwingyi, barring the Japanese line of retreat and compelling them to cross to the west bank of the Irrawaddy to escape, and subsequently to recross it lower down. By 2 May the Division's tank brigade reached Prome. Next day a Punjabi battalion pushed forward to Kamagale, a village twenty miles further on, and it was to this unit that the Section was now attached.

The retreating Japanese were reduced to about 6000. But they were well armed and had fought a clever rearguard action against 7 Division, which had lost contact. If they were allowed to cross the river north of Prome they could seriously threaten 20 Division's line of communication. The Punjabi battalion was dug in on the east bank in a flank protection role, and their position was selected to suit a perfect SRU setup. This time the Section had brought with it two 2-man canoes.

On arrival, Elder reconnoitred the river, and arranged with the commanding officer of the Punjabis to establish his perimeter in conjunction with the Section. The canoes were then assembled, and the SRU men carried out offensive river patrols throughout the night. Each 2-man canoe was armed with bren guns, carbines and M3 pistols. They also took with them duck calls and torches. The duck calls were used for signalling between the Section, but communication with the Punjabis was by hailing. Infuriatingly, soon after the last SRU patrol returned to base just before dawn, four boatloads of Japanese appeared on the stretch of river they had been patrolling.

Elder accordingly asked the CO of the Punjabis to position an ambush party on some cliffs on the west bank to shoot up any Japanese trying to cross. This was done, a platoon being escorted across the river that evening. The Section then resumed their watchful vigil in their canoes. After an hour and a half the first patrol returned to base with nothing to report. The second patrol, however, soon sighted two enemy boats 300 yards away and set off in pursuit. But the Japanese ran in towards the cliffs where the river narrowed and became fast-running. The SRU men alerted the ambush party, who shot them up successfully. The third patrol then set out, and an hour later they sighted three Japanese boats landing troops half a mile to the northwards. Approaching stealthily, the patrol opened fire and inflicted a number of casualties, forcing the enemy to abandon his boats and equipment.

The fourth patrol went directly across the river to lie in wait in the shadows cast by the cliffs. After some ninety minutes had elapsed, a large boatload of Japanese troops appeared, and was promptly engaged at ten yards range by the patrol with their bren guns and carbines. The only reply was a solitary pistol shot. There were some twenty Japanese on board, none of whom survived, the corpse-laden boat being found later aground down river.

At the same time as this was happening, a small boat containing four Japanese landed near the Section's base. They were spotted approaching, and the SRU men opened fire, killing a Japanese warrant officer and wounding two others. The fourth was pursued by Aircraftman Cobb, who was slightly wounded by an enemy grenade hurled at him. They also captured a light machine-gun and a Japanese flag.

After careful reconnoitring, the area was now found to be clear of the enemy. Since there was nothing further required of the Section, they reported back to Divisional headquarters. There they were instructed to join up with 100 Indian Infantry Brigade, which had been ordered to clear the west bank of the Irrawaddy from Prome to Bassein, a distance of some 200 miles. The brigadier planned to do this with a battalion of Gurkhas supported by mountain artillery and sappers. The SRU Section was to accompany the leading company of Gurkhas, and maintain patrols on the river night and day to ensure that supplies arrived at their forward position every day.

They started by collecting various river craft which the sappers made into rafts for transporting the Gurkhas' supplies and subsequent reinforcements. They also reconnoitred a possible harbour for the vessels, channels for the passage of gunboats, and landing places for the first crossing of the forward company. Work then came to a halt for several days until the obscure situation regarding the retreating enemy farther north could be clarified.

When this had been resolved, the operation got under way again, and the Section, now accompanied by an SBS group, set off down river. They were jointly manning three Mark VI powered canoes, a 'storm boat' mounting two Browning machine-guns, and three rafts of stores for the leading Gurkha company. After covering a distance of some fifteen miles, although continuously plagued by engine trouble, they moored to the bank for the night and set up river patrols in both directions.

Next day they journeyed on for another fifteen miles and reached the village of Thalidaw, where they were again held up, this time for three days because of uncertainty about enemy movements to the northward. They spent the time profitably carrying out reconnaissances to enable the Gurkhas to set up ambushes for Japanese stragglers. At this point, however, orders came for the Section to withdraw, and they returned by river to brigade headquarters. There the brigadier asked Elder and the group leader of the SBS if it was possible to continue operations having regard to personnel, equipment and conditions on the river now that the monsoon had started. Their advice was that operations were not feasible, especially as these would involve troops new to river work, and because severe squalls were becoming more and more frequent, during which one of their boats had been completely swamped.

By now Rangoon had fallen and, except for isolated units, the principal remnants of the Japanese armies were trapped east of the Irrawaddy. The battle for Burma was virtually over, and the work of the SRU at an end. By the beginning of June they were all assembled back in Hammanheil Camp. Wright noted proudly in his final report before he was flown back to Canada, having turned the unit over to Muldoon, that: 'Forty men went into Burma and forty men came out.' They had not suffered a single casualty.

Early in July the Commander-in-Chief, East Indies Fleet told the Chief of Combined Operations that as there was no further requirement for them, the unit should now be disbanded, and on the 26th of that month disbandment was approved by the Admiralty.

One final footnote might be considered to be not without interest. In December 1945, with World War II at an end, the Admiralty approved payment of a 'Special Duty Allowance' to former members of the Sea Reconnaissance Unit. Lieutenants RN and above and their equivalent were to be paid two shillings and sixpence (12½ pence) a day; Sub-Lieutenants RN and their equivalent two shillings (10 pence); and ratings and other ranks one shilling and sixpence (7½ pence); to be in addition to their Combined Operations Allowance already credited, back-dated to 1 April 1944 – but subject to Income Tax!

# III

## The Tragedy of Operation 'Checkmate'

Although Combined Operations personnel do not fall within the category of 'irregular' units as defined by those that were administered by DDOD(I)*, a certain of their minor activities resembled those of the latter, in particular an operation code-named 'Checkmate'. This was not to land secret agents clandestinely in enemy-occupied territory, but was purely offensive in character, having much in common with the exploits of the Royal Marine Boom Patrol Detachment's 'Cockleshell Heroes', referred to earlier on.

The aim of Operation 'Checkmate', carried out by a handful of inordinately brave volunteers, was to destroy German shipping in Norway. Unhappily, like the Dieppe raid, although a minor operation, it was ill-conceived, badly attempted, accomplished little, and ended in tragedy which could not have been foreseen by those who finally approved the plan.

In 1943 Norwegian-manned motor torpedo boats, working from a base in the Shetlands, were raiding enemy supply ships creeping up and down the 'Inner Leads', the channels between the mainland and the islands which for long stretches fringe the Norwegian coast. Working in pairs, the MTBs lay up at night among the numerous fjords and islands to ambush passing German convoys.

> Besides attacking the enemy's coastal traffic, the MTBs played a prominent part in the clandestine operations which were such a marked feature of the Norwegian people's resistance to the German occupation. They frequently landed stores and arms for sabotage purposes, picked up resistance leaders and brought them to Britain, and supplied or relieved the coast-watchers who reported enemy shipping movements. In addition, they carried out countless other crepuscular undertakings designed to harass and annoy the enemy, and force him to retain large forces in the country for security purposes.†

* Deputy Director of the Operations Division/Irregular).
† Roskill, *The War at Sea,* Vol. III, Part II, HMSO.

In April 1943 the outline plan for Operation 'Checkmate' was approved by the Chief of Combined Operations. Six all ranks of 14 Commando under Sub-Lieutenant John Godwin, RNVR were to cross the North Sea in a Norwegian-manned MTB towing a coble. When south of Bokn Island, some twelve miles north of Stavanger, the force would embark in the coble, which would be equipped with two canoes and rations for a month, while the MTB returned home. The party would then proceed to a hideout near Kongshamn, in the northern part of Bokn Island. Intelligence reports indicated that there were no Germans in that area, but a coast defence battery was sited at the island's southern extremity.

An observation post would be established on a 290 ft hill near the hideout to keep a watch for passing shipping and any that might anchor in Karm Sound. It was known that enemy convoys frequently passed up and down this stretch of water. If a convoy was seen to anchor off Kopervik, a small port on the east coast of Karmoy Island, halfway up Karm Sound, the coble carrying the canoes would move within striking distance after dark and they would attack the ships with limpet charges. If no target was offered in the Kopervik area but enemy shipping was seen concentrating in Haugesund anchorage, the latter would be attacked there through Karm Sound. In due course the 'Checkmate' party would be withdrawn by MTB, which would call at a fixed rendezvous at Sammungsoy, on the Urter Island group, on receipt of a signal on D + 11, and again on D + 18 if they had not been picked up on the first occasion.

When the plan was discussed with Godwin by Colonel Neville, Royal Marines, chief naval planner at Combined Operations headquarters, they considered the case of shipping lying off Kopervik, and the latter agreed that it looked a promising little operation if Godwin was sufficiently cunning and skilful.

Neville wrote later in his comments:

In the plan as now set out, it is stated that whereas enemy shipping used to lie at Kopervik, intelligence reports indicate that it now more frequently lies in Haugesund, at the northern exit of the Sound; and in paragraph 9 proposes a plan for attacking shipping at Kopervik, merely stating that if shipping is in Haugesund an alternative plan will be required. In other words, the main plan is produced for what is stated to be the most unlikely condition, and a very lightly sketched alternative plan for what is stated to be the most likely condition. I do

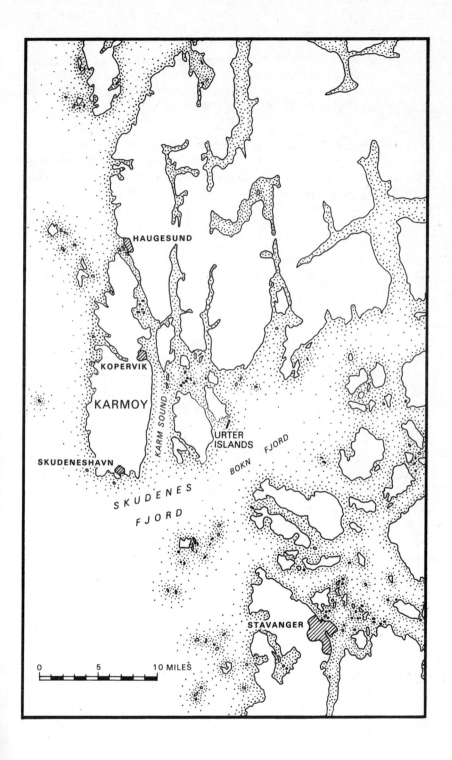

HAUGESUND

KOPERVIK

KARMOY

KARM SOUND

URTER
ISLANDS

SKUDENESHAVN

BOKN FJORD

S K U D E N E S

F J O R D

STAVANGER

0        5        10 MILES

not suggest that the alternative plan for the attack on Haugesund proper is by any means impossible, but it is plainly considerably more difficult. It seems we might almost just as well deposit Godwin and his crew in their hideout and set them to get on with it.

It would appear therefore that Neville was not entirely happy with the plan, but assumed that any doubtful aspects of it would be cleared up before the operation was launched. In the event, the final orders were issued by the Admiral Commanding Orkneys and Shetlands (ACOS), Vice-Admiral Lionel Wells, who was responsible for staging these raids on the enemy's Norwegian coastwise shipping from his headquarters at Lyness.

Haugesund lies roughly midway between Stavanger and Bergen. It is an irregularly built town, partly on the mainland and partly on the islands of Risoy and Hasseloy. The port possessed inner and outer harbours, and a torpedo boom had been placed partly across the northern entrance – thus an approach from the south was more suitable. As well as being a coaling station, Haugesund was equipped with oil fuel tanks, and was an important port of call for coastal convoys. The latter were frequent, and a typical convoy might include two motor vessels of 3,000 tons, two under 1,000 tons, and two coasters – sometimes a vessel of up to 8,000-9,000 tons.

Enemy patrol boats operated from Stavanger, Haugesund and Skudesnes, at the southern tip of Karmoy, and consisted of whalers, trawlers and ex-Norwegian torpedo boats. There were also machine-gun posts at Haugesund and Kopervik and in the surrounding area, and anti-torpedo booms.

As mentioned, the 'Checkmate' force was to consist of one Norwegian MTB towing a coble carrying two folding canoes and an inflatable dinghy. In addition to Godwin, there would be four naval personnel from 14 Commando, one naval rating lent from the base at Lerwick, and one telegraphist. With them they would take 20 limpet charges per canoe, personal arms and ammunition, equipment and clothing, and food, water and medical stores to last ten days. No radio was included because of the weight of the batteries, and the possibility that transmissions might be detected.

A slim, fair-haired young man, Sub-Lieutenant Godwin had been born in Buenos Aires in 1919, his family having settled in the Argentine early in the century. He had travelled to England especially to join the Navy, and as soon as he could volunteered for

Combined Operations. His companions for 'Checkmate' were 28-year old Petty Officer Harold Hiscock, official number LT/JX.18666500, a Patrol Service rating hailing from Northumberland; Sergeant Victor Cox, 5671612, aged 25 of the Somerset Light Infantry and 12 Commando; Ordinary Seaman Keith Mayor, C/JX.36347100, 20 from Preston; Ordinary Seaman Andrew West, D/JX.36326400, of Glasgow; Ordinary Seaman Neville Burgess, C/JX.33454700, 20, of Beverley, Yorkshire; and Petty Officer Motor Mechanic Alfred Roe, a 36-year old Londoner and the oldest man in the party, lent from the naval base at Lerwick.

14 Commando, to which nearly all belonged, was a special raiding outfit officially formed in December 1942 as the result of an urgent War Office memorandum, to be trained in Arctic warfare and to attack northern Luftwaffe bases. 'On account of the security value the establishment was not subjected to normal procedure, and passed on a very high level at the special request of the Chief of Combined Operations.' It was commanded by Lieutenant-Colonel E.A.M. Wedderburn of the Royal Scots, and in addition to four other army officers, included three naval officers: Lieutenant-Commander A. Glen, RNVR, Lieutenant A. Courtauld, RNVR, and Sub-Lieutenant Godwin; and a naval section of one petty officer and fifteen ordinary seamen. Four officers and twenty other ranks of the Canadian Army, all chosen for their experience in mountaineering or snow conditions, or for their knowledge of canoeing, were also attached to the Commando.

After assembling at HMS *Dorlin*, a special establishment concerned with the development of small craft at Loch Moidart, in Scotland, the naval party came to London and started training with kyaks at the Marshall Street swimming baths. Godwin and two army officers also came to London to undergo a short course of specialist training. Meanwhile the Commando had been formed into two troops and accommodated at Beauly, in Invernesshire, one troop to go into training in the Commando Mountain and Snow Warfare Camp at Braemar, the other on Balta, in the Shetland Islands. In January 1943, however, the latter troop was withdrawn to Loch Carron as being more suitable for training because of the bad weather at Balta.

In February 1943 a party from the Commando carried out Operation 'Crackers'. The latter formed part of an on-going operation code-named 'Omnibus', conducted by ACOS with his

special 'Northern Force', which included 12 and 14 Commandoes.*
'Omnibus' was a series of raids and attacks to be carried out from
MTBs against the Norwegian coast between Latitudes 59 and 63
degrees North to destroy enemy defence positions. More than thirty
targets had been specified, to include gun positions, watch posts,
RDF stations, and seaplane and patrol boat bases between
Stavanger and Andalsnes. Parties of from twelve to twenty-four men
were to be landed, certain personnel simply to lie up and observe.
Curiously, an unknown authority at Combined Operations
headquarters noted on the plans, however, that the effect of these
raids on the enemy war machine would not be very great! The
general idea was to disrupt the iron ore trade.

The party which carried out Operation 'Crackers' consisted of
two officers – Captain K. Waggett of the Middlesex Regiment, and
Sub-Lieutenant Godwin – with fourteen other ranks. On 22
February they embarked at Lerwick in two Norwegian MTBs,
picked up an agent at Krakhellesund next day, then went on to a
place called Gjeitory where the MTBs lay up in concealment. The
task of the force was to attack enemy shipping, lay mines in Sogne
Fjord, and collect and bring back one of our secret agents.

The places to be attacked formed entrances to the Inner Leads.
One target was a watch post at a point called Tungodden and, after
lying up for two days to make sure that the presence of the raiding
party had not been detected, Godwin and two others, Ordinary
Seaman West and Sergeant Bjernsted of the Norwegian army, set
out in a three-man canoe to reconnoitre the post. But it was
deserted, and after cautiously approaching the place, they found
that it had been previously shot up by our MTBs and subsequently
abandoned by the enemy.

The force duly carried out a number of reconnaissances of the
fjord, laid their mines in its waters, and collected the secret agent,
but after a nine-day stay, bad weather compelled them to return to
Lerwick. Based on their experience, it was considered that a
sabotage party would be able to lie up for long periods. 'Crackers'
therefore had a direct bearing on 'Checkmate'.

Soon afterwards a representative of Combined Operations
headquarters visited ACOS to discuss future overall plans, one of

* 12 Commando, formed chiefly of men from Irish and Welsh regiments in 1941
had already carried out many raids against enemy-occupied territory, including
the Lofoten Islands and Bruneval.

which was the limpet attack on enemy shipping at Haugesund, scheduled to take place at the end of April. Godwin was selected to command, and thus 'Checkmate' was set in motion. Its leader was confident of success, after which it was planned to carry out similar operations. No one had the slightest inkling of how in fact it would end.

Soon after midnight on 28 April, *MTB 626* under the command of Lieutenant K. Bøgeberg, Royal Norwegian Naval Reserve, slipped from the jetty at Lerwick, in which harbour rehearsals had been conducted, and picked up the coble, known officially as an LCP(M) (Landing Craft Personnel, Mechanised). With the latter in tow, she then headed across the North Sea at 15 knots. There was a light northerly wind, the sea was calm and visibility good. By 2200 the following evening the vessels arrived off the small island of Utsira, and finally hove to some five miles from the entrance to Skudesnes fjord.

By then a swell had got up, which made it difficult to transfer Godwin and his party and their stores into the coble. Thus it was about two o'clock in the morning of 30 April when the coble finally cast off and headed towards Bokn Island. The MTB retired to seaward at slow speed in case the smaller boat should get into difficulty. But all seemed to be well, and no enemy ships or aircraft were sighted. That was the last anyone from this country saw of the 'Checkmate' party.

The first rendezvous for the pickup was to have been made on 9 May, but because of bad weather no MTB could be sent until the 17th. This was *MTB 626* again, which circled Urter Island closely but saw no sign of life. Three subsequent attempts to pick up the party were made: on 23 and 26 May and 4 June. On the last occasion *MTB 653* commanded by Lieutenant Eerling Matland, RNNR went to the Urter group and cruised all round the islands, flashing lamp signals and hailing. A house was seen by the shore, but there was no sign of life. On 5 June it was decided that the party must be considered lost, and the next of kin were informed that the men were 'Missing from a hazardous operation'.

On 3 May, unknown of course to anyone in this country, an entry was made in the German Naval War Diary to this effect:

Karm Sound is again opened for traffic of small, independently sailing vessels and fishing smacks. An explosion occurred in a minelaying vessel alongside the quay at Kopervik, presumably through sabotage. The boat is lying with her stern on the bottom.

A more detailed German record expanded this item of news by adding that at 0430 on 3 May the minesweeper *M5207* alongside the quay at Kopervik reported three explosions and began to sink. At 0530 came a fourth explosion. A diver was sent down but could not discover the cause. On 10 May the sunken minesweeper was spotted and reported by a British reconnaissance aircraft. Two days earlier, after the local population had been accused of sabotaging the vessel, the Germans issued a decree prohibiting rowing boats from moving at night, warning that any such would be fired on.

On 13 May the German Naval War Diary recorded that a large open motorboat had been seized near Skudesneshavn on the previous day, and that a search for the crew was in progress. Two days later the Diary recorded that: 'Three men of the British motorboat found on the 13th have been captured.' And, next day:

> The remaining crew of the British motorboat, consisting of one officer and three enlisted men (Britons) was taken prisoner on the island of Urter. This squad carried out the adhesive mine plot against a minelayer in Kopervik on May 3.

On the 18th the Diary noted that: 'The minesweeper which was sunk by sabotage in the harbour of Kopervik has been raised and is being transferred to Stavanger.'

Almost a month later, on 12 June, the Chief of Combined Operations in England was informed that a small boat had arrived from the Norwegian coast the night before, and its occupant reported that seven Englishmen had been taken prisoner by the enemy on the island which was the rendezvous for the withdrawal of the 'Checkmate' force. On 13 June the War Office told Colonel Neville that the commanding officer of one of the Norwegian-manned MTBs on his return from a raiding mission reported that a fisherman had informed him that seven Englishmen had been taken prisoner 'two or three weeks ago' at the 'Checkmate' rendezvous. On the 14th Admiral Wells wrote to Lord Mountbatten, then Chief of Combined Operations, saying that it was good news that the party was alive and well, and adding: 'If I know anything of young Godwin we might well hear of him spending Christmas in Stockholm.'

He could not have been more wrong.

For the story of what actually happened we must return to 15 May and the office of Korvettenkapitän Hermann Jung, Harbour Commandant of Haugesund, who was interrogating a somewhat dispirited Sub-Lieutenant John Godwin. Present and taking notes was Jung's adjutant, Leutnant Grodler. By now there was more to add to the brief accounts in the German Naval War Diary about the sabotage of minesweeper *M5207*.

> At three o'clock in the afternoon on May 12, following up a report by the Norwegian police, a German naval patrol from Haugesund discovered a motorboat near a place called Sussert, at the southern end of Karmoy, hauled halfway up a stony beach. There was fuel in the boat, and a fuse found in the reserve fuel tank which indicated that an unsuccessful attempt had been made to destroy the craft. The patrol found provisions and a Norwegian chart on which had been marked the positions of batteries and bases. The boat was taken to Kopervik, and later sent up to Bergen. A search was then started.
>
> In the afternoon of May 14 an army patrol found three members of the crew of the boat, all ratings, at a place called Hervik. On the following day one officer and three ratings were found by a naval search patrol from Haugesund. These were the four who attacked the minesweeper, Godwin claiming that he had personally attached the mines to her hull.

In reply to his interrogator's questions Godwin gave his name, rank, date and place of birth, and also with surprising frankness volunteered the information that he belonged to Combined Operations. He then went on to relate that he had been sent with six ratings in a landing craft towed by an MTB to attack merchant ships at Kopervik with limpet mines. Arriving at a point four miles west of the southern tip of Karmoy Island at 2200 on 30 April, the craft cast off and proceeded under her own power. Just south of Karmoy the motor broke down, so that it was not until 0700 on 1 May that they reached the southern part of Bokn Island. There was a German coastal battery sited at that point and they could see men cleaning the guns. They remained the whole day in the same position.

During the night they concealed the coble in the cliffs and three of the party remained behind with it. Then Godwin and the other three ratings embarked in the canoes and paddled up the east coast of Bokn, entered Karm Sound from the north and continued on until they reached Dua, a point just north-east of Kopervik. They remained on the beach there the whole day and watched for ships, but did not find anything at Kopervik worth attacking, and saw nothing coming through Karm Sound. They stayed there for the whole of 1 and 2 May. In Kopervik they saw only one minesweeper lying at the steamer quay. In the absence of any other shipping they decided to attack her.

At 0300 on the night of 2/3 May they proceeded in the two canoes to the minesweeper and attached four magnetic limpet mines to her hull, and then withdrew. As they had lost time in waiting at Dua, they decided to return to base. They still had some limpet charges left, which they threw overboard.

The next two days were spent in the observation post on Bokn. On the night of 3/4 May they again embarked in their canoes and proceeded southwards down the east coast of Bokn, and stayed throughout the 4th on the southern tip of the island. They could not find the coble, so decided that as the MTB had not come to collect them, they would go to Urter Island to try to find a seaworthy Norwegian boat in which they could get back to England.

On the night of 4/5 May they proceeded in their canoes up the coast of Korneay, and in the forenoon of the 5th reached the south-west corner of that islet. On the night of 5/6 they got as far as the south-west entrance to Neavade, another small islet, and next night reacher Urter where they remained until captured. During the whole of this time they were looking for an opportunity to seize a Norwegian boat. Because of bad weather and stormy seas they saw no chance of getting any further in their canoes, and stayed for four days hidden among the cliffs. Then they moved into a small empty house where they found some Norwegian provisions. There was only one Norwegian fisherman on the island.

Towards evening on 15 May the lookout they had posted reported the arrival of two motorboats. Out of one came eight German naval ratings who made straight for their hideout. Taken completely by surprise, they put up their hands and were made prisoner. Godwin declared that he knew nothing about the limpet charges, only how to operate them. In England they had been instructed as a last resort to go to the island of Urter, from which they would have been picked up by MTB.

Assuming that Godwin was telling the truth, and there is no reason to suppose otherwise as the German navy was not usually given to the use of torture in its initial interrogation of captured prisoners, it would appear that Godwin's method of carrying out his attack did not at all follow the original plan approved by Combined Operations headquarters, even with Kopervik as the prime target. Thus he divided his force at the outset, and left behind the coble in which the whole party should have proceeded to the north of Bokn Island, and was himself absent for several days although he had no means of communication with the three men looking after the boat.

To have covered the whole distance up the east coast of Bokn Island in canoes and entered Karm Sound from the north, instead of lying up for a day or two in the chosen hideout on the hill to observe shipping movements, then moving across the Sound at night, seems the height of folly – and the target not worth risking capture for. Since the Germans found the coble beached near Skudesneshavn, on Karmoy Island, the question has to be asked: how did it get there? Did the party he left behind in Bokn Island lose heart, decide the operation had failed, and attempt to return to England in the coble? Lastly, how did the Germans know that the survivors would be found on Urter Island?

The answers will never now be known.

Security seems to have been very poor, for by admitting that their party expected to be picked up by MTB from Urter Island, they jeopardised the safety of their would-be rescuers. Enemy aircraft and surface warships would have been on the lookout for them ready to pounce.

Tragically for the 'Checkmate' party, Hitler had in the previous October issued his *Kommandobefehl*, or what came to be known as his 'extermination order'. This directed that, 'Sabotage troops of the British and their hirelings, whether in uniform or not, whether with or without arms, be killed to the last man in battle or in flight, *or, if captured indirectly, handed over to the SS.*' (My italics).

Korvettenkapitän Jung referred the whole matter to his senior officer, the Admiral Commanding the West Coast of Norway, and accordingly as ordered turned the prisoners over to the SD (*Sicherheitsdienst*, or SS Security Service). In complete negation of the provisions of the Geneva Convention, no word regarding the capture and whereabouts of Godwin and his men was ever made known by the German authorities, since after the *Kommandobefehl* the Germans refused all such captives the status of prisoner of war.*

---

* There were a few Allied prisoners in German hands for whom not even MI9

The rest of their story and eventual fate has therefore had to be pieced together from a number of sources, some of which tell conflicting accounts.

What seems to be certain is that after their capture, Godwin and his party were kept at Haugesund for almost a month before they were collected by the SD and taken to a civilian prison at Grini, some five miles north-west of Oslo, where they arrived on 12 June.

The prison was run partly by quislings and partly by the Gestapo. A report said to have been received in Stockholm in March 1945 from a former inmate of the gaol stated that five (sic) British prisoners of war arrived at the prison and were put into two cells, one on the ground floor and one on the first floor. Norwegians in the prison soon made contact with them. The Britons said that they had arrived from England in a fast boat at a fjord in the Westland where they had sunk some German ships. They then went to another fjord and damaged another enemy ship. Their own boat was then sunk and they were taken prisoner.

The author of the report went on to state that the Britons 'only got fresh air when the Germans had time; this was after the other prisoners had been locked up for the night, and lasted for only five to ten minutes.' They were frequently interrogated and subjected to anti-British propaganda. They were kept in Grini until the end of August. A former French inmate stated that the party wore khaki uniforms.

This information is confirmed in part by a statement made in 1945 by a Norwegian named Fenrik Rosenqvist, who himself had at one time been imprisoned in Grini. According to this man, Godwin and six ratings were brought into the prison in the autumn of 1942 (sic), having been captured at Kopervik. Godwin, one petty officer and two ratings had been captured in uniform, while three were wearing civilian clothes which they had apparently donned with the intention of trying to cross into Sweden.

The party was at first separated during the preliminary period of interrogation, then congregated in one cell where they were well treated, being taken out for exercise in the evenings, but completely isolated from all other prisoners. They were evidently the object of

---

was able to do anything, because they were kept hidden away from communication with the outside world; no prisoner in the Lubianka or the Bastille, or the deepest dungeon of a robber baron in the Dark Ages, was more firmly shut in'. MI9 – *Escape & Evasion*, Foot and Langley.

considerable interest to the Gestapo, for the SS Brigadeführer used to interrogate them personally, and it was understood from Godwin that Fehlis, the Gestapo chief, insisted that they were really Norwegians pretending to be British. They remained in their cell for sixteen months, when they were transferred to Germany.

As will be seen, despite a number of discrepancies, the Stockholm report and Rosenqvist's statement agree in essentials. The second part of the latter's deposition which deals with subsequent events concerning the 'Checkmate' party will be referred to later.

An earlier report received in this country from the British military attaché in Stockholm dated 7 July 1943, stated that Lieutenant John Gowen (sic) and six men who had been taken prisoner at Haugesund were 'still detained at Grini without comfort or exercise'. Their subsequent transfer to a prisoner of war camp was expected. He gave the list of detainees as follows:

Sub-Lieutenant John Gowen RNVR
Petty Officer H. Hiscock, C/JX.35454700
Ordinary Seaman N.D. Burgess, JX.35326400
Ordinary Seaman A.D. West, 36347100
Ordinary Seaman K. Mayor, of 14 Commando
Sergeant V. Cox, 5761612 of 12 Commando.

He added that as well as the above, the Naval Officer in Charge, Lerwick lent a petty officer motor mechanic (unnamed but obviously Petty Officer Alfred Roe).

As will be seen, Godwin's name was incorrectly spelt, and the official numbers of the ratings were also wrong. But these were only some of the errors that continually crop up throughout the whole story and add to confusion. The cause seems to have been a complete lack of liaison between Combined Operations who initiated Operation 'Checkmate', MI9 who apparently did the best they could with the meagre information available to them, the fact that the party was described as Commandos – and thus assumed, even in 1945, to be Royal Marines – and the paucity of information available to the British naval and military attachés in Stockholm, who should have been provided with a full list of the missing men, including ranks, ratings and official numbers, in the first place by Combined Operations headquarters, and instructed to pursue enquiries from whatever sources were open to them.

On 22 December 1943 the British Foreign Office requested Berne to ask the German government to supply full information regarding the above. At that time protests were being made about the alleged shooting of British Commandos, notably those taken prisoner in the latter part of 1942 who had participated in Operations 'Musketoon' and 'Freshman'.

Operation 'Musketoon' had been staged by a party of between twelve and twenty officers and men of No 2 Commando, accompanied by a number of Norwegians, with the object of destroying a hydro-electric power station at Glomfjord, a few miles south of Narvik, which was supplying power to an important aluminium plant providing the Germans with aluminium for aircraft production and other military uses. The operation had succeeded in destroying part of the plant, but eight of the raiders – including the two officers – had been captured by a German patrol. 'After being taken to Germany, the officers were shot in accordance with Hitler's order.'

Operation 'Freshman' was a more ambitious affair. It was known that German scientists were engaged in atomic research, for which they needed supplies of heavy water. This was being produced at a plant in the small town of Rjukan, in southern Norway. In October/November 1942 it was planned to land forty Commandos in two teams by glider to destroy the plant. The advance party landed safely, but in bad weather the gliders carrying the main body crash-landed on the nearby Hardanger plateau. The survivors were rounded up by German ski patrols, the injured killed and the rest shot after interrogation

The information asked for about the 'Checkmate' party was never forthcoming. Subsequently it was reported that they had arrived at Grini on 12 June and left on 23 September. This is confirmed in the first part of a report made in 1945 by a Mr Erik Johansen, a repatriated Norwegian prisoner of war, who stated that:

> Andrew West of 70 Camden Street, Glasgow; Jack Cox, Keith Mayor from Newfoundland; 'Trilby' Row of London; 'Shorty' Hiscock; 'Porky' Burgess from Scotland; and John Goodwin [sic], belonging to the Commandos, were sent out to raid on the west coast of Norway and taken prisoner at Kopervik.
>
> At that time they were in military uniform, but they were accused by the Germans of being civilians, and even of being Norwegians. They admitted they had a few civilian belongings, but not so much they could justly hide their uniforms. They were sent on to Germany in September 1943.

On 7 July 1943 Captain Denham, the British Naval Attaché in Stockholm, reported having received from Oslo the statement mentioned above regarding 'Lieutenant Gowen' and his companions. Two days later MI9 told Combined Operations headquarters that three members of the Commandos who had been 'staying for a week on the small island of Urter, south-west of Haugesund' were taken prisoner on or about 10 June. The Norwegian informant who had betrayed their presence was paid 10,000 kroner by the Germans. There is, however, no confirmation of such betrayal from German records. On 17 August MI9 learned that the 'Checkmate' party had been moved from Grini, and in December 1943 the International Red Cross was asked to make enquiries about them. No further information was forthcoming from this source.

Thus far, ignoring the more obvious errors, it seems clear that the 'Checkmate' party, after being retained at Haugesund for about a month until they could be collected by the SD, were first of all incarcerated in a civilian gaol near Oslo where the local Gestapo chief tried to get them to admit that they were really Norwegians. Their treatment up to then was probably reasonably humane, as it was for the other inmates of the prison, who may well have been ordinary petty criminals. It is also fairly clear that the length of their stay at Grini was about three months.

Much worse was now to follow.

For the story of what happened to the 'Checkmate' party during the next sixteen months we have to rely on the accounts of a number of former inmates of the concentration camp at Sachsenhausen, near Oranienburg, one of the original such camps. All these accounts came to light only after the end of the war in Europe. Because they were made at different times and to different people, it is difficult to present them in chronological order, but a coherent story does eventually emerge.

On 17 May 1945 the British naval attaché in Stockholm signalled to the Admiralty:

We learn that a Lieutenant John Godwin, RNVR and eight ratings were picked out and shot by an SS Commission at Sachsenhausen on the night of 2 February 1945. Their clothes and belongings were sold next day.

Two days later Captain Denham wrote to the Admiralty, enclosing the reports by the Norwegian Fenrik Rosenqvist, already mentioned, and an extract from 'a vague report' by a Doctor Henry Meyer, MD of Aabenraa, in Denmark.

Continuing his story which, as will be recalled, told first of all of the arrival of the 'Checkmate' party at Grini, Rosenqvist had gone on to state that the party arrived at Oranienburg (Sachsenhausen) in September or October 1943, and were allocated numbers in the region of 71900. They were believed to be the only British in the camp. During the first month they were treated as ordinary political prisoners and put to work in the kitchen, which was considered fairly favourable treatment. But at the end of December 1943 they were suddenly taken by the Rapporte Führer to a *Straf* (punishment) Company without any reason being given. It was understood, however, that the Rapporte Führer's house had been bombed by the RAF during an air raid, and that this was his idea of exacting revenge.

> Their treatment now was very much harder, and they were forced to put on German army boots to test and made to march 48 kilometres (30 miles) every day. Their food ration was 300 grammes (about 10 ounces) of bread and a litre of turnip soup. The physical exertion was such as to bring about a state of exhaustion. Many others died under the strain, but the British endured this treatment for the whole of 1944.

During the night of 2/3 February Rosenqvist was awakened by the sound of shooting. Next morning he learned that approximately 100 prisoners had been taken to the gas chambers and killed, among them six of the British. The reason for the shooting, he was told, was that on the way to execution a Pole had produced a knife with which he stabbed and killed the *Oberscharführer*, and that in the resulting turmoil the guards opened fire. The remaining British prisoner was named Alfred 'Row' and he had been in hospital, where he was still at the end of March. Rosenqvist stated that the names of the six Britons were recorded as *Tot Wahrend Des Transports* (Dead while in transit).

The Danish doctor, Meyer, stated that while at Oranienburg he had become good friends with the eight (sic) British prisoners of war, including Lieutenant Godwin, and that the latter had been captured in civilian clothes while trying to escape from Norway. 'Every time there was an attack on Berlin these men were subjected to some form of reprisal.' Meyer added that he had worked as a surgeon in different concentration camps as well as Sachsenhausen.

On 23 June 1945 Headquarters, Allied Land Forces, Norway, wrote to the Admiralty forwarding the report from Mr Erik Johansen (the first part of which dealing with the arrival of the 'Checkmate' party at Grini has also been previously mentioned). A list enclosed with the report named the following as being members of the party:

Victor John Cox, Dorset, born 18 December 1918
John Godwin, Buenos Aires, born 13 December 1919
Harold Hiscock, Northumberland, born 26 July 1915
Keith Mayor, Preston, born 27 September 1923
Alfred J. Roe, London, born 26 October 1907
Andrew West, Glasgow
Neville Burgess, Beverley, born 23 December 1923.

All arrived at Grini on 12 June 1943 and left on 23 September 1943. Cox, Godwin, Hiscock, Roe, West and Burgess were killed at Sachsenhausen on 2 February 1945. Mayor was transferred at an unknown date to Belsen, since when all trace has been lost.

In the second part of his report Johansen stated that the party arrived at Sachsenhausen in September 1943. He saw them arrive and noted that they were made to wait at the entrance for two and a half hours. They were wearing naval uniforms with shoulder flashes. They were put in an isolation and punishment camp (inside the main camp), but the Norwegians managed to smuggle food and tobacco to them. The inmates of the punishment camp were criminals from within the camp itself and from outside, at least fifty per cent of whom were homosexuals. Also in the camp were men condemned to death and awaiting execution.

'The punishment exercise was three hours *Straf* from 0400, which consisted of goose-stepping, lying down, rolling in the soil and rabbit-jumping.' The men were not allowed into the barracks except for a half hour for dinner. From 0700 to 1700 they were forced to march on a trial track wearing shoes, including female, which were usually a size or two smaller than their own. They marched on an average from 48 to 52 kilometres a day carrying a pack weighing between 50 lbs and 90 lbs. The track was made up of sections of cobblestones, sand, gravel, concrete, water, etc. They had to march in all kinds of weather, from sunshine to pouring rain, and in temperatures ranging from more than 100 degrees Fahrenheit to 20 degrees below zero.

All of them lost weight and grew weak, but Johansen and a fellow

Norwegian prisoner named Leif Jensen secretly collected weekly supplies of food, tobacco and money for them, so that the Britons remained in fairly good condition, except 'Trilby' Row, who developed kidney trouble and 'layed up' for about three months.

The British prisoners were compelled to wear a large letter 'E', about twelve inches square, on their backs, and another some eight inches square on their chests in addition to other numbers. But they concealed these by 'carrying another jacket on top', and in the evenings managed to slip through to the Norwegian barracks by bribing the block orderly. The Norwegians were their special friends, but the SS in charge of the camp were their tormentors.

When news was received at the beginning of February that the Russians had reached the Oder, two former German prisoners of war now in SS uniform, appeared at midnight one night and ordered the Britons to accompany them. They said it was not necessary to take any kit with them as they would get clothes where they were going. But the British knew at once what was about to happen. For the two ex-prisoners in SS uniform belonged to the so-called *Sonderkommission* (Special Commission). Andrew West wrote a short note to his mother, which Jensen hid and subsequently delivered to the British Legation in Stockholm.

> When the boys left barracks their last words were: 'They have taken everything from us but not our spirit. God Save the King!' [recorded Johansen]. They were taken through the camp entrance and turned left to the place of execution. Lieutenant Godwin now suddenly knocks down one of the attending *Oberscharführers*, snatches his revolver and kills him, and severely wounded another.

The British prisoners were ultimately shot fighting. Keith Mayor was not among those brought for execution. He begged to be allowed to accompany the others, but was refused. He was placed in another isolation block, and the Norwegians continued to smuggle food and tobacco to him. 'Trilby' Roe was also listed for execution, but was in hospital and apparently there was not time to collect him, as approximately 400 to 500 prisoners were fetched from different parts of the camp for execution. Roe was later sent to Belsen.

> All the SS were dead drunk. Godwin was the leader, and a great comrade and a shining example for the rest. When they were in difficulty, he stood punishment on their behalf.

Another report referring to the 'Checkmate' personnel stated that in February a panic took place in the camp owing to the approach of the Russians to the Oder, and Godwin and at least five other ranks were murdered by the Germans.

In a second letter to the British Legation in Stockholm, Johansen wrote that after the events he had previously described he met a Norwegian prisoner who was wearing Godwin's jacket with his number. Johansen examined the jacket and found in a secret pocket a number on a strip of grey linen, the letter 'E' and the number 7178 alongside a small brown triangle. The prisoner said that he had obtained the jacket from the hospital at Sachsenhausen, which had received it from the *Effektenkammer*. It was bloodstained, and in several places there were what appeared to be patched-up bullet holes.

On 16 April 1945 the British military attaché in Stockholm wrote to MI9 to say that a Captain H. Hogermann of the Norwegian merchant navy had written to him about the 'Checkmate' party 'as they were my close friends in Sachsenhausen'. They were captured, he said, after they had blown up a German cruiser in Narvik (sic). They were 'Lieutenant Godwin; A.T. Roe, 28 Northern Road, Slough; Neville Arthur Burgess, Flemminggate 55, Beverley, Yorkshire; Andrew West, 70 Camden Street, Glasgow C.5; Jack Cox, North Cadbury, Yeovilton; Harold Hiscock, Trinity Bay, Newfoundland'.

Later the military attaché reported having received a visit from Leif Jensen, who had been in Sachsenhausen since 1941. Jensen stated that there were 26,000 in the camp, of whom 2,300 were Norwegians. Between February and the date of the final Russian advance on Berlin, 8,000 were liquidated. Some months after the capture of the 'Checkmate' party their cases were investigated by the Gestapo and they were adjudged to be saboteurs. They were then singled out for outrageous treatment – marches for endurance tests of military equipment and endurance drugs. Their morale held out superbly and they earned the high regard of the Norwegian prisoners, who were better treated and had their own medical officer and medical supplies. The British were not allowed to write or receive letters.

Jensen stated that an air raid alarm was sounded as the 'Checkmate' party were leaving (for execution), and a scrimmage which caused delay might have allowed one or more to break away. 'But no one was allowed to go near the place next day except a clearing-up squad; but there were shot marks, and one German NCO wounded.'

On 3 July 1945 Lieutenant-Colonel Wade, Research Officer to the United Nations War Crimes Commission, sent the Director of Naval Intelligence the following deposition by a German prisoner of war named Hans Christian Witt, who had been confined in Sachsenhausen concentration camp.

> In the year 1944 on my return to the concentration camp at Sachsenhausen, I met in the Punishment Company about fourteen Englishmen who had been held there by the SS against the law of any country. To avoid any difficulties they were classified as Norwegians and isolated in the camp under the worst treatment. From morning till late at night they had to break in new shoes for the SS shoe factory of the camp on a stretch of road approximately 50 kilometres, sometimes with a valise of 10 or 15 kilogrammes. All came from the crew of an E-boat or S-boat which landed in Norway. The lieutenant was an Englishman who had lived in the Argentine.
>
> Two of my English friends, Andrew West, 74 Camden Street, Glasgow, and Jack Cox from Wales, asked me to inform the English authorities about their whereabouts if I was successful enough to escape and get to the British. In 1944 two of the prisoners were conveyed to Natzweiler Elsas, a *Sonderlager* (special camp) of the worst possible type, where they had to work in a quarry with Norwegians, Poles, Russians, Czechoslovaks and German political prisoners. Responsible for the treatment of the English prisoners of war are SS Standartenführer Kaindl, SS Untersturmführer Hohne, SS Obersturmführer Cornelius of the *Sonderkommission* (Special commission) of Sachsenhausen, subordinate directly to the Reichsfuhrer SS.

The War Office stated that it was hoped that these men would be brought before a War Crimes Military Court. There is no record, however, of any of these being tracked down.

On 30 March 1945 the Admiralty wrote to Mrs Cotter, Godwin's aunt who was living in England, to tell her that her nephew was a prisoner-of-war, believed to be well!

In June of that year the Commodore of the Royal Naval Barracks at Devonport wrote to Mrs Mayor, mother of Keith, forwarding on to her a farewell letter Keith had written on the night he thought he was going to be executed, sent on from the British Legation in Stockholm. This may well in fact have been the letter said by Johansen to have been written by Andrew West.

When Mrs Mayor wrote to the Commodore asking for further information about her missing son, her letter was passed to the Admiralty. On 10 October 1945 she received a reply from the Secretary of the Admiralty as follows:

> I have to inform you that according to information recently received in the Admiralty, your son, Keith Mayor, was a member of a party made up of one naval officer and four other ratings and an army sergeant who were landed in Norway in April 1943 on a most secret operation. Your son was not a paratrooper. Nothing more was heard of the party until March 1945 when information was received that they had been captured in Norway shortly after landing and had been in German hands since that time. Evidence furnished in May 1945 by two Norwegians who had been confined in Sachsenhausen concentration camp indicated that your son had been shot at that camp on 2 February. It was to one of these men that your son entrusted his farewell letter to you which was enclosed in the letter from the Commodore, RN Barracks, Devonport dated 19 June 1945. Additional evidence since received shows in fact your son was omitted from the party by mistake and so lived on to be transferred to Belsen concentration camp, where he was subsequently shot.

Regret was expressed at the added distress 'which publicity of this case must cause.'

Five days later the Admiralty wrote again, confirming the death of Mayor in Belsen four days before its liberation. Belsen was in fact liberated on 11 April 1945. It was reported that Roe had also been transferred thence from Sachsenhausen, and met his death there between 15 February and the date of liberation.

One other document relating to the 'Checkmate' party may be quoted. Dated 12 January 1944, it was signed by a Major Reichel and addressed to the Chief of OKW (Oberkommando der Wehrmacht) – Field Marshal Keitel. 'For exploitation for propaganda purposes the following cases come into consideration.' Then follow details of various Allied 'guerilla acts' in North Africa, the attack on the *Tirpitz*, and 'the blowing up of ships in Haugesund on 28 April 1943 and following days; a number of German ships sunk in Oslo harbour and at Hoppernvik (sic) in the Haugesund by adhesive mines.'

Referring to the latter, the document went on to state that:

> After an intensive search by the army and police, a number of those responsible were captured on the Haugesund in uniform on 15 May

1943 with the co-operation of Norwegian civilians. They were:–
  1. John Godwin, born 13.12. 1919, Buenos Aires
  2. Seaman Neville Burgess, 23.1.24, Beverley
  3. Seaman Keith Mayor, 27.9.23, Preston
  4. Seaman Andrew West, 25.4.22, Glasgow
  5. Sgt Victor Cox, 18.12.1918, Buckhorn Weston, nr Gillingham, Dorset.

They had instructions to sink ships with adhesive mines. Nos 1 and 2 and 3 and 4 in two canoes blew up and sank a mine-locating craft off Koppernvik (sic) Haugesund. They then returned to the three others who had remained in charge of a motorboat. They then cruised for a fortnight among the islands waiting to be fetched by a MTB in which they had arrived. The men were 'camouflaged with naval oilskins'. Godwin said he had only occasionally made himself understood to passing Norwegian fishermen by signs as none of them could speak Norwegian. They obtained food in exchange for coffee, tobacco and chocolate.

Infringements of International Law not yet proved. After intensive interrogation by the Army, handed over to the security police, and from thence to Sachsenhausen concentration camp.

Presumably OKW acquiesced in their subsequent fate in accordance with the Hitler order.

Thus, to summarise the melancholy story of the 'Checkmate' party: after their capture at Haugesund following their sinking of the solitary German minesweeper at Kopervik, they were treated reasonably well until they were turned over to the SD. No evidence of torture at Grini prison has come to light, but once transferred to Sachsenhausen they were treated with the utmost brutality by the SS, and befriended only by a handful of courageous Norwegians.

During their months of confinement in Sachsenhausen, officer and men together, living on turnip gruel and a little bread, and marching thirty miles a day seven days a week to test boots for the German army, deprived of letters from home and forbidden to write any themselves, aware that their relatives knew nothing of their whereabouts and uncertain of their own ultimate fate, their spirits remained unquenchably high.

At the last when they were being led to execution in the gas chamber, we have the story that Godwin himself seized a pistol from one of the SS guards and shot the man before the whole party was mown down where they stood.

Keith Mayor, whose name had somehow been translated into 'Meyer', which to the SS meant that he must be Jewish, bereft of his comrades, was transferred to Belsen, there to be murdered in cold blood. Alfred Roe, the petty officer motor mechanic, who seems from the first to have been shanghai'd into the expedition, and sick in the camp hospital on the night of the death of his companions, was also transferred to Belsen as soon as he was fit enough to be moved, and there himself murdered.

Yet, ghastly as was the fate of this little party of Combined Operations personnel, there were other Allied prisoners of the Nazis who suffered perhaps even more at the hands of the infamous SD, although in less drawn-out a fashion. In September 1944 forty-seven British, American and Dutch airmen, all officers, were murdered in Mauthausen concentration camp. According to an eye-witness, this is how it was done:

> The forty-seven officers were led barefooted to the quarry ... At the bottom of the steps the guards loaded stones on the backs of those poor men and they had to carry them to the top. The first journey was made with stones weighing about 60 lbs and accompanied with blows ... The second journey the stones were still heavier, and whenever the poor wretches sank under their burden they were kicked and hit with a bludgeon ... In the evening twenty-one bodies were strewn along the road. The twenty-six others died the following morning.*

The last word in the 'Checkmate' story appeared in the *Supplement to the London Gazette* of 9 October 1945 which announced that 'Temporary Lieutenant John Godwin, RNVR had been awarded a Mention in Despatches (Posthumous) "For great gallantry and inspiring example whilst a prisoner of war in German hands in Norway and afterwards at Sachsenhausen, near Oranienburg, Germany, 1942-45." '

Perhaps a more enduring memorial to Godwin and his companions is to be found on a plaque at Sachsenhausen which reads:

> Seven British sailors, the crew of an MTB in Norwegian waters were held in fascist custody. They were confined to this cell for a month and on the night of 1/2 February 1945 were murdered by the SS.

Yet even here, there are inaccuracies. Godwin did not fall into German hands until 1943, and there is no record of the 'Checkmate' party being imprisoned in a single cell at Sachsenhausen.

Theirs was a fate that after 1942 might well have befallen captured members of any British 'irregular' unit.

---

* Quoted in *The Rise and Fall of the Third Reich*, Wm L. Shirer, Secker & Warburg, 1960.

# IV

## Clandestine 'Boating Parties'

On a black and moonless December night in 1943 an Italian-manned *MAS* boat* under British control crept in on silenced engines towards the enemy-held Ligurian coast near the little town of Sestri Levante, on the eastern side of the Gulf of Genoa. Allied intelligence had reported this area of the peacetime Italian Riviera to be well guarded by batteries of low and high-angle guns, radar posts, and armed coast-watchers in pillboxes; while enemy surface craft up to destroyer size prowled along the coastline. Powerfully escorted enemy convoys could also be encountered. Since British light coastal forces often lay in wait for these, there was the additional risk of being blown out of the water by a friendly vessel if one was tardy in flashing the correct recognition signal.

The mission of the *MAS* boat was to land two SOE agents to infiltrate themselves into the countryside and establish liaison with Partisan bands operating in that part of northern Italy. The pinpoint selected for the landing was a minor outcrop of rock, behind which a steep climb up the bed of a small stream afforded a path inland.

To ferry the agents ashore and land them as quietly as possible, the black inflated rubber dinghy carried on the after deck of the *MAS* boat was manhandled gently over the side and carefully loaded with their luggage, which included a weighty wireless transmitter and its associated batteries – transistors then being unknown. Passengers and crew then cautiously lowered themselves down into the bobbing craft. The latter were a British army major and a sergeant. Overseeing the whole clandestine operation and responsible for navigating the *MAS* boat to and from this inconspicuous pinpoint was a short, dark-haired young lieutenant of the Royal Naval Reserve named Tom Maxted.

While far from being his first such operation, it was still a comparatively new venture for Major Andrew Croft, who now

* (*Motoscafi Antisommergibili*, or motor anti-submarine boat).

gingerly seated himself in the dinghy and took up the paddles. The sergeant, gripping a sub-machine-gun, crouched at the forward end to act as lookout and guide. After whispered farewells had been exchanged, the major swiftly but quietly paddled away, the dinghy being almost immediately lost to sight in the gloom, and the gentle lap-lap of the small waves against its sides soon fading.

After paddling northwards on a converging course with the coast for what seemed hours to the apprehensive passengers, but in reality was only some fifteen minutes, no sign of the landing place could be seen among the darker shadows cast by the craggy cliffs towering above. Croft therefore manoeuvred the dinghy round and began to paddle back along the shoreline.

It had not been expected that the task of finding the correct landing place would be easy at night, despite prolonged and careful study of maps and aerial reconnaissance photographs. Nevertheless Croft and Maxted had estimated that it should take the dinghy party no more than twenty minutes to reach the shore and disembark the passengers, and another twenty to return. A brief extension of time had been allowed for in case of unforeseen difficulty, after which the *MAS* boat with its nervous Italian crew would be able to wait no longer, since it was vitally important that the vessel should be well clear of the enemy coast by daylight.

When a further ten minutes had elapsed with still no sign of the landing place, a brief worried conference took place in the dinghy. No one, however, seemed inclined to abort the mission, so Croft resumed paddling. Then at last, as if in response to their unspoken prayers, the sergeant spotted a pale line of phosphorescence marking surf away to port, and after a few quick strokes of the paddles, the dinghy grounded gently on the tiny beach.

The sergeant jumped ashore, quickly and efficiently reconnoitred the immediate vicinity, then returned to the boat to report all clear. The passengers and their gear were speedily disembarked, there were handshakes all round, and as soon as the agents had melted into the darkness, the dinghy shoved off for the return trip.

During the waiting period the *MAS* boat had been lying hove to about a thousand yards from the shore. Along with the Italians, Maxted was becoming increasingly apprehensive, wondering what had happened to the dinghy and, more importantly, how long it would be before the presence of their craft was detected by the unseen enemy. Meanwhile Croft and his companion paddled directly out to sea until they were able to make out the darker silhouette of the *MAS* boat against the night sky. Minutes later they and their dinghy were alongside, had been safely re-embarked, and their mother ship was on its way southward to base at full speed. The whole operation had in fact taken just under an hour.

Some weeks later the two agents they had landed were in wireless communication with their headquarters in North Africa, thus marking the successful outcome of one of the many such sorties to the enemy-held coasts of Italy and France which played no inconsiderable part in bringing about the final downfall of the Third Reich.

*

Lieutenant Maxted's involvement with the Navy's clandestine boating organisation known by the cover name of 'African Coastal Flotilla' began after he had been serving for almost two years in ships of the Home Fleet. Born in 1920, he had trained as a Merchant Navy cadet in HMS *Worcester*, and then joined the Shaw Savill Line. As a midshipman in the Royal Naval Reserve, in which he had enrolled in 1937, he had been called up at the outbreak of war and appointed to the armed merchant cruiser *Circassia*.

First of the Anchor Line's new motor ships, the *Circassia*, after being requisitioned and armed by the Admiralty, became a unit of the Northern Patrol. The task of the special squadron of armed merchant cruisers employed on this patrol was to enforce the Allied blockade against Germany by intercepting enemy merchantmen, and stopping and examining for contraband all neutral vessels entering or leaving the northern approaches to the British Isles and the North Sea. Maxted had been one of her boarding officers, and earned promotion to the rank of sub-lieutenant. In mid-1941 when the need for the Northern Patrol lapsed and the *Circassia*, along with the rest of her consorts, was transferred to convoy escort duties, Maxted was appointed to the Home Fleet flagship HMS *King George V*.

Life as a junior officer in a battleship, however, lacked excitement, and Maxted was not at all displeased when one day early in 1942 he and Francis Cosens, a fellow RNR sub-lieutenant, were summoned to the Admiralty. There the pair were interviewed by an RNVR lieutenant named Patrick Whinney representing the

Deputy Director of the Operations Division (Irregular) (DDOD(I)), who told them that two RNR officers with a knowledge of navigation were required for special service, the nature of which he was not at liberty to disclose at that stage, but which, he hinted, might well prove hazardous. Both men promptly volunteered.

DDOD(I) was a retired naval officer who had been seconded from the Secret Intelligence Service to the Admiralty to take charge of the clandestine sea operations involved in restoring our shattered intelligence organisations in enemy-occupied Europe. He was in the process of acquiring a fleet of suitable surface craft from any available source and volunteer personnel to man them. His operations, initially conducted across the Channel and North Sea, had started soon after the fall of France and, working from Gibraltar, were being extended to the western Mediterranean.

At this point it is necessary briefly to mention the existence of certain other 'irregular' organisations which had come into existence since the outbreak of war with which DDOD(I) was to become involved, all working more or less independently of each other and with different aims. The most important of these was Combined Operations, which was concerned with all manner of offensive activities, from small raids on enemy-held coasts to large scale assault landings. Then there was Special Operations Executive (SOE), whose brief in Churchill's own picturesque phrase was to 'set Europe ablaze'. Specifically, the task of SOE was to encourage the people of the occupied countries to harass the German war effort at every possible point by sabotage, subversion, go-slow process and armed raids, and to aid the build-up, arming and training of resistance forces ready to rise up in the final overthrow of the enemy.

Thirdly was the agency known as MI9, whose function was to establish and operate escape routes for survivors of the British armed forces left behind after Dunkirk, evaders from that and subsequent operations, shot-down Allied airmen, and those lucky enough to escape from prisoner-of-war camps.

The provision of suitable craft by the Navy for Combined Operations was not difficult, but considerably more so for the smaller organisations, particularly as the Admiralty decreed that it alone should control all clandestine sea operations in home waters. While DDOD(I) was eventually appointed to co-ordinate these, the aims of his own organisation and those of SOE were quite different.

Thus intelligence agents needed to be landed as quietly and unobtrusively as possible to melt unobserved into a hostile countryside, while SOE's object was to stir up trouble. DDOD(I)'s vessels were increasingly to be used on behalf of SOE and MI9 – the former having made a start with their own.

Under the terms of the French armistice, the Germans had occupied the northern half of that country together with a 70-mile coastal strip of the southern half, so that they possessed all the ports. The French government therefore moved to Vichy, which then served as the capital of the unoccupied zone. Other armistice terms included the demilitarisation of zones in southern France, Tunisia, Algeria and French Somaliland, together with the naval bases of Toulon, Bizerta, Ajaccio and Oran, and Italo-German Armistice Commissions were soon established in all the important towns in those territories. The security forces in the unoccupied zone of France consisted of the gendarmerie, assisted by an unpleasantly pro-Nazi militia known as the *Milice*. In addition, southern France was full of Gestapo agents with whom the latter worked closely.

While the RAF eventually succeeded in establishing an efficient system for dropping agents – mostly SOE – and supplies into occupied Europe, aircraft and aircrews were not readily available at first. Reception committees had to be organised by resistance workers, and safe landing and pick-up points chosen and marked out. Landing aircraft was dangerous and difficult and called for complicated planning as well as dependence on the weather, and was therefore used sparingly. It was also difficult to take people out by air in an emergency over and above the number of 'bodies' allowed for.

More in the way of passengers, stores and equipment could be carried by sea. On a moonless night a disguised vessel, such as a fishing boat of local appearance and apparently innocent function, could make an almost silent approach to a small deserted beach or previously reconnoitred pinpoint, anywhere along a hostile coastline. Apart from the risk of encountering inquisitive enemy patrol craft, the only brake on such seaborne expeditions was the weather.

As mentioned earlier, DDOD(I) had begun operations across the Channel in mid-1940, transporting agents to and from enemy-occupied Europe in a varied assortment of craft, ranging from a former Breton tunny-fishing vessel to a number of requisitioned motor gunboats originally being built for the Turkish navy.* Also working from Gibraltar at this time was a small Polish naval mission whose principal object was to maintain contact with intelligence cells established by a number of Polish officers after the defeat of their country in several French cities where there were Polish communities, notably Toulouse, Clermont Ferrand, Lyons, Limoges and Vichy itself, and put ashore agents, arms and stores.

For these clandestine trips to pinpoints along the southern coast of France, two 20-ton ex-Spanish sardine boats, called feluccas, were being used, captained by two young Polish naval officers, Lieutenants Buchowski and Kadulski. But after their underground organisation had been betrayed to the enemy in 1941, they in these small and uncomfortable craft continued to work for DDOD(I), SOE and MI9. Among the many SOE agents they landed, both men and women, was the famous Odette Sansom, afterwards to be awarded the George Cross.

British submarines based on Gibraltar and making runs to take supplies to beleaguered Malta were sometimes pressed into service to drop off agents en route. But by and large the Admiralty was understandably reluctant to risk valuable warships on such missions.

Also briefly employed from Gibraltar on similar agent-landing operations had been an extraordinary vessel known as HMS *Fidelity*. A 2,400-ton armed French merchantman named *Le Rhin*, employed by the French colonial intelligence service, she had been seized at Marseilles by a French naval officer serving in her, who persuaded the crew to sail her to England to serve with the Royal Navy as a 'Fighting French' ship. After being commissioned under the White Ensign as a special service vessel, the crew given new identities and the ship renamed, she was acquired by DDOD(I) for clandestine work in the western Mediterranean. Because of her size, however, she was found to be unsuitable for this role, and later as a 'Q-ship', still under command of the fiery Corsican who originally shanghai'd her, she was sunk by a U-boat off West Africa while escorting a convoy to the Far East.

Another acquisition to DDOD(I)'s 'private navy' for employment overseas was the trawler *Tarana*. A former French fishing vessel, she had been taken over by the Navy to serve in the Auxiliary Patrol, which had been formed to keep watch in the

* See *The Secret Navies*, A. Cecil Hampshire, Wm Kimber, 1978.

Channel during the threat of German invasion. Overhauled and fitted with concealed guns, and captained by Lieutenant-Commander E.B. 'Nobby' Clark, RNR with a volunteer crew, she was sailed to Gibraltar early in 1942.

Prior to her arrival, however, DDOD(I)'s clandestine sea operations in the western Mediterranean had also been concerned with a plan conceived by Winston Churchill. Since the British Chiefs of Staff considered an Allied invasion of Europe impracticable before, at least, 1943, Churchill had pressed on President Roosevelt the desirability of Anglo-American intervention in French North Africa, to prevent German occupation of that territory which might draw in Spain and Portugal on the side of the Axis. North African bases would also be required from which to attack Germany and eliminate Italy.

Churchill code-named his original plan Operation 'Gymnast', and it hinged largely upon the defeat of Rommel by General Auchinleck in the Western Desert. 'Gymnast' was later overtaken by a larger scheme called 'Super Gymnast', and finally altered to Operation 'Torch', the Allied invasion of French North Africa which took place in 1942.

Thus in order to sound out possible French reaction to an American landing in North Africa – as British standing was at a low ebb because of the events at Oran, Dakar and in Syria – it was necessary to infiltrate agents along the Algerian coast to contact the French Underground. Information was needed about French military strength, also the general feeling among navy and army officers. A more strategic purpose was to survey the coastline for possible Allied landings. At that time the specialist organisation known as 'COPP', (Combined Operations Pilotage Parties) which was later formed for the purpose of carrying out such surveys prior to an amphibious assault, had not then come into being.

Engaged in this tricky work was the ex-Scottish Fishery Protection vessel *Minna*, requisitioned by the Navy during the invasion scare and now forming part of the Gibraltar Auxiliary Patrol, and temporarily borrowed by DDOD(I) from that organisation. The ship's officers included one of DDOD(I)'s early recruits, Lieutenant Donald MacCallum, RNR, who personally commanded the boatwork between the *Minna* and the shore.

The choice of pinpointing the coast was limited to rocky or exposed landings, and it was necessary for the *Minna* to heave to for upwards of a quarter of a mile off shore because of her large silhouette and unsilenced engines. In those days surfboats for special operations had not then been designed. Thus in order to land and pick up passengers, MacCallum himself sometimes swam ashore with a line by means of which a small boat could be hauled in to the beach. On more than one occasion the *Minna* was attacked by enemy aircraft while on her trips to and from the coast, but she fortunately managed to escape unscathed. Under an intriguingly laconic citation which gave away very little, MacCallum was subsequently awarded the DSC.

After spending a short period at the organisation's London headquarters, Maxted and Cosens arrived at Gibraltar in a troopship in the late summer of 1942 to begin the tasks for which they had been recruited. Present on 'the Rock' at that time were representatives of three of the agencies already mentioned – SOE, MI9 and DDOD(I)'s own setup, all of which were involved in clandestine operations to the south-western coast of France. Maxted and Cosens found that they were to work with the two Polish officers, Buchowski and Kadulski, and use their feluccas. The Poles, who by then were feeling the strain, were not displeased at this turn of events.

In order to avoid repetition it will be convenient to recount in some detail the experiences of Maxted, since they were typical of those undergone by the men engaged on these difficult and dangerous operations which, in the words of the DDOD(I), 'called for qualities of leadership, endurance, determination and navigational skill out of the ordinary'.

Maxted's first trip was in the felucca *Seawolf*. Like her sister vessel *Seadog*, she was a craft of wooden construction, some 38 feet long, narrow beamed, with a short raked mast and lateen sail. She had been fitted with a diesel engine which gave her a top speed of some $6\frac{1}{2}$ to 7 knots. Accommodation on board was meagre in the extreme. Forward was a small compartment containing four cots; amidships was the wheelhouse, which afforded just sufficient room for the helmsman with another man standing beside him; and right aft was a tiny cabin, only slightly larger than a cupboard, containing one bunk, which was shared turn and turn about by the two officers.

There was no mess room, no 'heads' (lavatory) or washing facilities of any kind. The crews' natural functions were usually performed directly over the side while holding on to the shrouds with one hand. Passengers, however, could use a bucket, and females accorded the privacy of the engine compartment. Hot meals could be cooked when conditions permitted on a tiny, coal-fired galley stove housed in a hutch. A small wooden dinghy was carried upside down on deck, together with one or two 40-gallon drums of diesel oil. For armament the *Seawolf* boasted an old Vickers .303-inch machine-gun, but she was not expected to put up much of a fight if challenged by an enemy warship.

The crew, apart from the two officers, consisted of a coxswain, motor mechanic, and two seamen, all volunteers. Navigational equipment included a compass, sextant and charts, and a good two-way radio was also carried. Throughout their clandestine voyages officers and men slopped around in civilian fishermen's rig of weather-stained jerseys or smocks, trousers and seaboots, although certain items of naval uniform were also taken along in case they should be seized as *francs tireurs*.

The average time taken to reach a pinpoint from Gibraltar was five or six days, but in the face of head seas and strong winds voyages could take much longer, much to the discomfiture of any apprehensive agent due to be 'exfiltrated' and on the run from the enemy, to whom even a few minutes of waiting could seem a lifetime. An average round trip covered a distance of up to about 1,400 miles, which involved some fourteen to sixteen days at sea. Life on board was very difficult, and in bad weather all hands quickly became soaked through, and they had to remain in their wet clothes since there was not a dry spot on board. During such times hot meals were out of the question, and they had to subsist on corned beef.

The weather in the Gulf of Lions, through which their clandestine voyages customarily took them, is notoriously bad. Even in mid-summer when fine weather can normally be expected, gales are apt to blow up without warning and raise heavy seas, while sudden changes in the weather can occur between areas only a few miles apart. In winter, conditions can become as bad as any to be encountered in the North Atlantic.

After embarking her passengers in Gilbraltar – known only to the crews of the feluccas as 'Joeys' – the vessel would leave harbour unobtrusively, and when about two miles out, all hands were required to set to work to paint the sides and deck structures in the colours normally favoured by local fishing craft, adding as a finishing touch a representation of the Spanish flag. On the last night of the return voyage to Gibraltar, the same procedure had to be gone through in reverse, substituting normal Navy grey paint and hoisting the White Ensign. Even so, on return to harbour, it was difficult to ward off the inquisitive who wanted to know how one had become so sunburnt and weatherbeaten. Questions such as these had to be adroitly parried since absolute secrecy was their only safeguard.

The following instructions (a) to an agent about to depart from the United Kingdom on a mission, and (b) to a reception committee composed of Resistance workers at the receiving end – the latter sent by wireless in code – are typical of usual procedure:

> (a) 'To Lise. Operation Clothier. Destination Auxerre. You will leave this country by plane for Gibraltar. You will then be taken by felucca to a point on the east of the Gulf of Lions where you will be received by certain members of our organisation who will assist you to contact – – – –'.

But agents could not always go by air, and sometimes had to take passage in a troopship.

> (b) 'No 57 for Michel. Repeat stand by tonight watchman bringing 6 agents independent. One ton materials to be sunk with line to buoy Pointe de l'Esquillon,* collect one ton tinned food. Maximum passengers return Pierrot and two others to leave space for RAF men embarking elsewhere. Signals: boat to shore Red M for Mother; shore to boat White O for Oscar.

In the late evening of the day on which Maxted started out on his first trip in the *Seawolf*, two agents, a man and a woman, arrived on board bringing with them, somewhat to Maxted's surprise, a bicycle. He was never to discover the reason, for security was so tight that there was rarely any converse between felucca crew and the 'Joeys' they carried. The less anyone knew about their business the better. Somehow the bicycle was stowed out of sight in the engine compartment, and with the rest of the agents' luggage tucked away, the *Seawolf* chugged quietly out of harbour. After a brief halt so that she could be painted in her false colours, the felucca set off on a course which would take her between the Balearic Islands and the Spanish mainland. This route was sometimes varied by going between the islands themselves.

Fortunately the weather remained fair and nothing untoward occurred to disturb the daily routine, although all hands remained very much on the alert. To the casual observer the *Seawolf* appeared to be just another scruffy fishing boat going about her leisurely and

---

* Sinking stores brought from Gibraltar and buoying them for later recovery was frequently resorted to in order to save time and reduce risks.

legitimate business.

Six days later she arrived off that stretch of the French coast in which was sited the designated pinpoint. It could hardly have been more hazardous. For the pinpoint was inside the bay of Cassis, a small seaside resort on the coast of Provence, almost equidistant between the great French naval base of Toulon and the equally large and busy port of Marseilles.

Waiting until darkness had fallen, the felucca began to creep stealthily into the bay with her engine just ticking over, the headlands on either side showing up starkly against the night sky. Distance off shore was always difficult to judge, but the vessel was invariably taken in as close as her captain dared in order to avoid a long dinghy row. Then the 'fisherman's anchor' was let go, enabling the felucca to ride gently to a rope cable. An axe was always kept handy in case it should become necessary to make a quick getaway.

The dinghy was quietly manhandled over the side, all orders being given in whispers. The two seamen who were to paddle it to the shore then climbed down, taking with them a boat's compass. The bicycle followed, an awkward object to stow since the boat was barely eight feet long, and lastly the two agents with the rest of their gear. The dinghy then shoved off and headed for the shore.

The landing went off without a hitch, and when the boat returned as noiselessly as it had departed, it was quickly hoisted on board, the anchor weighed, and the felucca stood out to sea. When about twenty miles off the coast, she hove to, and with the coming of daylight fishing nets were streamed. There the *Seawolf* was to remain for the whole of next day, to all intents and purposes a neutral fishing craft innocently following her normal occupation. That night, however, she was due to close the coast again, this time to take off two 'Joeys' and convey them to safety.

Around midnight, when all had become quiet and the coastline shrouded in darkness, the *Seawolf*'s crew hauled in their nets, the engine was started up, and she headed back towards the bay. This time if all went well she was to be met by a reception committee. The pinpoint was a small sandy beach inside a cove at the southern tip of the peninsula which formed one arm of the bay. From 0100 onwards the reception committee was to flash the agreed signal to seaward with a shaded torch every twenty minutes.

It was a warm still night, and as the felucca glided towards the cove, which was surrounded by high cliffs, the light breeze blowing off the land was redolent with the scent of pines and *maquis*.* To

* The shrub that gave its names to the Resistance movement.

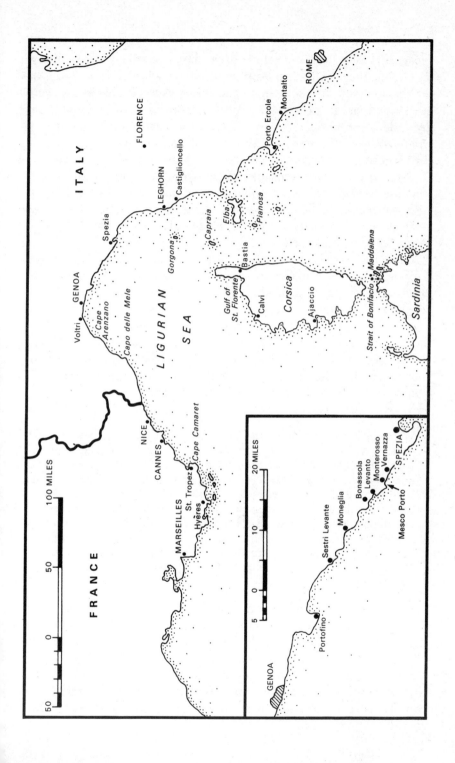

FRANCE

ITALY

FLORENCE

Spezia

LEGHORN

Castiglioncello

GENOA

Voltri

Cape Arenzano

Capo delle Mele

Gorgona

Capraia

Elba

Pianosa

Porto Ercole

Montalto

ROME

LIGURIAN SEA

NICE

CANNES

St. Tropez

Cape Camaret

Hyères

MARSEILLES

Gulf of St. Florente

Bastia

Calvi

Corsica

Ajaccio

Maddalena

Strait of Bonifacio

Sardinia

100 MILES

50

0

50

20 MILES

10

0

5

GENOA

Portofino

Sestri Levante

Moneglia

Bonassola

Levanto

Monterosso

Vernazza

SPEZIA

Mesco Porto

everyone's relief the expected torch signals blinked reassuringly, and after they had been answered, the anchor was let go, the dinghy lowered and sent in to the shore. Agreed passwords were exchanged as it neared the beach, and as soon as the boat grounded, the two agents were helped aboard. A brief whispered word of farewell, and it was away and heading back to the *Seawolf*, the reception committee having already faded into the landscape.

No time was lost in embarking the two agents, and hoisting and stowing the dinghy back on board, these tasks being accomplished with a speed and efficiency borne of long practice. The anchor was hove up, engine started, and the felucca ghosted out of the bay to begin her long haul back to Gibraltar.

While nothing went wrong on these two operations, it might well happen that after making an accurate landfall to effect a pickup at an obscure pinpoint somewhere along an unlighted and unfriendly coast on a cloudy or rainy night, no signals were seen from an expected reception committee, and the operation would reluctantly have to be abandoned. 'There were times,' recorded DDOD(I), 'when problems, handicaps and setbacks involved seemed insurmountable, but the morale of the felucca crews and their faith in the vital work being attempted remained unshaken.'

Maxted later recalled that:

> We always operated when there was no moon, so it was always pitch dark. Navigation was all-important. Reliance had to be placed on sun and star sights – no *Sight Reduction Tables* – only the old system of logs; and working out all these figures in a small boat in bad weather was murder. We used silhouettes of the land taken from the chart, and I used to make my own when on the coast. We used to creep in, the headlands showing up as we got nearer. Depths had to be taken with a leadline, and we had no chronometer. The worst part of all these operations was waiting for the dinghy to return. Sometimes it would be away for as much as two hours, but usually about an hour. I never left without the dinghy crew.

The feluccas they used, which were in fact the only boats available, were in a bad state of repair and the engines unreliable to a degree. They were invariably heavily loaded with extra fuel, passengers and special stores and equipment, and the task of nursing them in the appalling winter weather conditions of the north-western Mediterranean, and maintaining the morale of the passengers in conditions of acute discomfort called for special qualities in their commanding officers.

Maxted completed a number of trips from Gibraltar to the south of France in the *Seawolf*, which was the better and more seaworthy of the two feluccas, all of them to pinpoints in the area near Marseilles. On one occasion, having picked up two intelligence agents in that neighbourhood, he was ordered to call at another pinpoint near Perpignan. Close by the pickup rendezvous beach was a 'safe house' in which were crammed some thirty to forty 'parcels', as they were referred to by their French helpers, and who included evaders and escapers, shot-down RAF aircrew, and various wanted individuals known as *refracteurs* who were one jump ahead of the Gestapo and had to be taken off.

They had been awaiting the arrival of a rescue vessel for several days, and had reached the point where fear, tension, boredom and frustration erupted in a wave of reckless excitement when at last they saw the *Seawolf*'s dinghy approaching the shore where they were assembled. Maxted was appalled by the noise they were making, and feared that at any moment the whole area would be flooded with *Milice* and Gestapo agents.

Somehow, however, the whole party was safely ferried off to the waiting felucca, among them a man who had been in hospital with a broken leg. Pursued by the enemy, he had been helped to escape by friends. But in jumping out of the hospital window he had sustained a broken ankle. The rescued men had to be packed tightly in rows like sardines round the deck of the *Seawolf*, the injured man being propped against the wheelhouse, and they remained there for the entire voyage. If it had become necessary to hide them from view, a tarpaulin kept rolled up along the gunwale would have been pulled over them. In such tiny vessels as the *Seawolf* and *Seadog* there was no space below in which they could have been concealed.

Soon after leaving Perpignan the weather blew up rough, and soon all the passengers were severely seasick, many of them loudly lamenting that they had ever left the dubious security of dry land. The food situation also soon became critical, with only a little corned beef and a few biscuits remaining. Maxted therefore radioed Gibraltar for assistance, and was instructed to rendezvous with the *Minna*, which had now herself become a full-time unit of DDOD(I)'s clandestine Mediterranean flotilla. The two vessels duly met off the coast of Majorca, where Maxted's unhappy passengers were transferred to the trawler. She then provided the *Seawolf* with a welcome supply of bread, butter, fresh meat and other necessities. Since, as earlier mentioned, the felucca lacked lavatory or other sanitary facilities, her condition after this experience is best left to the imagination!

On more than one voyage when the *Seawolf*'s engine gave up the unequal struggle in heavy weather and conditions were too bad for hoisting the sail, she was forced to ride to a sea anchor during daylight in enemy waters. To her captain's normal anxieties was added the possibility of air attack or surface ship investigation, and the subsequent capture of himself and his crew in civilian clothes disguised as French or Spanish fishermen.

For most of the time Maxted was able to retain his own coxswain and crew.

> They were a fine bunch of lads and never hesitated to do anything. For us those felucca days are quite unforgettable. There were periods of boredom and great discomfort, but the sheer excitement and drama of those cloak and dagger operations made up for all the bad spots.

Cosens, too, had his share of hardships and excitement. Not only was the *Seadog*, in which he carried out a number of trips, a poor seaboat, she had been fitted with a particularly clumsy and temperamental engine of Swedish manufacture. This could only be got going with the aid of a blowlamp, was extremely noisy and once started, difficult to control.

Another officer recruited into DDOD(I)'s flotilla at about the same time as Maxted and Cosens was Lieutenant Marian Lukas of the Polish navy. His attempts in command of expeditions were less successful than those of his colleagues, but he was all the more determined and proved himself to be a resourceful leader and skilful seaman and navigator. Once when he had started out on an operation, engine defects developed which caused flames and sparks from the exhaust to become so conspicuous that he abandoned the attempt for fear of compromising the proceedings. Returning to harbour where another unit of the flotilla was lying incomplete for sea, he transferred his stores and equipment to her, landed his coxswain who had become unwell, sailed short-handed, and with no wireless completed the mission successfully.

On their return to Gibraltar at the conclusion of their 'expeditions', the captains of the feluccas retired to the Bristol Hotel, in which they were accommodated, to write out their individual reports for submission to DDOD(I)'s link on 'the Rock', Captain Charles Osborne, RNR, whose duty it was to pass on to them their orders in the first place. In addition to the more formal Navy-style 'report of proceedings', a private and more colourful account of events was always appended, which told the DDOD(I) far more, and enabled him to assess exactly the problems and dangers involved in an undertaking which could never be officially publicised. And indeed it is more than probable that post-war these individual reports have long since been consigned to the flames.

On the night of 7/8 November 1942 the Allied Invasion of North Africa was launched under its revised code name of Operation 'Torch'. From Casablanca to Algiers more than 100,000 British and American troops were initially landed to begin the drive to Tunis. In the words of General Eisenhower, Allied Supreme Commander, 'The minimum objective of the North African invasion was to seize the main ports along the coast, denying their use to the Axis as bases for submarines, and from them to operate eastwards towards the British desert forces.' For earlier, on 23 October, the Eighth Army had opened its offensive against Rommel at Alamein, the victorious outcome of which, following the 'Torch' landings, was eventually to lead to the final expulsion of the Axis forces in North Africa and open the way to landings in southern Europe.

Enemy reaction soon followed news of the landings. Unoccupied France was promptly overrun by the Germans, and the Italians moved into the coastal zone from the frontier to Marseilles. By January 1943 all clandestine felucca trips from Gibraltar to south-western France had been temporarily closed down.

Once the Allied landings had become stabilised, and Allied Force Headquarters firmly established in Algiers, DDOD(I)'s clandestine organisation in the western Mediterranean, now distinguished by the title of 'African Coastal Flotilla' – although no mention of the existence of any such unit appeared in any official naval publication – shifted its headquarters to that port from Gibraltar. The trawler *Tarana*, whose clandestine voyages, alternating and sometimes coinciding with, those of the feluccas – although to different pinpoints – had been undertaken largely on behalf of MI9, during which some distinguished 'parcels' had been successfully collected, was turned over by Clark to Lieutenant Jim Leslie, a fellow RNR officer recruited by DDOD(I) earlier in the year, and sailed to Algiers.

Clark was then directed to take over a former millionaire's yacht named *Sidi Efni* which, having fallen on evil times and ending her days in the Spanish coastal trade, had somehow become a British prize of war. She was so ancient and decrepit, although still retaining traces of her former internal baroque glory, that no reference to her appeared in Lloyd's Register. After being overhauled and having various alterations made to her in the dockyard at Gibraltar, she became the flotilla's base accommodation ship at Algiers.

That task accomplished, Clark was ordered back to the United Kingdom to commission and sail out to the Mediterranean DDOD(I)'s latest acquisition, the trawler *Prodigal*. One of eleven minesweepers designated the *Proctor* Class, built in Portugal for the Admiralty in 1941, she was diesel-driven, and armed with three 20mm guns and two light machine-guns. She was to be employed chiefly on clandestine operations in the Adriatic.

Unfortunately, the Allies lost the race for Tunisia by a narrow margin, into which country two days after the initial 'Torch' landings the Germans had rapidly begun air-lifting troops with the connivance of the Vichy-controlled Resident-General, Admiral Esteva. Having captured the coastal towns of Bougie, Djidjelli, Philipville and Bone, First Army spearheads did in fact thrust forward to within sixteen miles of Tunis, but our ultimate failure to reach and capture the place was due to a number of factors, not least that the 'First Army' was little more than a corps, and compelled to advance over 400 miles of mountainous roads in the worst possible winter weather. Shipping and land transport were inadequate, and rain and enemy bombing rendered available airfields unserviceable. Difficulties were also experienced with the French, whose senior officers were Vichy-minded.

Facing a new and formidable army under Colonel-General von Arnim, the First Army dug in along a sixty-mile front stretching southward through the mountains from the Tunisian coast while its strength was steadily built up. The small iron-ore port of Bone, the most easterly point reached in Tunisia, had been captured on 12 November by British paratroops, followed up shortly afterwards by Commandos landed from destroyers to take over the port and aerodrome.

Five days later the first Allied tanker was able to berth in its harbour, and landed 1,100 tons of badly needed petrol. By 8 January 172,000 tons of Allied shipping had used the port; more than 31,000 men had been landed; 4,500 vehicles disembarked, and more than 3,500 tons of war material landed in a single day. For the next three months, despite being bombed day and night, Bone became the principal forward supply base for the Allied armies. The defences fought back magnificently, and as one war correspondent wrote, 'Bone was a little Malta on its own, and the band of men who ran it as valiant as the men of Malta.' It was also to Bone that, after he had brought out the *Prodigal*, Clark was despatched to set up an advanced headquarters for the African Coastal Flotilla.

A few miles farther up the coast was the tiny port of Tabarka, base for the Commandos who, along with four troops of American Rangers, carried out raids against the enemy's flank outposts, cut his lines of communication, and patrolled in front of our own lines. Night after night urgently needed supplies of petrol, oil and lubricants, lifeblood of a modern army, together with rations were ferried up from Bone by landing craft.

In charge of the place, which boasted only a couple of 'hards' normally used by fishing craft in peace-time, and the disembarkation and forwarding of the supplies to the front line was volunteer 58-year-old Lieutenant Kongstaff of the RNVR Special Branch, members of which were not usually appointed to an actively combatant role. Imbued with enormous fighting spirit, and in his element as self-style NOIC (Naval Officer in Charge), Tabarka, with these initials boldly stencilled on his steel helmet, Longstaff was daily to be seen superintending the work of his 'parish' in a White Ensign-emblazoned and furiously driven jeep, closely pursued by low-flying, cannon-firing Messerschmitts.

While Cosens was ordered back to England to take over another new addition to DDOD(I)'s slowly growing and painfully acquired flotilla, this time a British-built version of the feluccas *Seawolf* and *Seadog*, named *Seahawk* and fitted with twin high-speed diesels, and also destined to be employed in the Adriatic, Maxted found himself in charge of yet another temporary newcomer. Named *Welcome*, she was a gaff-rigged Spanish fishing vessel of some 15 tons. In her Maxted carried out a number of operations along the North African coast, chiefly to pick up agents from points further east and return them to Algiers. The task of these 'Joeys', some of whom had been infiltrated long before the Allied landings, had been to obtain information regarding enemy military strength and his rapidly changing order of battle.

Clandestine operations were also started by the ACF to the Italian islands and mainland and to Corsica. But these operations presented even greater difficulties than those mounted from Gibraltar, since the limited craft available for requisitioning along the North African coast were in even more ramshackle condition than the Spanish feluccas. No engine spares were available, and nobody possessed the technical knowledge to effect lasting repairs to the engines of Italian manufacture, with the result that exasperating delays and mechanical breakdowns were the principal features in the early attempts to penetrate Italy. 'Much of the work of the flotilla during this period therefore consisted of nursing leaky and neglected craft from Bone to Algiers under sail or in tow in attempts to replace or manufacture at Algiers some spare part essential to the rusting and worn-out engines.'

Meanwhile the enemy occupation of Vichy France had enhanced the difficulties of operations to that country, and time after time expeditions from Algiers involving long voyages were frustrated by the arrest of intelligence reception committees, or their failure to penetrate the banned coastal areas and keep their appointments.

This was the experience of Maxted when he set off from Algiers in the tiny *Welcome* to pick up a couple of agents at a pinpoint in south-western France. He was well on the way to carry out this rescue mission when he was suddenly recalled by wireless. And to make sure that he received the news that the mission had been aborted, an RAF aircraft hastily despatched from Algiers dropped a confirmatory message which informed him that the luckless agents had been arrested.

His next mission, to transport arms to the Maquis in Corsica, was more successful. Creeping silently after dark into the rugged bay of Porto, he ran the *Welcome*'s bows up on to a small beach, where the guns and ammunition were speedily unloaded by the delighted Corsicans. On her way back to Algiers next morning, 'we were buzzed by a German aircraft,' reported Maxted, 'but he went away.'

Two other officers of the flotilla, one a pioneer in its formation and the other a comparative newcomer, also managed to bring off a couple of notable operations against odds. Thus Lieutenant Walter Gervaise, RNR, a considerably older man than his colleagues, took a local-type craft to the northern coast of Sicily to land an agent just prior to the Allied invasion of that island. Delayed by bad weather en route, his vessel was attacked – not by a German but an Allied aircraft – during which his coxswain was severely wounded in the hand. Lacking proper medical kit, Gervaise rendered first aid,

Felucca *Seawolf*

Lieutenant T. H. Max
RNR

ML576 after being at
by an allied fighter-b

completed the mission successfully, and tended the coxswain during the vessel's return voyage so expertly that his treatment saved the man from losing his hand or worse.

Lieutenant Charles Irwin, RNR, who had joined the ACF early in 1942, set out in another local craft to land an agent on the northern tip of Corsica. This involved a voyage of more than a thousand miles during which the weather became foul and, by an unhappy coincidence, his vessel was also attacked by the trigger-happy pilot of an Allied fighter, fortunately without loss. Despite the imposition of bombing restrictions in response to DDOD(I)'s protests to AFHQ at Algiers, a number of such incidents continued to occur, with consequent adverse effect on the morale of the flotilla crews.

In this connection it has to be borne in mind that in conducting his clandestine activities, which played an important part in the successful prosecution of the war, DDOD(I) was responsible for obtaining, manning, fuelling, victualling, repairing and operating his own vessels, and arranging for them to carry out their designated tasks almost independently of any local naval authority, and in complete secrecy if the latter were to succeed. At the same time a workable liaison with commanders on the spot had to be maintained in the face of prejudice and an understandable dislike of any organisation which smacked of being a 'private navy'. When other agencies were also involved in seaborne operations, things were made infinitely more difficult, and there were times when the sympathy and understanding of local naval authorities became so alienated that they came to regard irregular operations with a mixture of ridicule, impatience and hostility.

When the *Welcome* inevitably succumbed to her defects and had to be discarded, Maxted was given another 'crazy craft', requisitioned at Bone by Patrick Whinney who had been sent out from England to track down and obtain suitable vessels from local sources. Named *Annunciada*, she was of the felucca type, lateen rigged and some 45 feet long. Prior to the coming of war to North Africa she had been employed in trundling small quantities of sand around the coast. Her former owner thoughtfully fitted up some crude bunks for her new naval owners, and also supplied a cast-iron cooker which could be carried on deck. Maxted's task now was to ferry plastic explosives, ammunition and a variety of special equipment by night to the Commandos and Rangers operating from Tabarka, dodging prowling enemy E-boats en route.

If his vessel happened to be unlucky enough to be caught in

Tabarka in daylight there were other hazards to be endured. On one occasion the little *Annunciada* was attacked with machine-gun fire by enemy fighter-bombers, but except for some perforated oil drums, managed to escape without damage or casualties. Bone, too, was no haven of rest. During one of the many daylight raids on that long-suffering port while the *Annunciada* was lying alongside a jetty formerly used for loading iron ore, a bomb came whistling down which, if it had exploded, would have blown the tiny vessel to smithereens. Instead, by a miracle, it hit a nearby crane jib and split open, shedding its sinister contents all over the jetty.

By the early spring of 1943 the Tunisian campaign had passed its climax, and plans were already being formulated for the next objective, the invasion of Sicily, referred to by Churchill as striking at 'the soft underbelly of the Axis.' The speedy occupation of that island, the fall from power of Mussolini, and the subsequent Allied invasion of the Italian mainland at Reggio and Salerno have already been mentioned. The Salerno landings took place on 9 September 1943 and were so fiercely contested by the Germans that it was not until 1 October that Naples, only thirty miles away, was captured. Despite the defection of their ally, the Germans had prepared a number of formidable defence lines up the 'leg' of Italy, and their stubborn resistance, coupled with the fact that the Allies had to fight their way over mountainous country in atrocious weather conditions was to turn the campaign into one of the most difficult and arduous of the war.

Corsica had been fully occupied by the Italians since 1942, but by 9 September the Germans had taken control of all ports and bases in that island. Three days after the Salerno landings, Hitler, faced with impending battles on the Russian front, ordered Sardinia to be evacuated. Accordingly the Germans began transferring their forces to Corsica.

The Resistance movement in the latter island had been aided by SOE agents sent in from Algiers, some by sea and others by air. The Partisans, or Maquis, who called themselves the 'Front National' although mostly Communists, numbered about 10,000. When Italy surrendered, it seemed likely that the majority of the Italian troops would side with them, and in fact with the aid of its former Italian garrison the Maquis were able to capture Bastia.

Meanwhile the Germans had completed the transfer of their forces from Sardinia into Corsica which, since the Allies were fully engaged at Salerno, they were able to do with little interference.

More than 25,000 troops with a considerable number of tanks, guns and vehicles were ferried across the Strait of Bonifacio, and in due course Bastia was retaken. Hardly had their evacuation of Sardinia been completed than a handful of American and Italian officers landed in that island, which therefore fell to the Allies with hardly a shot being fired.

By then Hitler had ordered Corsica also to be evacuated, and the Germans now started to leave that island by air and sea. Meanwhile Free French forces had begun to arrive in their own warships, an infantry company of the *Bataillon de Choc* (French shock troops) being transported from Algiers to Ajaccio overnight in the French submarine *Casabianca*. The latter vessel had escaped from Toulon on the morning of the day on which the French fleet there was scuttled after the German occupation of Vichy France. Because of defective torpedo tubes she was useless for naval purposes, but she had a large carrying capacity. Prior to playing this important part in the liberation of Corsica, she had also been used for secretly landing agents and arms in that island.

By the evening of 3 October when French troops were approaching Bastia, the Germans had practically completed their evacuation. As with Sicily, the move had been organised and carried out with great efficiency. More than 27,000 troops were air-lifted to the Italian mainland and the island of Elba, and the remainder, together with guns, tanks, vehicles, equipment and stores, transhipped by sea. But not without loss, the enemy's vessels being successfully attacked by our submarines and light coastal forces, and his transport aircraft by bombing attacks on Italian airfields. By 4 October Corsica was clear of Germans, the first *département* of France to be liberated.

As soon as the German evacuation of Sardinia became known, the ACF began preparing to move forward to that island. Whinney was ordered by DDOD(I) to proceed to Maddalena and organise operations out of that port. Short-range expeditions were to be staged to the Italian west coast and the intervening islands, the Gulf of Genoa and as far west as Marseilles. Whinney took with him the two Gibraltar feluccas and a newer acquisition in the form of *ML576* which had been wheedled out of Coastal Forces. But new tactics had to be adopted, and the feluccas superseded by fresh and more efficient craft, for much work lay ahead for the flotilla.

DDOD(I)'s organisation was not the only one to take advantage of the new strategic striking position. Light coastal forces in the shape of eleven motor torpedo boats and Fairmile motor launches of the 7th MTB Flotilla were moved up from Messina to Maddalena, and a Senior Officer Inshore Squadron (SOIS) appointed to take charge of the new base in the person of Captain Norman Dickinson, RN. As Senior Naval Officer (Landing) (SNOL) at Bougie during Operation 'Torch', Dickinson had had his headquarters ship *Karanja* sunk under him by enemy bombing. His next task had been to take charge of the Commando operations staged from Tabarka. When the North African campaign ended, Dickinson was appointed a SNOL at the Sicily landings, and again at Salerno. Now he was to become 'father' to the miscellaneous organisations, clandestine and otherwise, which were hastening to set up shop in Maddalena.

Included among these 'irregular' units were SOE, OSS, MI9, and a Free French clandestine agency representing the French Deuxième Bureau. Another organisation which was considering staging activities in that area was 30 Commando. Modelled on the *Abwehrkommando* of Admiral Canaris, the function of this unit was to act as armed and expert looters, penetrating behind the enemy lines in advance of our leading troops, capturing key enemy personnel if possible, and important documents and equipment before these could be destroyed. The Commando had operated successfully throughout the North African campaign, in Sicily and at Salerno, and its leader was considering the advisability of putting a section into the newly acquired base, from which raids could be made behind the enemy lines along the Italian coast.

But Maddalena was not to function for long as a forward base. Now that Corsica had been liberated, the port of Bastia at the north-eastern tip of that island, although greatly damaged in the recent fighting, offered better facilities for staging operations to the Italian mainland as well as considerably shortening the length of the voyages involved. It was only 82 kilometres to the nearest point on the Italian mainland and 160 to southern France.

First to arrive in Corsica, however, initially at Ajaccio in the small SOE-operated vessel *MFV2017* was a unit of that organisation known as the 'Balaclava Mission'. Its cover name, however, was ISSU-6 (Inter-Service Signals Unit). With his vessel loaded with supplies and equipment – which included two motor cycles – and enough stores to last for six weeks, the leader of the Mission, which totalled just eight sailors and three soldiers, two of them American, was Major Andrew Croft of the Essex Regiment.

In command of *MFV2017*, which had previously been working from a base in the Helford river to Brittany on behalf of SOE, was a black-bearded Channel Islander named John Newton who held the rank of Temporary Boom Skipper, RNR. Described by his colleagues as 'a proper old pirate', Newton, along with one of the petty officers of the trawler, had just been decorated with the DSC ,and DSM respectively 'for bravery, resource and undaunted devotion to duty' in recognition of their Brittany operations. Newton and his crew were further to distinguish themselves during the forthcoming months in the Mediterranean.

Even for SOE, Andrew Croft had had a diverse career. Born in 1906, he had been at Lancing, first head boy of Stowe, three years at Christchurch, and was awarded the Polar Medal in one Arctic expedition; wintered as ADC to a maharajah; back in the far north next summer on another; learned to fly and ski; had more than a smattering of ten languages, and was secretary to the Director of the Fitzwilliam Museum when the war began.*

Croft had also served in Norway as intelligence officer with the Independent Companies, and for twelve months as Assistant Military Attaché in Stockholm before joining SOE. He and his mission were to be closely associated with the ACF. The cover story for ISSU-6 was that it was a Commando training unit, specifically, training the *Bataillon de Choc* in boatwork.

Croft decided that the small sheltered harbour of Calvi, on the west coast of the island and a $2\frac{1}{2}$ hour drive from Bastia, would be most suitable for training his boats' crews, and accordingly he set up a subsidiary base there. Representatives of various other clandestine organisations had now arrived in Calvi and, under the chairmanship of SOIS – himself about to move up from Maddalena – a conference was held of all interested parties to discuss procedures and work out a *modus operandi*. Besides ACF, SOE, OSS, MI9, ISSU-6 and the French Deuxième Bureau, they also included representatives of the French High Command, French First Army Corps, French Navy, *Bataillon de Choc*, the US 2677th Headquarter Company† and 30 Commando.

It was decided that a naval officer with a knowledge of MTBs, PT boats and other similar craft was needed to collate

* *SOE in France*, M.R.D. Foot, HMSO.
† A special reconnaissance unit composed of Americans of Italian extraction.

requirements and advise on types of boats, etc., and to liaise between individual units and SOIS. Any organisations not satisfied with his decisions had the right of appeal direct to the latter. As a result Whinney was appointed the co-ordinating authority, and Lieutenant Davies of 30 Commando seconded from that unit as Joint Intelligence Officer, his commanding officer having decided after all to confine the Commando's attentions to the Adriatic.

Whinney had had plenty of experience. After previous service in the Royal Navy in the early 1930s, he had been re-entered in the RNVR soon after the outbreak of war. In 1940 he had been recruited into the clandestine organisation of DDOD(I) and had carried out a number of operations to the enemy-held coast of northern France. He was then loaned to SOE for a spell before rejoining DDOD(I)'s headquarters in London. It was he who had been responsible for obtaining the feluccas *Seadog* and *Seawolf* for the operations from Gibraltar, and subsequently various craft along the North African coast. DDOD(I) had now appointed him to take charge of ACF operations from Bastia.

By late October all the different organisations were settling down in Bastia, which was now becoming a thoroughly polyglot town, with British, Americans, French, Italians and Corsicans rubbing shoulders amicably together, the Americans having also taken over the airfields. The ACF officers and Croft's mission were allotted accommodation in two separate villas behind the town and close to each other, their respective ratings and other ranks having their own separate messes. SOIS established his headquarters in a former convent, where Whinney was able to set up a good operations room furnished with maps, a joint intelligence library, and other necessary equipment for the use of all concerned.

Insofar as their operations were seaborne, all these very mixed organisations other than the French came under the command of SOIS as the naval representative of Allied Force Headquarters. That they were able to function smoothly was due in no small measure to the personality of Captain Dickinson, known to all as 'Uncle Dickie'.

After DDOD(I) had himself paid a visit to Corsica, the new ACF setup was organised as follows:–

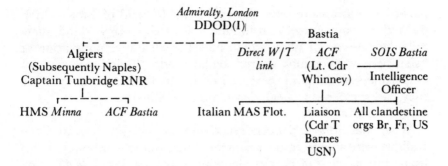

(Captain Tunbridge had relieved Captain Osborne, who had formerly been DDOD(I)'s link man at Gibraltar and Algiers).

Normal naval activities carried on by the coastal forces based on Bastia were the responsibility of the 7th MTB Flotilla, whose area of operations ranged from the River Tiber to La Spezia. This meant that to avoid being attacked by our own side, advance information regarding clandestine expeditions to planned pinpoints in the north and west had also to be passed to Allied submarines and other warships working in that area. To placate US susceptibilities a flotilla of American PT boats under Commander Tom Barnes, USN, was attached to the Coastal Force base at Bastia. From time to time these craft, too, would be co-opted for clandestine operations. Since they were the first to be fitted with effective radar, the 7th Flotilla's MTBs frequently sallied forth on their forays with their senior officer directing operations from a PT boat.

As the campaign in Italy moved gradually northwards, enemy opposition stiffened. Because of Allied dominance by sea and air, German forces relied to a very considerable extent on coastal traffic. Supplies were transported by sea from France and northern Italy in convoys, and these were now strengthened by the addition of large landing craft armed with 88mm guns. Convoys and escort craft hugged the coastline so closely that radar did not reveal them until visibility distance had been reached.

Enemy destroyers constituted the greatest threat to the operations of the clandestine 'boating parties'. The north-eastern sector of the Ligurian Sea was heavily patrolled by these vessels, together with E and R-boats, and criss-crossed by their supply convoys. Since our coastal forces were constantly attacking the latter, close liaison was necessary, as has been mentioned, when clandestine operations were being staged at the same time. Another hazard to movements was the enemy-held island of Elba, which flanked the routes they had to follow. Capraia, a tiny island a few miles north-west of Elba, which had a small native population of fishermen, was actually 'shared' by both sides. Periodically a party of Germans would land there and set up an observation post. After they had vacated it or been driven out, an Allied party from Bastia would move in.

When Sardinia had been evacuated by the Germans and the Italians were able to resume control of that island – although it was by no means clear of Fascist elements – two flotillas of *MAS* boats with their crews had been left behind. Following the Italian armistice, an agreement had been signed with the British naval Commander-in-Chief, Mediterranean regarding the employment of Italian warships and merchantmen on the side of the Allies. Whinney therefore now asked for these boats to be turned over to the ACF as being more suitable than the scratch craft he had and any local ones that might be available, and this was duly arranged. 'Co-operation with the Italians after a moderately sticky start,' he afterwards reported, 'worked remarkably well once we had been to sea two or three times.' One operation which had already been carried out in *ML576*, during which Maxted landed two OSS agents at Castiglioncello, near Leghorn, had shown up her unsuitability for clandestine work.

The *MAS* boats were 65 feet long, displaced some 20 to 25 tons, and were powered by two Isotta Fraschini petrol engines to give a speed of from 42 to 47 knots; also two silent auxiliaries. Carrying a crew of ten, they were armed with one 13.2mm machine-gun, normally carried two side-firing torpedoes and six depth charges, and with extra fuel tanks had a range of about 200 miles. They were, however, poor sea boats, very noisy on their main engines and slow on the auxiliaries, when they could only wallow along due to their stepped hulls at six knots. Fast and of small silhouette, they were suitable for operations not involving the transport of large numbers, and to pinpoints not more than 150 miles from base. Their only navigational aid was a small magnetic compass, which became unstable at high speeds; the bridge/wheelhouse was small and cramped, and accommodation meagre. Between three and six of these craft were usually available for ACF operations.

The most active of their commanding officers, who soon earned the liking and respect of their Allies, were Lieutenant Kusolich (known to all as 'Ginger' because of his fiery thatch), related to a well known Triestini shipping family; and Lieutenant the Marchese Centurioni, a typical Roman noble. 'They were all for the stiff upper lip,' recalled Maxted, 'and used to bark their orders at their crews, and clout them if they were slow to obey.' But not all our former enemies were to be trusted, as will be seen.

The American PT boats which, as mentioned, were also frequently lent from the Coastal Forces to which they were attached, were several knots slower than the *MAS* boats when at full speed, but could run almost silently at 15 knots. Of 46 tons displacement, they were better equipped and carried radar. Well armed, they were good sea boats, had a greater fuel capacity and more endurance, but were more conspicuous in silhouette.

The British Fairmile 'B' type motor launches, of which *576* was one, were slow, more heavily armed, had a bulky silhouette, and thus could only operate under cover of darkness over relatively short distances. In MacCallum's view, 'they had a remote chance of evading detection by discreet, if undignified, withdrawal.'

As to the work in which the 'boating parties' operating from Bastia were now to be engaged, it was varied and with different aims. Something like 74,000 Allied prisoners-of-war were known to be confined in various camps throughout Italy at the time of the armistice, and it was regarded as urgent to get as many as possible of these away before they could be transferred to Germany. Following news of the Italian surrender, some camps had been opened by the guards and their inmates invited to make their own getaway, but AFHQ had also issued a 'stand fast' order in the expectation either that these would be quickly overrun or that the Italians would prevent the prisoners' removal. This had put many off, while others joined up with the Partisans. Thus escape organisations needed to be set up.

It was also important to promote and support resistance in Italy, which might have received a setback following the spectacular rescue of Mussolini by German SS glider troops from the mountain prison in which he had been held, and his Hitler-backed declaration that he now headed a 'Fascist Republican' government. Thus a network of agents had to be established throughout German-occupied Italy to obtain intelligence about defences and the rear dispositions of enemy units, establish contact with, and arm and encourage, the Partisans, harass the Germans, and collect prisoners-of-war and shot-down Allied aircrews.

The clandestine voyages now to be undertaken on behalf of the various agencies involved were normally confined to non-moon periods. As they took all night to complete, they imposed a considerable strain on nerves and physique. Weather conditions also restricted their frequency, the Italian *MAS* boat crews being particularly affected by stress and the vicious movements of their craft in a seaway. In fact it sometimes happened that an Italian captain would collapse completely, leaving the ACF officer to assume command and bring the boat back safely.

For most of November 1943 the weather was so bad that less than half a dozen sorties could be carried out even by the Coastal Forces. But the different agencies were fully occupied in planning and organising their future operations; indoctrinating the officers and crews of the *MAS* boats at Maddalena; exercising shore parties in the skills of handling rubber dinghies by day and night in all weathers, studying landing techniques, the use of reception lights, etc., and undergoing weapon training; and co-ordinating arrangements with the Americans and French, the chief aim of the latter, who were working for their own ends now that victory seemed certain for the Allies, being to effect the early recapture of Elba. In planning this they needed accurate information regarding enemy defences and troop dispositions, a task to be carried out through the Deuxième Bureau.

Evidence of German intentions to retaliate against this nest of 'bandits', as they referred to the Coastal Force craft which were attacking their convoys, was soon forthcoming when on 24 November their bombers raided Bastia. Unfortunately the fire of the Italian AA gunners who were supposed to defend the harbour with their 75mm guns was so ineffective that the MTBs and PT boats were forced to put to sea, pursued by enemy bombs.

Later on, as will be seen, when the weather improved and Coastal Forces stepped up their attacks, the German Naval War Diary recorded that the *Kriegsmarine* had been forced to ask the High Command of the Army and Air Force to 'eliminate' the place because the navy was unable to. Unhappily for Dönitz and his local naval commanders, the Wehrmacht and Luftwaffe were too busy elsewhere to do more than stage the occasional air raid. Nevertheless, on several occasions German naval forces did carry out hit and run bombardments against the port.

In mid-December they actually caused an invasion scare in Bastia. Two days earlier, with enemy aircraft circling overhead, three German destroyers had appeared off the coast trying to shell the 'Y' station. At the time the port found itself virtually isolated because heavy rains had broken down bridges and flooded roads. The airfields were waterlogged and aircraft unable to take off. Two American PT boats and a merchant vessel on passage between Maddalena and Bastia were sunk. Sardinia was full of Fascists, and an attempted coup d'état by them was reported to have been nipped in the bud. But in fact no invasion attempt was made, and enemy sea and air activity again became spasmodic.

Enemy mines also constituted an ever-present danger. On 23 December an Italian landing craft suddenly blew up in the new harbour at Bastia, probably due to a magnetic mine dropped during an enemy air raid. On the last day of the month there was an even worse disaster when a minesweeper and a landing craft approaching the port were blown up by mines, the latter with a heavy loss of life, most of the victims being RAF and RN personnel.

Once Advanced AFHQ had moved to Naples, SOE followed suit, to set up its Italian organisation, No 1 Special Force, code-named 'Maryland', at Monopoli, between Bari and Brindisi on the Adriatic coast, to promote and support resistance in that country. In command of the naval section was Commander Gerard Holdsworth, RNVR, who had run the Helford river flotilla in the operations to Brittany, and was responsible for *MFV2017*. From Monopoli SOE agents, some of them women, were flown to Corsica and turned over to the Balaclava Mission for onward transit by sea.

Normally these and other Joeys, who were regarded as very 'hot potatoes' indeed and had to be carefully watched throughout their nail-biting periods of waiting, were accommodated in an old *citadelle* overlooking the Gulf of St Florent, a few miles from Bastia.

Except for an early attempt, using one of the Coastal Force MTBs, to land four French officers on Elba to ascertain the strength of the enemy garrison, the state of the defences and the general feeling of the inhabitants, which literally foundered when their dinghy sank on the way to the shore, the first operation involving the ACF was planned for 28 November after three SOE agents had arrived from Algiers. They were to be put ashore near Spezia.

In an operation code-named 'Valentine', the agents were to be transported in *ML576* with Whinney as senior officer. Croft and Sergeant Arnold were to go along to row the agents ashore. The rubber boats used on these trips were of three types and could carry up to six people. They were fitted with special crutches, or rowlocks, secured to the sides of the dinghy by bosticked patches. The oars were of wood, paddle-shaped, and the boats camouflaged to show no 'loom'.

Unfortunately the weather turned out to be so rough that the expedition had to be postponed. On 1 December *ML576* started off, but after two hours at sea conditions became so bad that she was forced to return to harbour. Next day the operation was mounted for the third time, this time in *MAS541* commanded by Lieutenant Kusolich, Whinney again being the ACF senior officer. As the night was very dark and the pinpoint difficult to find, the *MAS* boat had to reduce speed to ten knots in order to search the shoreline.

When she finally hove to off the hoped-for position, the Italian crew merely heaved the rubber dinghy over the side, tying it to the rail so ineptly that it was unable to rise and fall with the waves, and then stood and gaped while Croft and Arnold struggled to free the boat and get the agents and their wireless set and personal gear down into it. Since the pinpoint was almost within earshot of an important enemy naval base, their exasperation could only be expressed in furious whispers.

By now the south-westerly wind had blown up a nasty sea, but fortunately the dinghy behaved well. For the first forty minutes they could find no possible landing place. Then, by good fortune, a natural rock formation sloping into the water was discovered, and the agents and their equipment were landed dry on its lee side. When they were seen to be safely on their way, the dinghy shoved off on its return journey to the *MAS* boat, signalling its approach by shaded torch. Although the latter was lying with stopped engines barely 200 yards from the shore, she could hardly be seen. As soon as Croft, Arnold and the dinghy had been re-embarked, the *MAS* boat headed away from the coast on her auxiliary motors until it was safe to increase to full speed. But because of the rough seas this had to be reduced to fifteen knots. Operation 'Valentine' was the first of many to be carried out by 'Ginger' Kusolich in *MAS541*.

The ACF officers who for the next seven or eight months were to act as senior officers and navigators for the clandestine operations staged from Corsica – they totalled more than fifty for SOE alone, of which five were on behalf of 'A' Force – included besides Whinney and Maxted, Lieutenant Fergus Dempster, RNR; Sub-Lieutenant Ronald Boyle, RNVR, who had joined the flotilla in 1943 with no experience of irregular operations; Lieutenant 'Doughboy' Dow, RNVR, who was later to lose his life on an expedition that ended in disaster; and, early in 1944, Donald MacCallum, now promoted to lieutenant-commander; and Lieutenant Brian Smith, RNR. In April MacCallum took over from Whinney as commanding officer at Bastia when the latter's health broke down and he had to return to the United Kingdom. In every clandestine operation the ACF officer was the key figure, the man in charge, who alone knew where 'Joeys' were to be landed and was responsible for navigation to and from the pinpoint.

The ACF had their own surfboat crews, who were always used on operations, except those conducted on behalf of SOE, when Croft preferred to take along his own men. All volunteers, they were a mixed collection of ratings recruited by DDOD(I) from various sources. They included two petty officers, Munro and Bates; two leading seamen, Luff and Marchant; two able seamen, Alex Izzard and Clarence Hall, and Seaman John Woolston, and Stoker Edwin Woodroff. Woolston was a Patrol Service rating, but the others came from normal naval general service. All, including their officers, characterised by the Director of Naval Intelligence as 'outstanding representatives of an irregular naval flotilla which has performed hazardous duties for all three Services since the fall of France,' were eventually to be awarded British and French decorations under the laconic and uncommunicative citation: 'For gallantry, enterprise, and undaunted devotion to duty on hazardous operations.'

During its ten months in Corsica the Balaclava unit's operational personnel never numbered more than a dozen officers and men. Besides Croft, these consisted of Lieutenant (jg) Fisher Howe, USNR, later relieved by Captain Ken Carson, US Army, both of OSS; Skipper John Newton, Petty Officer Sam Smalley, former mate of a Grimsby trawler; Leading Seaman Robihson; Seamen Miles, McDuff, Ashton and Chalmers; Sergeants Arnold and Coltman (the latter of whom had served for four years in the Foreign Legion), and Corporal Bourne-Newton of the Royal Engineers. Also working with them at Bastia was Captain Peter Fowler of 'A' Force.

Although weather conditions continued to restrict clandestine operations during December, a special expedition was staged on the 28th of that month at the urgent request of OSS in Algiers, who wanted two agents to be put ashore in a 'blind landing' in the St Tropez area of southern France. Croft and Seaman Miles went along as the shore party, and Maxted was the senior officer in a *MAS* boat.

The party left Bastia at 1930 that evening and, as the weather had taken a turn for the better, the boat was able to maintain an average speed of 35 knots until 2330 when she was within fifteen miles of the French coast. Unfortunately the high speed had affected her compass, and this resulted in a positional error. Since the area was reported to be well defended, with two enemy batteries guarding the approach to the three-quarter mile strip of rocky coastline, the final silent approach which had to be made on auxiliary motors took almost five hours, so that when she eventually reached the pinpoint the time was 0430.

Croft and Miles with the two agents embarked in the dinghy and duly set off for the shore. Luckily the landing place turned out to be ideal, with overhanging cliffs to hide the dinghy's approach, and nearby a wooded exit. Croft held the dinghy offshore while Miles waded in to carry out a brief reconnaissance, returning to report that all was clear. The dinghy then beached, and the agents landed and scurried away inland.

But Croft and Miles now found themselves faced with a long pull back to the *MAS* boat, which had shifted its position by about a mile. Fortunately, as they were nearing the end of the no-moon period, it was a clear bright night. The boat left the target area at 0530 and had to crawl along for forty minutes before it was considered safe to open up her main engines. She was still only twenty-five miles from the coast when daylight came, and five hours later she arrived safely back in Bastia.

During each full moon period Whinney flew to Algiers to work out with DDOD(I)'s representative the following month's schedule of operations, known to all as the 'Sked', so that AFHQ, and particularly the staff of the naval Commander-in-Chief, Mediterranean could be kept informed. As soon as the moon waned, operations really got going, and a list of those carried out in the latter half of January 1944 gives some idea of the strain imposed on boats and crews. Each operation was given its own special code name, but security was difficult because of the many nationalities taking part in them.

Thus on 15 January came Operation 'Big Game'. This involved *MAS541* taking stores to be landed on the tiny island of Gorgona, some twenty miles off Leghorn, where a forward observation post had been established by SOE. On the 17th, in Operation 'Richmond', *PT215* with *PT203* in support was to land four agents and stores south of Porto Ercole, seventy miles north of Rome. During the outward journey, however, *PT203* broke down and had to return to harbour. Although two enemy vessels were detected on her radar, *PT215* was able to dodge them and complete her mission.

Next day *MAS541* landed two American officers and stores on a small beach in Elba, the latter being a target due to figure increasingly on the list during the forthcoming weeks. On the same day, in Operation 'Chicago', Coastal Force craft landed and re-embarked a reconnaissance party of fifteen US Rangers on the island of Pianosa, south of Elba. On the 19th, in Operation 'Fragrant', *MAS541* tried to land four SOE agents, two men and two women, at Moneglia, north of Spezia, but had to bring them back because – owing once again to the unreliability of the *MAS* boat's compass caused by her high speed – the boat arrived late in the target area. Flown to Bastia from 'Maryland' at the end of December, having been unable to get through Eighth Army lines, the agents had been waiting to be taken on ever since.

'Fragrant' had first been tried in fact as early as 2 January, using a PT boat, taking along in addition a small SIS party who were also due to be landed near Moneglia, Maxted being the senior officer. Unfortunately the noise of the PT boat's engines alerted the enemy coast defences, and soon two approaching E-boats were detected on her radar. There was nothing for it but to abandon the operation and make for home at top speed.

Next night the party set off again in another PT boat with Whinney in charge, and Croft and Coltman as dinghy party. Yet again things went wrong. The boat was late on schedule, and according to her radar had hove to no more than 300 yards from shore; in fact the distance was nearer 1,400. In their heavily overloaded dinghy, with six people and the agents' equipment aboard, Croft and Coltman had to make an exhausting row along a precipitous coastline in almost pitch darkness during their search for a practicable landing place. But they could find none, certainly nothing that women could tackle, so this attempt, too, had to be abandoned. During the struggle to get back to the PT boat three of the dinghy's oars were broken.

Since this took place at the end of the no-moon period, any fresh attempts had to be postponed for a time, and Captain Dick Cooper, the conducting officer who had brought the agents from 'Maryland', took them down to Calvi for a rest and to settle their jittery nerves. Now arose a further complication. The women agents were called Fiammetta and Anna; while the men were Ranieri, an Italian, and their wireless operator Martin, a

Canadian. Both men were in love with Fiammetta and fiercely jealous of one another, while Martin appeared to be a sick man. The party returned gloomily to Bastia.

On the 21st Operation 'Fragrant' was again mounted, this time in *MAS543*. Maxted was the senior officer, Newton and Robinson the shore party, and Croft and Cooper accompanied the agents. But after five hours at sea *543*'s engines failed due to a broken petrol pipe, and she had to return to harbour.

Two days later Anna complained of feeling unwell, and on the 24th because of her sickness and low morale, it was decided not to land either of the women, and they were flown back to Italy, Cooper being only too happy to be rid of them. Then Martin complained of a bad heart and announced that he was too ill to proceed. Accordingly Operation 'Fragrant' was called off altogether. It was probably just as well, since Ranieri was later found to be a Fascist!

Meanwhile other operations had continued to go forward. On the 20th, in 'Richmond II', *MAS541* with *543* in support landed six agents near Porto Ercole, and embarked seven others and an escaped British prisoner-of-war. More of the latter had been expected, but they failed to show up because they feared that they were walking into a trap set by Italian Fascists. As a senior officer Fergus Dempster was particularly unlucky in this respect, and DDOD(I) afterwards recorded:

> His patience and morale were severely tested, since a number of his operations were on behalf of MI9, and although the expeditions were invariably faultless from a naval viewpoint, on frequent occasions the escaped prisoners-of-war failed to arrive at the pinpoint, with the result that Dempster, after a troublesome passage, had a gruelling voyage back empty-handed.

In Operation 'Possum' on the 21st, *MAS507* landed stores for the Allied forward position on Capraia; on the 22nd came Operation 'Barley', when *MAS543* landed two agents south of Leghorn. On that same night also *MAS541* had tried to land agents south of Sestri Levante, was fired on by an enemy patrol vessel but managed to evade. On the 27th came 'Possum' again – this code name was used more than once with a figure added to denote its sequence in the series, since the landing of personnel and stores on Capraia became a routine requirement – and also Operation 'Ladbroke' on behalf of Balaclava.

In the latter *MAS541* was to land two French SOE agents at a

Admiral Burrough talking to Major General Evelegh

Allied invasion convoy en route for North Africa

Italian Mas boat

British MTB

A US PT boat

point south of Cannes, on the French Riviera. The conducting party consisted of Croft, Bourne-Newton and Seaman Ashton – the two latter on their first operation. Maxted was in charge, and this time he was accompanied by Sub-Lieutenant Boyle, who was also making his first trip.

It was considered particularly important to infiltrate these agents, who had spent several weeks in Corsica being instructed in the tricky business of dinghy handling, landing techniques, the selection of potential landing areas and so on, in order to instruct other agents of their own choosing, and studying aerial pictures of the French coast between Marseilles and Menton.

*MAS541* left Bastia at 1715 in the afternoon of the 27th, but once again her compass proved to be faulty and she had to heave to three times on the outward journey for a positional check. The French coast was sighted at 2100, but as this was earlier than intended she had to cruise round for two hours. Then began a search for the small village near which was the pinpoint, but after creeping along for several hours on auxiliary motors, the area could not be located. At 0500 with daylight not far off, the operation had to be abandoned.

Next night Operation 'Tail Lamp II' was staged. In this expedition *MAS509* was to land two SOE agents at a pinpoint near Voltri, another extremely hazardous area in view of the proximity of the shipbuilding yards of Genoa. Maxted was again in charge, and Croft, Coltman, Seaman Miles and Captain Carson went along as dinghy and conducting party – Coltman and Miles for instructional purposes. *509* left Bastia at 1800 in perfect weather conditions, with a calm sea and no wind, and duly arrived off the pinpoint half an hour after midnight. Dinghy and agents were preparing to disembark when suddenly white flares burst overhead to illuminate the scene, and the *MAS* boat was peremptorily challenged by signal lamp. Since the challengers comprised more than one vessel there was no time to stand on ceremony, and *509* turned tail and fled for home at top speed, pursued by enemy gunfire.

Simultaneously with 'Tail Lamp II', Operation 'Furtive' was being staged. In this operation *MAS543* was to collect two SIS agents and important mail they were bringing with them from a point west of Cape Camaret, near St Tropez. The coastline in the vicinity of the pinpoint was rocky with a backdrop of rugged cliffs, and the area was policed by a German land patrol. The dinghy had to approach the shore with extreme caution, and, in order to avoid the enemy patrol, the agents were forced to lower themselves down the cliff face by rope. But they managed to descend safely, and they and their mail were successfully taken off.

This particular pinpoint off Cape Camaret was to become very familiar to Tom Maxted, for once a month he was scheduled to call there, either to land or pick up a courier – sometimes only a suitcase. 'In the end,' he said, 'I could find the place blindfolded.'

On the 29th came the eighth expedition in the 'Possum' series, when *MFV2017* landed stores on Capraia; and on the next night a second attempt was made to infiltrate 'Ladbroke's' French SOE agents. Embarked in *PT209*, with *PT217* as diversionary craft, Maxted as senior officer, and Croft, Smalley, Newton and Chalmers (the latter under instruction) as dinghy party, they left Bastia at 1730.

But 'Ladbroke' seemed doomed to failure. This time, however, there was no mistake about the pinpoint, and a perfect landfall was made shortly before midnight. The shore party was being readied when suddenly two E-boats were picked up on the radar. They were moving north-eastwards and obviously on a patrol leg which would take them past the pinpoint. Since it appeared that they would be patrolling this stretch of coast all night, and visibility had dropped to about 200 yards, Croft suggested that *PT217* should carry out her diversion and draw off the enemy while the dinghy party nipped in with the agents. But her captain was unwilling to take the risk, and suggested instead that the agents should be put into the dinghy and left to find their own way. Croft indignantly refused, and said that he would accept full responsibility if the shore party should become stranded in France. But still the Americans would not budge, and 'Ladbroke' had finally to be called off.

This was not the only occasion when the captains of American boats, inexperienced in this type of work, demurred at approaching landfalls and pinpoints after enemy patrols had been detected in the vicinity. But the tact, example and determination of the ACF officers usually overcame their scruples and prevailed upon them to complete the operation.

On the last night of the month came a repeat of 'Tail Lamp II'. This time *PT217* with another American boat to back her up was to land three agents at the hairy pinpoint of Voltri, near Genoa. Whinney was the senior officer, and Croft, Coltman, Miles and

Ashton the shore party. The PT boats departed from Bastia soon after 1900, and were back by 0830 the following morning, with broad grins on the faces of all hands to testify to the success this time of the operation. But another expedition, code-named 'X-Two', staged the same night, in which two SIS agents were to have been put shore along the mainland of Italy, failed because there was no reception committee.

During the nine moonless nights of February, fifteen operations were carried out, and in March another nineteen on its eleven dark nights. That so many clandestine expeditions were being staged might give the impression that almost more secret agents were being landed in Italy than fighting troops! In fact, however, more than half the operations carried out on behalf of the agencies concerned failed for various reasons. Some were staged to Elba on behalf of the French Deuxième Bureau prior to the successful invasion of that island; others for the purpose of exfiltrating agents due for relief or on the run from the enemy, and escapers and evaders. The usual number of 'Joeys' landed was two, of which one was the all-important radio operator.

As to the campaign on the Italian mainland, this had developed into a slow and painful advance over difficult terrain against a determined and resourceful enemy, skilled in the exploitation of natural obstacles by mines and demolitions. When this trend became apparent, the only method of frustrating the enemy's intentions of compelling the Allies to fight a slow and costly frontal battle up the 'leg' of Italy, was to stage amphibious landings on the coast behind his lines.

Accordingly, on 21 January, an Allied landing took place at Anzio in order to capture Rome and turn the enemy's flank. Unfortunately it was not sufficiently exploited, and little more was done than establish a bridgehead, while the enemy's defensive lines were still intact. Nevertheless, the overall campaign was fulfilling its primary task of containing as many enemy formations in Italy as possible, and drawing in supplies and reinforcements needed on the Eastern front and against the impending assault from the West. Any irregular operations which would weaken the Germans in Italy, destroy their lines of communication, and tie up forces needed elsewhere were therefore of considerable value.

In addition to the failure of some of the clandestine operations carried out from Bastia during February and March, both months were marked by other misfortunes.

On the night of 18 February, despite poor weather, four operations were mounted, code-named 'Jolly', 'Benello', 'Youngstown' and 'Doughboy'. In Operation 'Jolly', which turned out to be anything but that, *MAS509* was to put an SIS agent ashore at a pinpoint near Capo delle Mele, on the western side of the Gulf of Genoa. But sea conditions became so bad that she had to turn back.

Operations 'Benello' and 'Youngstown', staged on behalf of 'A' Force, were also difficult. *MAS546* was to land two parties, each of two agents, at different pinpoints near world-famous Portofino on its great promontory. Maxted was the senior officer, Captain Fowler the conducting officer, and one of ACF's surfboat crews the dinghymen. This time *546*'s steering gear broke down before the first pinpoint was reached, but an emergency tiller was rigged up, and the operations successfully completed. The return voyage, however, was made in such heavy weather, handicapped by the faulty steering gear, that considerable concern was felt at the base for her safety. When she finally reached harbour with the signs of the battering she had received plainly visible, 'Uncle Dickie' himself was on the jetty to welcome her back.

In Operation 'Doughboy', *ML576* took three French agents and their wireless set to be landed on Elba on behalf of the Deuxième Bureau. Lieutenant Dow was in charge, Captain Carson accompanied the agents, and Seaman Smalley and Corporal Bourne-Newton constituted the dinghy party. All went well in spite of the weather conditions and the difficulties of manoeuvring a rubber dinghy crammed with excitable and apprehensive Frenchmen and their bulky radio equipment in a choppy sea on a pitch black night. When, two days later, the agents made contact with Bastia, Croft recorded that: 'This success was celebrated that night in French headquarters with a great party with singsongs round the piano, football, etc.'

On the 21st he took charge of a more unusual expedition. 'Maryland' had acquired an Italian *motosilurante*, or MS boat, and in this craft, commanded by an RNVR sub-lieutenant, eight Italian Commandos were to be landed in the Moneglia area near Spezia. The MS boat was a 63-ton vessel powered by three Isotta Fraschini engines and capable of a top speed of 34 knots. She brought her own dinghy party, but Croft's knowledge and experience was essential to the success of the venture – which it triumphantly turned out to be. Not only were the Commandos slipped ashore safely and unseen, Croft had time to nose around and make his own private reconnaissance of the area.

When they got back to Bastia, however, they found the base plunged in gloom caused by the loss of *MAS546* with heavy casualties, who included Dickinson's staff officer (intelligence). What had happened was that on the 21st the American ARB (Air/Sea Rescue Boat) *P403* set off to carry out Operation 'Possum XI', this time to land a reconnaissance party on Capraia to investigate an enemy raid on the island which had taken place the day before. She was followed up a little later by *MAS546*, temporarily commanded by her chief petty officer, a capable individual, bringing more personnel from Bastia. After disembarking the party, she was moving away from the jetty with her engines full astern when she exploded an acoustic mine and sank immediately. Five survivors were fished out of the water and taken ashore by the local inhabitants.

As soon as news of the disaster was received in Bastia, *ARB P402* with a medical officer and Whinney in charge was despatched to Capraia to bring back the survivors. Since it was thought to be unsafe for the ARB to berth alongside the jetty, the badly injured men had to be ferried from the shore in small boats. But somehow the task was accomplished, and *P402* came safely back to Bastia next morning.

It was considered that the mine which destroyed *MAS546* had probably been laid earlier, either by the Germans on leaving, or dropped from an enemy aircraft, and fitted with an arming delay, since Maxted was sure that on a previous visit to Capraia his boat had actually 'clipped' a mine when leaving the jetty.

At daylight on the 23rd Maxted set off in *ML576* to carry out Operation 'Possum XII', but its sad mission this time was to collect and bring back the bodies of the victims of the disaster to *MAS546* which had been picked up at Capraia. Ironically enough, the motor launch was attacked en route by three American Mitchell fighter-bombers from Corsica. The first dropped a stick of bombs, which fortunately missed; the second came in to machine-gun the launch, but his aim was bad; and the third opened fire with 75mm cannon, blowing two big holes in the side of the vessel, putting her engines out of action and wounding her telegraphist.

Lieutenant Durston, RNVR, her commanding officer, had ordered recognition signals to be fired the moment it became apparent that the aircraft intended to attack, but it was only after carrying out their runs that the trigger-happy pilots flew off, leaving the ML in a bad way. She was bullet-scarred, taking in water, her engines were out of action, and she was drifting off a lee shore. Hammocks and other gear had to be used as an improvised collision mat to plug the hole opened below the waterline, and the motor mechanic eventually managed to start one engine. Slowly the crippled launch made her way back to Bastia, fortunately without further incident.

Later on that day the offending airmen came over to the base from their airfield to look at the damage wrought by their cannon fire. Shamefacedly they explained that there were three buttons on their joysticks by means of which their armament could be fired – 1 for bombs; 2 for machine-guns, and 3 for cannon. Each swore that somehow he had pressed the wrong tit!

Thirty-two operations had originally been scheduled for March; of which, as already mentioned, fifteen were unsuccessful and four failed on account of the weather. But the chief features of the month were the loss of *MAS541* with the popular 'Ginger' Kusolich and Lieutenant 'Doughboy' Dow, and the terrible outcome of Operation 'Ginny'.

Because weather conditions became favourable about the middle of the month, it was decided to recommence operations on the 17th, a day earlier than anticipated, and in fact no less than six were staged that night. Three of them, code-named 'Anstey', 'Zeal' and 'Flack', were carried out in one trip by 'Maryland's' *MS24* with Croft in charge on behalf of the Deuxième Bureau, when ten agents were landed near Genoa. The fourth operation, called 'Amloch', to land five SOE agents at Castiglioncello, was carried out by *MAS541* with Maxted in charge, and three of Croft's men as dinghy party.

While these were all completed successfully without incident, the fifth and sixth, code-named 'Sand' and 'Mario', in which three agents were to be landed by *MAS543* near Levanto, another pinpoint perilously close to Spezia, ran into trouble. Sub-Lieutenant Boyle was the senior officer, and in view of the importance of this particular operation, Boyle himself took charge of the surfboat work. *543*'s arrival off the pinpoint had been delayed because she had been forced to make an extensive detour to avoid two large enemy patrol vessels in the vicinity, which left little time before moonrise.

While the boatwork was in progress between ship and shore, two E-boats approached from the north, and were joined soon afterwards by a third from the south. It now became a race between the return of the surfboat and the inevitable sighting of *543* if she remained in her hove-to position. Moonrise, the arrival of the surfboat alongside, and a challenge from the E-boats occurred simultaneously. Fortunately, however, the enemy was hesitant and challenged three times before opening fire with inaccurate starshell and tracer. Meanwhile Boyle and the dinghy crew were scrambling aboard the *MAS* boat to the accompaniment of screams of *Motor principali*! as the Italian motor mechanic made frantic efforts to start her main engines. Within split seconds these broke into a roar, the boat leapt ahead, and had reached 40 knots just as the enemy found the range. *543* returned safely to Bastia with only superficial damage and no casualties.

Four operations in the 'Big Game' series were carried out during the month, all except the final one on the 27th being routine trips to land stores and special equipment on Gorgona. Sadly the last one, carried out by Coastal Force craft, was to bring back two wounded and three dead SOE agents who had been shot in a raid on the island mounted by the Germans the night before.

Two other operations involving the ACF were code-named 'Pre-Balkis' and 'Balkis'. In the former, staged on the 16th, *MAS543* landed and re-embarked a reconnaissance party on the island of Pianosa. As a result, two days later, came Operation 'Balkis' when two French *chasseurs* escorted by Coastal Force craft raided the island and took 120 Italian prisoners.

On the 21st, Operation 'Cadex' was staged on behalf of the Deuxième Bureau, in which *MAS541* with Dow as senior officer was to land two French Commando officers with explosives to carry out a demolition raid near Cape Arenzano, some ten miles west of Genoa. But from this operation no one ever returned, and once again the base at Bastia was plunged into gloom. An aerial reconnaissance was flown next day over the pinpoint, but could find no trace of the missing craft and returned with a negative report. The only explanation of *541*'s disappearance seemed to be either that she had hit a mine en route, or that she had been blown to pieces by accident during the handling of the explosives she was carrying.

In his monthly report of proceedings Dickinson wrote:

The non-return of *MAS541* with the conducting officer and two French officers was a serious loss. Her young Italian captain was one of the original officers to come to Bastia from Maddalena at my suggestion, and proved himself to be most capable and well liked by all.

On the same night that she disappeared, Operation 'Cromer' had been staged for the second time. Its object was to land an SOE woman agent near Marseilles. To shorten the journey, the operation had originally been scheduled to sail on the 19th from Calvi instead of Bastia, PT boats *206* and *210* being used for the purpose. Maxted was to be the senior officer, and Croft and a woman conducting officer were to have accompanied the agent, taking along Coltman and Miles as dinghy party. But the weather had been so bad that the operation had to be postponed.

On the 21st the expedition as originally constituted did set off, but soon after reaching the Gulf of Lions, *PT206* broke a propeller shaft, and the boats were compelled to turn back. Croft's entry in his log included a note that he thought women agents brought with them a 'hoodoo'. He would appear to have been justified for, like the earlier 'Ladbroke', Operation 'Cromer' was doomed to failure.

A third attempt to set out was made on the 24th, but was once again foiled by bad weather. On the fourth and last occasion, two days later, the pinpoint was reached without difficulty, and the dinghy crew of Ashton and Chalmers were preparing to set off for the shore with the agent, whose nerves must by now have become frayed to breaking point. But although signals were flashed from the 'reception party' as expected, they were not the right ones. The American captains became convinced that it was the Germans who were waiting on the beach; the dinghy was recovered and they accordingly discreetly withdrew from the scene. That was the end of Operation 'Cromer'.

On the 22nd 'Ginny' was mounted, and this was to end in a way that could not have been imagined. Staged by the OSS, fifteen officers and men from the 2677th Headquarters Company at Bastia were to be landed near Sestri Levante to blow up a railway tunnel on the main line between Spezia and Genoa. The party embarked in PT boats *210* and *214*, with Brian Smith as senior officer and an ACF dinghy crew. The landing was successfully effected, but while the PT boats were waiting to re-embark the raiders on their return, enemy patrol craft appeared and opened fire. The PT boats were therefore compelled to withdraw.

On their arrival back in Bastia next morning, Croft was consulted and asked if he could help to recover the raiding party, and it was agreed with MacCallum that an attempt should be made that night. Accordingly PT boats *204* and *207* set out just before 1800 with Boyle in charge, and Ashton and Chalmers taking along Balaclava's Goatley boat (an 11ft 6ins collapsible craft capable of carrying seven men) as well as their rubber dinghy. Since there was a pre-arranged routine with special signals for such an emergency, little trouble was anticipated unless enemy patrol vessels were again encountered. Unfortunately this is just what happened, hostile craft being sighted some four miles off the pinpoint, and the PT boats had to turn back.

On the 25th Operation 'Ginny A', as it had been code-named, was again mounted, this time with PT boats *208* and *214*. But although the coast was clear of enemy craft, and it was possible to send the dinghy ashore, there was no one at the pinpoint, and the expedition returned empty-handed.

It was not until after the end of the war in Europe in fact that the full story regarding the fate of the 'Ginny' party finally came to light. Before they could carry out their mission, they had all been captured by the Germans. Although they were in uniform and had no civilian clothes with them, they were executed by firing squad without trial two days later on the orders of General Anton Dostler, Commander of the LXXVth German Army Corps, under Hitler's 'extermination order' of October 1942. Dostler was condemned to death by a US Military Tribunal in Rome in October 1945.

In his monthly report for March, SOIS stressed that shortage of craft was becoming a serious problem, and during the latter part of the period nearly all clandestine operations were carried out with American PT boats. He was impressed with their efficiency and the willing co-operation of the personnel of the PT craft, but since these were selected at random as dictated by other operational requirements, there was little time to perfect the technique of special operations in individual craft, which enhanced difficulties. With the approach of summer and shorter nights it would be increasingly difficult to function unless very high speed craft were made available.

Then, early in April, occurred an event which was to result in the withdrawal of the Italian *MAS* boats which, since their arrival on the scene, had been used almost continuously.

Maddalena was their refitting and maintenance base, and it was from this port that *MAS505*, which thus far had played no part in special operations, sailed for Bastia on 10 April. She was commanded by Sub-Lieutenant Carlo Sorcinelli, and on board were two other Italian officers, Commander Marcello Pucci Boncambi and Lieutenant Primo Sarti, who were taking passage to Bastia. But she never arrived at her destination, and at first it was thought that she had been mined. Although the bare outlines of the story of what happened to her did become known, the full horrific account did not emerge until much later.

Whether the crew of *505* were Fascists, or simply did not relish the idea of risking their lives on hazardous operations for their former enemies, is not known. But soon after the boat left Maddalena they mutinied, shot the three officers and threw their bodies overboard, then headed for Santa Stefano, on the mainland, where they surrendered to the local German commander. Next day the boat was taken to Spezia and turned over to the harbour defence forces. Interrogated by the Germans, the crew revealed much useful information.

On 14 April the German Admiralty and the Admiral, Adriatic, were asked if any use could be made of *505*'s crew in the Adriatic as their presence in the Spezia area was no longer desired. Admiral, Adriatic, however, did not think it advisable to employ them in that sea in view of the general situation there, and on the 20th they were allocated to the First Naval Division. After the war they were tried by a military court.

When rumours of the mutiny on board *MAS505* did reach Bastia, the rest of the Italian boats were withdrawn from special operations, 'on account of the fact,' wrote Dickinson, 'that they might prove untrustworthy, as did *MAS505*. This risk was too great as valuable information might fall into enemy hands.'

Twenty-nine operations had been proposed for the month, of which twelve were successfully completed, four failed,and thirteen were postponed or did not materialise. Because of the shortage of available craft they were, as has been stated, all carried out by PT boats. Considerable enemy interference was experienced, and on several occasions enemy patrols were lying in wait at the pinpoint.

The first big operation of the period was 'Gooseberry', staged on the 18th on behalf of 'A' Force to pick up escaped prisoners-of-war at Montalto, a small coastal village some ninety miles north of Rome. PT boats *212* and *215* duly set off, with Peter Fowler, Dempster as senior officer, and Coltman, Miles and Ashton as dinghy party. But when they arrived at the pinpoint no reception lights were seen, and there was no one waiting. Then enemy aircraft began circling overhead, and when they started to drop flares, the PT boats were forced to leave.

On the 24th 'Gooseberry' was attempted for the second time, Dempster again in charge and the dinghy party as before. This time *PT214* was escorted by a motor gunboat from Coastal Forces. But again they were to be disappointed. There were no reception lights and no anxious escapers waiting, although the dinghy party risked going in twice to look for them. And yet again the enemy appeared to have been alerted. Flare-dropping aircraft arrived, and a coastal battery opened fire on the Allied vessels as they sped off into the night; but they got away unscathed.

Also mounted on the same night was Operation 'Youngstown', when PT boats *209* and *211* with Maxted in charge set off to land SIS agents at Portofino. But as they were nearing the pinpoint they sighted two enemy destroyers on patrol and had to retire. Two nights later came Operation 'Abraham' to land SIS agents at a point near Cape Camaret.

When this operation had first been mounted, enemy destroyers were encountered near the pinpoint, which opened fire without challenge, but the PT boats escaped without being hit. This time the area was found to be clear of hostile craft. The dinghy with agents and crew was duly sent off, but as it was approaching the beach an enemy shore patrol appeared and opened fire with rifles, one of the bullets going through a toolbox on which Maxted was standing to oversee the operation. The dinghy hastily returned while the PT boats laid down a smoke screen, behind which they made their escape.

The first success of the period came on the night of the 23rd when, in Operations 'Arctic' and 'Nostrum', PT boats *207* and *215* with Boyle as senior officer, landed three French agents on behalf of the Deuxième Bureau at separate pinpoints on the south-west coast of Elba, Skipper Newton and Seaman McDuff acting as surfboat's crew. So smoothly did this operation go off that the craft were back in Bastia before dawn next day. Four days later the same agents were safely exfiltrated in what SOIS described as 'the most outstanding operation of the month'.

Although they involved a shorter sea journey, expeditions to Elba were every bit as hazardous as those to pinpoints along the defended coasts of Italy and southern France. Detested by the local inhabitants, the island's garrison of Germans and Italian Fascists was daily expecting to be attacked by Allied forces; thus their coastal patrols, ashore and afloat, were always very much on the alert.

The weather outlook on the morning of the 27th appeared to be very unfavourable, with grey skies and rough seas, and it seemed doubtful whether the pre-arranged pickup of the 'Nostrum' agents could be made. But after a message had been received from the Frenchmen, '*Ici mer calme − mission terminée*', it was decided to go ahead. That evening therefore *PT218* escorted by *214* left Bastia, with Maxted in charge and Newton and McDuff as dinghy party. Rendezvous was to be made at the agreed pinpoint at 0130.

But when *218* was about to enter the bay her radar warned of the presence of an E- or R-boat. Nevertheless she cautiously continued, and eventually got between the enemy vessel and the shore. When in due course a shaded torch blinked out the expected signal from the waiting agents, Maxted and the Americans wondered if the enemy, too, had seen it. Newton was warned of the danger, but the 'bearded pirate' insisted on taking the dinghy in. Then ensued a lengthy and nail-biting wait, during which the enemy patrol craft made no move and appeared to be completely unaware of the dark and silent PT boat lying hove to only a few hundred yards away with her guns manned and trained in its direction.

At long last the dinghy reappeared and slid noiselessly alongside with the agents and all their gear and equipment. They were speedily embarked, and the engines started up. As the PT boat ghosted towards the open sea, Maxted longed to open fire on the enemy with all guns. 'But that sort of thing,' he noted, 'was strictly forbidden.' The French were delighted with the success of the operation, for the agents had brought back such valuable information that, after the island's capture, the invasion force commander was moved to comment, 'Never have French troops gone into the field with better intelligence.' Maxted and the dinghy crew were later awarded the Croix de Guerre.

Thirty-one operations were scheduled for May. Despite the fact that the weather turned out to be unusually severe for the time of year, twenty-one were successful. Four were unsuccessful and six others either cancelled or failed to materialise. The most notable feature, however, was the absence of enemy interference. For the first time Coastal Force MTBs were used in order to relieve the pressure on the American PT boats. They were considered to be very suitable for clandestine operations as they had a wide range and a good turn of speed, although slower than either the Italian or

American boats. There was considerable enemy coastal traffic along the western Italian seaboard, and on the coast of southern France the enemy had relit the lighthouses at Cape Camaret and Levant Island, albeit with reduced power.

To detail the month's operations in full would be tedious, although each was attended by a full measure of danger and excitement; but one or two may be considered worthy of mention. Thus on the 15th Operation 'Ashwater' was staged with the object of landing at Capo delle Mele, near the Italian border with France, three SOE agents brought by Cooper from 'Maryland'. The significance of various infiltrations which ACF effected in this area from time to time will become apparent in due course.

On this occasion the agents were to be taken in *MTB375*, with another going along as escort. Maxted was the senior officer, and Croft and Miles the dinghy crew. Unknown to the British vessels, their approach as they neared the coast had been picked up by enemy radar. In due course they hove to off the pinpoint, and the dinghy pushed off with the agents. But when it had got within fifty yards of the beach, a lorry full of German troops suddenly arrived in the road opposite, who jumped out and distributed themselves at various points along it. In spite of this, Croft was unwilling to give up, and turned away to look for another landing point. But on closing the beach again, footsteps were heard approaching, and it was soon evident that the whole area had become thoroughly alerted. Then coastal batteries opened fire with starshell, and the lights of the nearby village of Alassio switched on to illuminate the scene still further. There was nothing for it but to retire hastily.

Unhappily, 'Ashwater' was yet another of SOE's operations which seemed doomed from the outset. On the 17th it was tried again, this time in a couple of PT boats with Smith in charge. But by the time the boats were abreast of Cape Corse the weather had become so bad that they had to turn back. Two days later Cooper reported to Croft that the morale of his agents had slumped to zero and that they now had cold feet. It was agreed that they should be flown back to Monopoli, But at the last moment when the party had reached the airfield, the agents told Cooper that they had changed their minds and now wished to complete their mission, as they feared the humiliation facing them on their return to Italy. But 'Maryland' had had enough and ordered the operation to be cancelled.

June proved to be a momentous month. Considerable enemy opposition was met on almost all sorties made by the clandestine 'boating parties', and on two occasions dinghy parties had to be abandoned. Thirty-one operations had been proposed: seventeen did not materialise; ten were successful and four failed. Vessels used included American PT boats, British MTBs, American ARBs and, on one occasion each, *MAS509* and *MAS543*, whose crews had taken part in special operations earlier on and were considered to be trustworthy. Due to increasing enemy vigilance and a shortening of the coastline held by them, it was anticipated that clandestine operations would become more difficult, and in certain areas impossible.

At this point it is necessary once again to glance at the progress of the campaign in Italy. In May a breakout from the Allied bridgehead at Anzio had finally been achieved, and on 4 June Rome was captured. By the end of the month the climax of the Italian campaign had been reached.

Ever since the previous autumn the commanders of the Allied forces in Italy had been conscious of the importance of Elba to the enemy in keeping a protective watch on the coastal shipping supplying his army. Plans had earlier been prepared for the capture of the island, but these had to wait until the Allies penetrated to the north of Rome. It was decided that this should be a Free French operation, and that the troops should be provided from the 9th French Colonial Infantry Division, which was training in Corsica. Designated 'Force 255', the invasion force eventually comprised the equivalent of two regimental combat teams from the 9th Division, Commandos from the *Bataillon de Choc* and Goumiers, together with two British beach Commandos. The naval forces were commanded by Rear-Admiral Troubridge, a veteran of the North Africa and Sicily landings. Code-named Operation 'Brassard', the assault was scheduled for 17 June.

Unknown to the Allied planners, however, the evacuation of German forces from Elba had been prepared for the 13th. Although considered to have only limited value, the Führer had ordered the island to be defended to the last. But Kesselring, the German Commander-in-Chief in Italy, had decided that this could only be done by accepting heavy losses, which he was not prepared to do. Nevertheless the enemy garrison, numbering some 4,000, of whom about half were Italian Fascists, resisted for a time with such ferocity that Operation 'Brassard' was dubbed 'a bloody little sideshow'.

The island was captured in two days, by which time Pianosa had also been occupied. Although the evacuation of Elba by the Germans had been ordered for the night of 19 June, only a handful managed to escape to the mainland under cover of darkness, among them the German commandant. They lost more than 500 killed and over a thousand were taken prisoner. Noting in his private log the receipt of a message from 'Charles' in Elba (code name for the French secret agents' wireless operator) reporting on the 19th 'Mission terminated – awaiting instructions', Croft felt justified in adding:

> We have played a major role in the Allied landing on Elba, as the Charles Mission was put in four times and exfiltrated three times, once with enemy close on heels. In addition, we have maintained wireless contact and supplied and maintained equipment.

In Europe, Operation 'Overlord' was launched on 6 June, the news being toasted at Bastia in a special concoction originally devised on the occasion of a visit to the base of an Ensa party in April, and christened the 'Bastia Bracer'. On 10 June the Russians opened an offensive on a wide front which was to be long and victorious. And in mid-June preparations were begun for an assault on the south of France to open a second entry port through which American reinforcements could flow into France and link up with Eisenhower's armies in the north.

In this connection, it was vital that up-to-date intelligence should be obtained regarding possible landing places between Hyères and Cannes, and including such points as Cape Camaret, Port Cros, Levant Island, Cape Negre, Cavalaire and Pampelonne, where the Germans had built up defences and the coast was now heavily defended, and to strengthen contacts with the local Resistance. In the event this was the area chosen for the Allied landings in Operation 'Dragoon'.

A peep over the enemy's shoulder around this time would have been revealing. Thus in June 1944 the German Naval War Diary recorded that:

> Sea traffic off the Italian coast for carrying supplies to the front and bringing back most valuable industrial goods is becoming of ever-increasing, and perhaps decisive, importance because of the systematic destruction of traffic routes on land. Sea traffic is being hindered mainly by well known enemy air supremacy. Besides this, increasing damage has recently been inflicted along the west coast by enemy

torpedo boats operating every night along the entire coast up to the area Spezia, Genoa and Nice.

Then followed an impressive list of Axis vessels sunk or damaged in these encounters.

> Reconnaissance by the German Air Force and our own investigations [the diary continued] reveal that the enemy torpedo boat base and repair base is still at Maddalena, but the jumping-off point is almost without exception Bastia. The elimination of Bastia harbour as a MTB base by naval bombardment is impossible because suitable heavy artillery carriers are lacking and because of enemy air supremacy by day. Up to now night bombardments have not achieved lasting results, especially as MTBs were not encountered during night operations. Furthermore, short nights at present render any night operations impossible.
>
> Naval Staff is of the opinion that a single blow at enemy MTBs and their base at Bastia would for some time bring about considerable relief for the traffic off the Italian west coast, and thereby result in favouring the fighting on land by a temporary, and perhaps decisive, improvement in the supply situation.

The armed forces High Command and the High Command Air Operational Staff were asked to investigate the possibility of this. An immediate surprise blow, said the Naval Staff, was of decisive importance in order that the expected increase in supplies might have its effect on the present fighting.

But by mid-June the diary noted sadly that:

> Due to developments on land (the Allied capture of Rome) the necessity of increased supplies over the sea has disappeared. Only fuel in addition to cement will be transferred from Genoa to the south by waterway.

The Naval Staff appeared to be unaware that also from Bastia emanated the individuals responsible for the lamentation that:

> Italian soldiers and police are becoming more and more unreliable, with frequent desertions. Partisan activities behind the front line in the entire area of Italy are responsible for disturbances in the traffic and communications systems, as well as for casualties to German personnel.

*

Thus far little has been said about the work of the surfboat crews, or dinghy parties. These men, probably more than anyone except the agents themselves, were required to perform the most hazardous tasks in the dangerous business of inserting Allied agents at largely unknown pinpoints along stretches of enemy-held and heavily defended coast. Many of these were along the Italian Riviera, which is notable for its rocky and picturesque coastline, indented with small bays, and its background of mountains which in places slope precipitously to the sea. One convenient pinpoint, used on more than one occasion, was immediately below a villa perched high on the cliffs. No one knew, since the fact could not be detected by aerial reconnaissance, that it concealed a heavy German coastal gun, whose crew used the villa as their mess!

Their rubber dinghies, little more than nine feet in area when inflated, and equipped only with a pair of oars for propulsion, were crewed rarely by more than two men, one armed with a sub machine-gun acting as guide and lookout. They often had to row long distances in choppy seas on black and stormy nights to find a suitable spot in which their nervous passengers, usually encumbered with a heavy wireless set and other gear, could be dry-landed. Sometimes they had to feel their way over unseen reefs and through narrow channels lined with jagged rocks which, if scraped against, could hole their flimsy craft and leave them stranded. Missions to evacuate escaped prisoners-of-war entailed additional difficulties, since they might have to tow extra dinghies.

With them they usually had a compass, walkie-talkie radio, torch and batteries, and a haversack containing emergency rations and escape kit, which included a map of the surrounding area. They had to watch out for the correct signals of a reception committee, and when making a 'blind landing' were only too well aware of the possibility of running into an enemy ambush when they could be blasted out of the water by gunfire, or taken prisoner along with the agents to meet an unpleasant fate.

> There was always a fearful risk that accident, indiscretion, or treachery might betray a pre-arranged rendezvous to the enemy; in that case a ... warship and its crew might be lost in an attempt to bring out a single and not necessarily a valuable agent.*

A well established procedure was of course laid down to be followed if in emergency they had to be left behind. But, as Maxted had said of his earlier trips in the feluccas from Gibraltar, no commanding officer would ever willingly abandon his surfboat's crew.

During the forthcoming period, however, this was to happen in two different operations.

* *SOE in France*, M.R.D. Foot, HMSO, 1966.

On the night of 18 June, Operations 'Scram' and 'Ferret' were staged, both by the same craft and in the same place. The purpose of 'Ferret' was to land three SOE agents behind the enemy lines at Bonassola, twenty-five miles north of Spezia; and 'Scram' to keep a rendezvous at the same spot with a number of escaping prisoners-of-war. *ARB403* was the craft used with Smith as senior officer. A 'Maryland' conducting officer accompanied the agents, Fowler of 'A' Force to take charge of the escapers, and Sergeant Jones and Corporal Bourne-Newton were to man the dinghy. But en route the weather became so bad that the ARB had to turn back.

Next night *403* set off on a second attempt with the same party. This time the pinpoint was reached without difficulty, and Jones and Bourne-Newton departed for the shore with the agents. The operation promised to be a particularly hairy one. Dark rugged cliffs enfolded the area, and behind these the night sky was lit by the probing fingers of enemy searchlights and the red bursts of AA fire as Allied bombers droned overhead. The sea was rough, and the dinghymen had difficulty in finding a suitable landing place. Finally they discovered a gap in the rocks fringing the coastline which led to a small beach where they were able to disembark the agents. But a search of the neighbouring area failed to reveal any of the escaped prisoners-of-war they expected to find. After a brief wait they started to row back to the ARB.

They had covered about half the distance to where they thought she was lying, when a light began to blink from the point on shore they had just left. Jones reported this to Fowler on the walkie-talkie, who asked them to go back and investigate. This they did, but could find no one about although they heard movements in the undergrowth. Deciding that the light they had seen could not have been intended for them, they pushed off and headed for the ARB again.

Then they heard the sound of engines, which they thought came from an E-boat. Jones tried again to raise Fowler on the walkie-talkie, but could get no reply, and they continued to row. Eventually the saw the dark outline of a vessel they took to be *403*, but it was an enemy patrol craft, and they hastily paddled away. It had been arranged that the ARB would wait for them until 0400, but for some reason neither Jones nor Bourne-Newton was wearing a watch, and they estimated the time to be about 0300. They therefore continued to paddle about somewhat aimlessly, while noting that the mysterious signals they had seen earlier were still being flashed from the shore. To add to their worries, the walkie-talkie seemed to be no longer working and they could not get a peep put of it.

At last they stopped rowing to discuss their predicament. It seemed obvious that some emergency had arisen which had forced the ARB to retire and leave them behind. This left them with two alternatives: to return to the shore, scuttle the dinghy and try to contact the agents; or conceal themselves near the pinpoint and wait to be picked up by another boat. Yet the whole area appeared to have been alerted and was probably swarming with Germans. If they were caught they would probably be shot, for by now rumours of what had happened to the men of the 2677th Headquarters Company had filtered back to Bastia. Finally they decided to row back to base, although it was probably all of a hundred miles across open sea.

What had happened to *ARB403* was that while she was lying hove to, hostile craft had been sighted and she had to make a hurried withdrawal to seaward. When the enemy had disappeared, she cautiously returned to the pinpoint and continued to wait there for another hour and a quarter. But there was no sign of the dinghy party, and it was impossible to raise them on the radio. When daybreak came *403* was compelled to leave the coast.

After her arrival back in Bastia with the bad news, wireless contact was established with the agents she had landed, and they were instructed to try to find Jones and Bourne-Newton. Next day the agents sent a cipher message to Bastia, but no one could manage to decipher it. Then on the 23rd they sent another signal to say they considered the dinghy party to be safe since they had heard nothing to the contrary.

When Croft went to discuss with MacCallum the re-staging of an expedition which had failed to come off, he found the latter depressed because three members of his own surfboat crews had also been left behind in an ACF operation.

The latter was code-named 'Locust' when PT boat *310* escorted by *309* with Smith in charge had tried to land a party of SIS agents near Monterosso, close to Spezia, but had been driven off by gunfire from enemy destroyers and coastal craft when nearing the pinpoint. On the 21st 'Locust' had been tried again, using PT boats *309* escorted by *308*, again under Smith's charge. But they were prevented from reaching the pinpoint by heavy enemy coastal traffic. Finally on the 23rd *ARB403* escorted by *PT218*, with Smith still in charge, set out to land the agents at Moneglia, the pinpoint having been changed for security reasons.

In order to land the agents and their equipment, two surfboats had to be used, and while these were on their way inshore, *PT218* remained two or three miles out with the intention of drawing off any enemy forces which might appear. Some fifteen minutes after the surfboats had left, an enemy corvette, accompanied by several smaller vessels, was sighted about a mile to seaward, whereupon *403* edged to within 200 yards of the pinpoint. Four minutes later the enemy opened fire with starshell in the direction of *218*, but the bursts also illuminated the ARB, and she was forced to retire to the south-west pursued by 40 mm fire. After contacting and transferring to *218*, Smith ordered the ARB to return to base, and began to work round the stern of the enemy back towards the pinpoint.

When he had got close enough in, he tried to contact the senior surfboat by walkie-talkie, but was unsuccessful as their set had been damaged in the haste of landing. Soon afterwards the enemy challenged from the south-east and fired starshell again. Under cover of smoke, Smith retired to seaward, hastened by both 88 mm and 40 mm gunfire. When the PT boat was finally out of range, she stopped and all hands watched the enemy vessels firing at each other until the lateness of the hour compelled her to return to Bastia.

Fortunately, however, the dinghy crews were to be safely recovered.

At 0130 in the morning of the 24th Croft was awakened by a telephone call from the OSS and told that a message had been received from their station on Capraia reporting the arrival at that island of Jones and Bourne-Newton. Their own message to headquarters was simple and to the point: 'Beg to report safe arrival Capraia 1830GMT June 23.' A boat was at once sent off to bring them back to Bastia.

That night *PT305* with Brian Smith as senior officer, and escorted this time by four Coastal Force MTBs, set off to recover the 'Ferret' dinghy crew. The operation was code-named 'Essorbee' (unofficially standing for 'shit or bust!') for Smith was determined to bring them back himself since they had been left behind on an operation of which he had been in charge. Fortunately the weather was favourable, with low clouds, poor visibility and a moderate sea.

On arrival off the enemy coast, the support force remained to seaward, while Smith in *305* proceeded inshore until his radar indicated the presence of an enemy vessel off the pinpoint. 'Avoiding action was taken, and the target conformed,' he reported. Five minutes later he saw the expected and pre-arranged light signals from his crew, dashed in, embarked his men, and had *305* turned and pointing to seaward before the enemy opened fire with inaccurate starshell. The enemy fire was easily evaded, and the British force returned to base in triumph. Subsequent investigation revealed that the enemy ships engaged on the previous night formed the vanguard of a convoy which later anchored in the bay in which was sited the pinpoint.

Back in Bastia they also learned the full story of the epic row of Jones and Bourne-Newton from Bonassola.

After starting out on their long pull, the pair found themselves only four miles from the Italian coast at sunrise, but their tiny craft was not spotted. With them they had two full water bottles, two flasks of rum, two tins each of bully beef and 48-hour rations, and some bars of chocolate and chewing gum. Thus there was no shortage of water or provisions. Included in the dinghy's equipment was a compass, petrol lighters, escape knives, a torch and spare battery, walkie-talkie radio, a spare paddle and a foot pump, while for weapons they had a revolver and a Sten gun. They decided to row alternately in two-hour shifts.

Luckily the weather remained calm and the sea smooth, although during the day the sun grew uncomfortably hot. On the first morning they saw British bombers flying overhead and tried to signal to them, using the polished rum flasks as a makeshift heliograph. But their signals were not seen. Then an unpleasant visitor turned up in the shape of a large swordfish, which came nosing inquisitively round the dinghy. They watched its antics apprehensively, and when it seemed to be preparing to attack, they opened fire with revolver and Sten gun and drove it off.

At dawn on the second day they could see in the distance the tops of the mountains of Corsica, some twenty miles away, and by late afternoon they were within four miles of Cape Corse. But then they found the current set against them, which finally forced them to abandon all hope of reaching Corsica. They decided to head south-eastwards towards Capraia where they knew the Americans had a shore station.

By midnight they were so exhausted that they gave up, and both slept. At daybreak, finding themselves no further advanced, they

rowed southwards for a while, then turned east, and with the help
of the current made better progress. Late that afternoon the dinghy
grounded on a deserted beach on the coast of Capraia. After taking
a brief rest, they struggled round to the harbour where a fishing
boat towed them in. They had rowed 120 miles in 90 hours.

Two other important operations scheduled for the period failed
for different reasons. One of these, code-named 'Gorge II' ('Gorge I'
having been staged earlier on) was to land some SOE agents in the
St Tropez area of southern France; the other, 'Scram II' was to
bring off escapers from a pinpoint near Moneglia.

On the 24th 'Gorge II' was mounted in *PT556* with Boyle in
charge and Croft and Smalley as dinghy party. But compass defects
forced the boat's return. Launched again on the following night,
*556* being escorted this time by another PT boat, and with
Dempster taking charge, the pinpoint could not be found, and the
operation had to be abandoned.

Two nights later 'Scram II' was staged, when *PT306* accompanied
by a diversionary force of three of her consorts, with Dempster as
senior officer and Newton, Miles and Chalmers the dinghy party,
tried to reach the Moneglia area. But heavy enemy coastal traffic
prevented any approach. On the following night *MAS509* with the
same party set off to try again, but as she neared the coast the *MAS*
boat was spotted and shadowed by an enemy aircraft. The defence
forces were duly alerted, and in quick time two enemy surface
vessels appeared and attacked *509* at 250 yards range. Dodging
their gunfire, and with no escort in support, she had to flee for
home flat out, luckily without damage or casualties.

The end was now in sight for special operations from Bastia.
With the Allied armies astride northern Italy from Florence in the
west to Ancona on the Adriatic, the enemy was steadily being
driven back behind the River Arno and his 'Gothic Line'. The
shrinking enemy-held coast between Genoa and Spezia had
become very much alerted, and as strong enemy forces were being
encountered, it was decided to abandon attempts to carry out
clandestine operations on that particular stretch. Thus for the next
no-moon period only eleven operations were proposed. Of these
two did not eventuate, three were unsuccessful, and six succeeded –
but half the latter were routine trips to Capraia and Gorgona.

The story of these final operations, carried out in July before
SOIS ordered that no more should be attempted to Italy, clearly
reveal how the dangers were daily increasing.

Thus Operation 'Skid', staged on the 15th, led in fact to a minor sea battle. Its object was to extricate thirty Allied escaped prisoners-of-war, who were to be picked up at Vernazza, another pinpoint near Spezia, where a reception committee was expected. No ACF officer was needed, and the rescue party consisted of Peter Fowler with Balaclava's Arnold, Ashton and Chalmers acting as surfboats' crews. They were embarked in *MTB357* of Coastal Forces, which was escorted by two PT boats and Lieutenant Tony Blomfield, RN, senior officer of the flotilla, in his own MTB.

The boats arrived off the pinpoint at 2330, but as they began to close in an enemy convoy was spotted steaming along between the 'Skid' flotilla and the shore. Engines were stopped while they waited for the convoy and its escort to pass, then *MTB357* crept to within 800 yards of the shore to await the agreed signal from the reception committee; Blomfield's force meanwhile remaining to seaward.

One and a half hours went by with no signal, then Blomfield called up the CO of *357* on R/T and told him to leave as hostile craft had been sighted approaching. As the MTB was heading away from the shore, two vessels were sighted which were assumed to be two of her escorts, and she continued on course. But they were not what they seemed. They suddenly challenged her, and followed this up with an immediate burst of fire. *357* at once took evasive action on her main engines, while her attackers were engaged by Blomfield and his boats.

But the enemy was present in force, for soon there appeared two destroyers, a corvette and another E-boat. While *357* fled for home as fast as she could, Blomfield covered her retreat with a brisk rearguard action, during which the night sky was lit up with gun flashes and streams of coloured tracer. When the engagement was finally broken off, the British force had suffered a certain amount of damage and some slight casualties, while one E-boat was thought to have been destroyed.

Nine days later came Operation 'Kingston' in which *MAS543* with Boyle in charge tried to land two OSS agents at Mesco Porto, also near Spezia, in good weather and clear visibility. After dodging enemy patrols en route, the pinpoint was safely reached, and the surfboat launched. But it had not gone twenty yards when three E-boats came tearing up. Almost at once they opened rapid tracer fire at a range closing to 150 yards. There was no time to recall the dinghy party, so Boyle hastily retreated, zigzagging in the hope of drawing the enemy's attention from the boat.

For the next three hours he tried to return to the pinpoint, where much activity was in progress, the enemy vessels sweeping the sea and adjacent cliffs with searchlights. Meanwhile other actions were taking place on a large scale both north and south of the area. During intervals between the firing Boyle continued his efforts to close the pinpoint, and tried to contact the surfboat by walkie-talkie, but was continually driven off by fire from shore batteries and surface craft. Finally, just before dawn, the search had to be abandoned, and *543* returned to Bastia with the bad news.

Operation 'Kingston' was one of the rare occasions when a dinghy party was lost. For when on the following night Boyle returned with a strong supporting force to recover the dinghy and its occupants, they were not at the pinpoint or the pre-arranged rendezvous, and it could only be assumed – rightly as it so happened – that they had been captured by the enemy.

Operation 'Scram 3' had also been mounted on the night of the 24th, when *MTB378* with three of her consorts as escort landed a party of agents near Moneglia after an engagement with enemy craft, during which she sustained damage and casualties. Once again, however, the escapers who were to have been picked up at the pinpoint could not be found.

'Post Kingston' – Boyle's abortive attempt to recover his dinghy crew – was the last clandestine operation to be staged from Bastia.

On 3 August Croft and his Balaclava Mission moved to Calvi to await their dispersal order, and by the end of September the remnants of the Mission had 'petered out'. They had infiltrated nearly 100 agents to enemy and enemy-occupied countries – all of them delivered safely – and brought out nearly half that number on the return journey, in addition to taking in an unknown quantity of wireless sets, arms, ammunition and other supplies. No figures are available for DDOD(I)'s agents or those of other agencies.

Of DDOD(I)'s Adriatic operations there is also little record. After the Italian surrender, 'Nobby' Clark was ordered to set up a small operational base at Molfetta, some twenty miles north-west of Bari.

> At this time [he recalled] all sorts of 'private armies' were trying to make names for themselves and getting in each other's way. So the Flag Officer, Italy sent for me and told me to gather together the commanding officers of all these mobs. Then he laid down the law to them. No seaborne expeditions were to be staged except through me as his Staff Officer (Special Operations).

As mentioned earlier, Charles Irwin was one of the ACF officers transferred to the new base, and he played a leading part in fitting out newer and better local-type craft which now became available for operations to Dalmatia and the Italian Adriatic coast. At that time the attitude of Tito's Partisans towards any clandestine craft was suspicious and threatening.

Thus when Irwin was carrying out an early operation to the Jugoslav coast, bad weather caused him to miss his appointment with the reception committee waiting on shore. When he put into harbour for shelter, his ship was fired on, seized, searched, and he was interrogated and placed under arrest by the Partisans. Although unable to speak a word of the language, Irwin succeeded in convincing them of his identity and honesty of purpose. Thereafter, having established mutual confidence, he rendered valuable service to the Partisans by evacuating personnel from adjacent islands threatened by the enemy, reported the movements of the enemy-manned Jugoslav cruiser *Dalmatia* and destroyers, and finally embarked a large party of refugees, including women, for Italy. During the voyage his ship encountered gale-force winds and heavy seas. The pumps failed, the wireless was flooded and put out of action, and when she finally made harbour the ship was in a waterlogged condition.

On a subsequent operation to the northern Adriatic, Irwin's ship was attacked and machine-gunned by two enemy aircraft a few hours after leaving harbour. Two of his men were killed outright and the rest of the crew wounded, two of them critically. Irwin himself received shrapnel wounds in the body and limbs. He managed to get his ship into the nearest Allied port, where he and his crew were removed to a military hospital. Unshaken by this experience, he returned to his command on recovery and continued to run the gauntlet of enemy air and sea patrols while maintaining regular contact between an advanced post on the island of Vis, which was also Tito's headquarters, and underground organisations in other Adriatic islands. Those members of his crew who recovered accompanied him. Irwin was later to be awarded the DSO and each of his men the DSM.

Another ACF pioneer whom we met working from North Africa, and who transferred to the Adriatic was Lieutenant Gervaise, RNR. He had carried out eight major operations in local-type vessels and Coastal Force craft in the Mediterranean, and acted as senior officer of a member of sorties carried out on behalf of the French, who presented him with the Croix de Guerre. When the physical strain of operations in small craft appeared likely to affect his health, he was transferred to command of the trawler *Prodigal*. Yet even then he found himself almost continuously at sea with little rest, escorting supply ships between Bari, Brindisi and Vis. He was later awarded the DSC for 'gallant and distinguished service in special operations.'

Francis Cosens, also mentioned previously as having taken command of the *Seahawk*, the British-built, diesel-driven version of the Gibraltar feluccas, duly arrived with her in the Adriatic. Unfortunately she proved to be unsuitable for clandestine work. Nevertheless Cosens executed a number of operations involving precise navigation in her to pinpoints along the featureless coastline of the northern Adriatic with such skill and judgement as to win him a well-earned DSC.

Maxted, too, had a spell of service in the Adriatic after the base at Bastia closed down. Transferred to command of *MGB180* and operating from Ancona, he carried out a number of clandestine landings on the Dalmatian coast before finally returning to the United Kingdom in the spring of 1945. By then the Eighth Army had raced up the coast, capturing Padua, Venice and Treviso, and eventually established contact with Tito's forces at Monfalcone. The war in Italy was practically over, and the final collapse of the Third Reich not far off.

# Bibliography

*SOE in France*, M.R.D. Foot, HMSO, 1966.
*The War at Sea*, Vol. III, Pt. II, Roskill, HMSO, 1961.
*Sea Devils*, J.V. Borghese, Hutchinson, 1952.
*The Frogmen of Burma*, Lt. Cdr B.S. Wright, Wm. Kimber, 1970.
*Defeat into Victory*, Field Marshal Slim, Cassell, 1956.
*Crusade in Europe*, D. Eisenhower, Heinemann, 1948.
*MI9 – Escape and Evasion*, Foot & Langley, MacDonald Futura, 1980.
*The Partisans*, D. Mountfield, Hamlyn, 1979.
*Flag 4*, D. Pope, Wm. Kimber, 1954.
*Providence their Guide*, Major-General D. Lloyd-Owen, Harrap, 1980.
*The Filibusters*, J. Lodwick, Methuen, 1947.
*Dust upon the Sea*, W.E. Benyon-Tinker, Hodder & Stoughton, 1947.
*Fresh from the Laundry*, Ilka Chase, W.H. Allen, 1967.
*Despatches*, General Sir H. Maitland Wilson
*Naval Operations in the Aegean – Reports*, Commander-in-Chief, Levant.
*War Diary*, Flag Officer, Levant & Eastern Mediterranean, 1944/45.
Supplements to the London Gazette.
Admiralty, War Office and Defence papers in the Public Record Office.
German Naval Staff War Diary.

# Index